TURNING THE WHEEL

TURNING THE WHEEL

Henri Nouwen and and Our Search for God

Jonathan Bengtson and Gabrielle Earnshaw, editors

NOVALIS

ORBIS BOOKS

Maryknoll, New York 10545

Founded in 1970, Orbis Books endeavors to publish works that enlighten the mind, nourish the spirit, and challenge the conscience. The publishing arm of the Maryknoll Fathers and Brothers, Orbis seeks to explore the global dimensions of the Christian faith and mission, to invite dialogue with diverse cultures and religious traditions, and to serve the cause of reconciliation and peace. The books published reflect the views of their authors and do not represent the official position of the Maryknoll Society. To learn more about Maryknoll and Orbis Books, please visit our website at www.maryknoll.org.

Published by Orbis Books, Maryknoll, NY 10545–0308.

Published in Canada by Novalis Publishing Inc., 10 Lower Spadina Avenue, Suite 400, Toronto, Ontario, Canada M5V 2Z2.
Phone: 1–800–387–7164; Fax: 1–800–204–4140;
E-mail: books@novalis.ca; www.novalis.ca

For more information about Henri Nouwen, his work, and the work of the Henry Nouwen Society, visit www.HenriNouwen.org.

Manufactured in the United States of America.
Manuscript editing and typesetting by Joan Weber Laflamme.

Library of Congress Cataloging-in-Publication Data

Turning the wheel : Henri Nouwen and our search for God / edited by Jonathan Bengtson and Gabrielle Earnshaw.
    p. cm.
    ISBN 978–1–57075–727–3
    1. Nouwen, Henri J. M. I. Bengtson, Jonathan. II. Earnshaw, Gabrielle.
    BX4705.N87T87 2007
    282.092–dc22
    [B]
                            2007015912

Library and Archives Canada Cataloguing in Publication Data

BX4705.N87T87 2007a   282.092   C2007–905390–4
Novalis ISBN 978–2–89507–959–0

For Heiko Willms

Contents

Introduction

Nathan Ball

> *I have always been fascinated by these wagon wheels with their wide rims, strong wooden spokes, and big hubs. These wheels help me to understand the importance of a life lived from the center. When I move along the rim, I can reach one spoke after the other, but when I stay at the hub I am in touch with all the spokes at once.*
>
> —HENRI NOUWEN

The dream that produced these conference proceedings began in an informal conversation among friends: Gabrielle Earnshaw, archivist of the Henri Nouwen Archive and Research Collection; Jonathan Bengtson, chief librarian of the Kelly Library; and Sue Mosteller and myself from the Henri Nouwen Legacy Trust. We were asking ourselves, "How can we give thanks for and celebrate Henri's life and legacy to mark the tenth anniversary of his death? How can we nurture a sustained conversation about the ongoing relevance of Henri's spiritual teaching?"

This conversation spawned the idea of a major international gathering and, within minutes, Gabrielle and Jonathan eagerly proposed that the Henri Nouwen Archives at the University of St. Michael's College host a three-day conference. The dates were set, May 18 to 20, 2006, and the planning began. Several partners enthusiastically signed on: Regis College from the Toronto School of Theology at the University of Toronto; L'Arche Daybreak, the community where Henri lived during the last ten years of his life; and the Henri Nouwen Societies of the Netherlands, the United States, and Canada. The dream would become a reality!

Right from the beginning we wanted the conference to explore the search for God in the Christian spiritual life by examining themes that Henri had worked with during his lifetime and that still resonate for Christians today. We felt challenged to hold together, as Henri did in his lifetime, the academic and the pastoral, so that scholars, ministers, university students, and spiritual seekers would each find a place in the circle of those who would gather. We decided on the conference theme: "Turning the Wheel, Henri Nouwen and Our Search for God."

The response to our call for papers was surprising both in the numbers who responded and in the themes suggested. Registrations came from women and men of all ages, students, ordained and lay people, professors, authors, doctoral students, and those who claimed that Henri, through his books, was their spiritual director. Most Christian denominations were represented: Baptist, Roman Catholic, Episcopalian and Anglican, Presbyterian, Lutheran, United Church of Christ and United Church of Canada, Protestant, Evangelical, and Greek Orthodox, and others. People came from Hong Kong, Germany, the Netherlands, Canada, the United States, Colombia, England, and Scotland. The breadth of representation reminded us again of the remarkable reach of Henri's life and writings. It was truly representative of the people of God.

Henri's former community of L'Arche Daybreak, north of Toronto, launched the gathering by welcoming over 100 conference participants for a community retreat day in its beautiful chapel, The Dayspring. This was followed by a visit to Henri's grave, where Henri's brother Paul spoke in the context of a prayer service. Back at the university in downtown Toronto, 235 people spent the next two days together listening, sharing, singing, praying, laughing, taking notes, discussing, and meeting new friends.

The keynote and lecture and workshop presentations in this book capture the breadth and depth not only of Henri's inspiration during his lifetime, but also of the very fruitful and continually expanding legacy he left. The presentations variously challenge the mind, stimulate the imagination, and touch the heart.

Henri loved Luke's story of the road to Emmaus. Cleopas and another disciple were returning after the shocking and demoralizing experience of Jesus' crucifixion. En route, they met the risen Jesus without knowing who he was, but later, sharing a meal with him, they recognized him—and he vanished! They said to one another, "Were not our hearts burning within us while he was talking with us on the road, while he was opening the scriptures to us?" (Lk 24:32).

The fact that *our* hearts were burning within us as we celebrated Henri's life and legacy during the conference is our most powerful testimony to the spiritual gifts that Henri left us. But our hearts were burning too because of the scholarly and inspirational presentations of those who offered us the fruits of their research and their life-search. To each of those more than forty-five people we are deeply grateful.

We are grateful too for the superb quality of the whole conference. Gabrielle Earnshaw and Jonathan Bengtson directed and inspired a strong team of volunteers who were keen and competent and who attended to every detail. Colette Halferty was a brilliant conference coordinator. This event simply would not have happened without the dedication and hard work of these people.

Henri's abiding desire was that each and every person live out of a deep personal knowledge of his or her identity as the beloved of God. May this book, with its many voices, bring you ever closer to that one voice of unique and personal love.

A Brother's Memorial

Paul Nouwen

This memorial was given at Henri Nouwen's gravesite, May 18, 2006, King City, Ontario, Canada.

Ten years ago we also stood here with many people, family, colleagues, friends from all over the world, and especially the core members of L'Arche Daybreak, around Henri's coffin. We have the feeling that it all happened yesterday because it was so impressive and intense.

Henri was born in 1932 in a little town in Holland. I came two years later. We grew up in a peaceful family, until World War II started in 1940. Our country was occupied, and we suffered hard times. Toward the end of the war, my brother Laurent and my sister Laurien were born.

At the age of eight Henri showed great interest in becoming a priest and performed ceremonies in a makeshift chapel in our home just beside the room where my father was hidden from enemy soldiers who were looking for him.

My parents noticed how, day by day, the inner voice of God was speaking strongly to Henri and how his vocation to the priesthood was born.

Henri's search for God had begun, a restless looking for the great Father. It brought him to his studies in Holland and to his teaching at several universities in the United States, as well as his many visits to many countries all over the world–from South America to the Ukraine. And then the inner voice of God spoke again and brought him here to become a pastor, looking after people who were vulnerable indeed but strongly beloved children of God. L'Arche became his home, where he tried to be a beloved man himself. Still he went on traveling, always on the way to find the Father.

Luckily he had time to write and to preach in order to get into the minds and hearts of many people all over the world, and now even increasingly. He spoke and wrote in a simple, not really academic language that moves the hearts of vulnerable people, whom we all are. He was the wounded healer. He wanted us to believe that we are the beloved children of God whoever we are.

And in the parable of the prodigal son Henri did not wish to be only the son who was forgiven by his father. No, he finally decided to become like the father himself.

Now, in these last ten years since his death in a hospital in Holland, he is with the Father. At the time of his death my father, and my siblings and I, realized that Henri wanted to be buried here, close to those he loved and for whom he was the pastor. So his final destination was King City, Ontario. King reminds me of the kingdom of God.

And now, ten years later, we dare to say that his life was not that short because it was so full and because he lives on through his books and prayers. He gives support to many people in this world who are looking for the love of God and perhaps not knowing who God is. His message for all of us is this: Do not say that you cannot find God, but do your utmost so that God can find you!

We are very grateful to those who organized this very special day here and the days that are to follow. We thank you too, Henri, for your fruitful life, and your life as a servant leader.

1

We Are Weak and Strong as God Is Merciful and Just

Henri Nouwen and the Search for God in Western Culture

Mary Jo Leddy

These reflections are neither those of an expert on the thought of Henri Nouwen nor those of someone who knew him personally. Unlike many of those present, I do not have even a single "Henri" story to tell! However, I have been engaged by some of his insights and concerns and have pondered their significance within the more recent history of the search for God in Western culture.

Let me attempt to situate Nouwen's writings within a basic consideration of the correlation between our image of the human person and our image of God. On the one hand, when our spirituality is shaped by an experience of human weakness, we can imagine God as merciful and compassionate. So too, when we have an image of God as the Compassionate One, we can more easily embrace the fundamental weakness of the human person.

On the other hand, when we experience the possibility and imperative of human strength, we can imagine God as just—as holding us to account for our power. So too, when we have an image of God as just, we can more easily admit the burden of human responsibility. As God is both merciful and compassionate, we human beings are both weak and strong.[1]

I suggest that it is helpful to situate Nouwen's insights and developments in Western culture within this correlation between the images of the divine and human.

The Culture of Modernity and the Search for God

The culture of modernity in the West was shaped by a belief in the power of human reason. From the time of the Enlightenment an increasing number of persons were convinced that just as reason could build new technologies, so too reason would be able to reshape society for the better, to understand and improve economics. As modernity began to build a new culture, it also destroyed the medieval culture built on a respect for tradition and authority, on the values of community and the common good.

With the advent of modernity, the autonomous individual, who acted on the basis of conscience and reason, was released from attachments and loyalties to real communities. Community became more of an ideal that could be realized when rational people worked out sensible contracts and reasons for being together. Although many of the first modern thinkers remained practicing Christians, their belief in the power of reason would ultimately reduce and restrict the realm of religious faith. The emphasis on human freedom would inevitably challenge the more classical image of God as all powerful and all knowing. This image of God was diminished in order to make room for human initiative.

As reason established itself as the foundation of politics and economics, faith was increasingly relegated to the realm of feeling and emotion. Those who lived primarily by emotions (women, the mentally retarded, the uncivilized) were defined as inferior human beings. Those shaped by the culture of modernity no longer looked on the world as a sacrament of the divine, a place of awe and mystery. The world was taken for granted; it was a thing to be worked on and improved. This modern confidence was, in retrospect, astonishing. Just as human beings could understand how a clock worked and how it could be fixed if it was broken, they could also understand how the world worked and how it could be fixed when broken. This arrogance extended even to the human person: social scientists assumed they could understand what makes people tick and how they could be fixed, improved upon. Professionals became the new ruling class and controlled the world through specialized knowledge. The modern faith in reason became a general attitude that could be translated into popular terms as *If you just think hard enough and work smart enough, things will get better.*

The greatest threat to this world view came from what was not known, what or who could not be understood, what or who could not be improved. Rather than probe these limits of modernity, some theologians tried to make faith more reasonable. Others affirmed faith as a special feeling, a special way of knowing. Eventually, a philosophical critique of modernity would emerge in the various forms of Marxism, Freudian psychology, and Existentialism. However, the greatest and most telling critiques came from life itself. The eruption of war and barbarity in the heart of modern, civilized Europe cast a grave shadow over the light of reason.

I also think that a living critique of modernity comes from the witness of the L'Arche communities founded by Jean Vanier. It is through the commitment of these communities to real and not ideal people, to people who seem less reasonable than most, that a critique of the values of modernity is proclaimed. Within L'Arche, human beings are not valued on the basis of reason but through the eyes of faith and love. Wisdom rather than reason becomes the guide for deciding who or what is of value.

Nouwen and the Modern World View

I think that Henri Nouwen was profoundly shaped by the modern world view. He understood it, intellectually and emotionally, and he was a very effective critic of it. In his early writings we read his critique of the kind of psychology that tries to "fix" people, with the kind of counselors who protect themselves from the suffering of "clients" with the mantra of "clinical distance." He was not impressed by the efforts of professional ministers to become "qualified." In short, he was not comfortable with the modern thought boxes that tried to keep life and God within manageable limits.

Many of his reflections seem to circle around the question of the basis for the relationship between the minister and the one cared for. He rejected the model of the strong minister who served the weak person. He also rejected the image of God associated with more professional models of ministry—an image of God as untouched by suffering, as distant and in control. Nouwen's concerns had already been articulated by some theologians in the wake of the massive crisis of two world wars. Before he was hanged by the Nazis, German theologian Dietrich Bonhoeffer said, "Only a suffering God can save us now." Some theologians even said that only a powerless God could be credible after the social experience of such destructive power.

Henri Nouwen began to articulate shared weakness and vulnerability as the authentic basis for relationship between human beings. He urged the professional minister to realize that he or she was a "wounded healer." When the minister and the individual are each able to be weak, then this becomes the basis for community. Through solidarity in suffering, the mercy and compassion of God become present. The minister, Nouwen said, is called to be with another, not to be over another. This is an immensely liberating insight for those who experienced the particular forms of oppression in the modern world view. What a relief not to have to be strong, all together, in control. What a relief not to feel the burden of fixing the world, other people, and even oneself. What a relief not to feel the constant pressure to improve upon what has been given. What a blessing to experience that you are beloved, not because you are strong but simply because you are. This insight was liberating for Henri Nouwen, and because he was able to share it through his writings and talks, it became liberating for countless other people. He spoke about the primacy of the heart rather than the priorities of reason, and this led him to places and people of the heart. His heart would lead him to communities that were real rather than ideal. According to Nouwen, the heart was not unreasonable, but it was a deeper way of knowing that put reason in its proper place.

As he spoke about his own weaknesses, he became a witness to the mercy and compassion of God. He described his own search for God in great personal detail. Some may say he gave us too much information about himself. However, I think it was precisely the particularity of his writings that made them so universally accessible. In this he is an example of a literary maxim: the more particular and located the writing, the more universal its meaning. Think of the great Russian novels and the detailed description of the snow, the sky, the flowers in the spring. Even though the characters have names we do not recognize and live in a landscape we will never visit, we can identify with people who are located in a particular place and are shaped by it, with people who have real names and particular struggles.

Henri Nouwen did not write about the idea of weakness, the idea of God's mercy. He described what Bronwyn Wallace called "the stubborn particularities of grace," and this is why he spoke to so many and speaks to us now. Nevertheless, there was a price to be paid for this form of bearing witness. It was a bold and risky venture and seemed to afflict him with the burden of self-reflection. In this he was similar to Thomas Merton, who never quite escaped the mirror provided by his own self-awareness. Both Nouwen and Merton began with the experience of the self. In this they are alike, and in this they are both children of modernity. This is why they were able to speak to the deep search for God, which all the discoveries of modernity had not found. However, they did not begin with the experience of the imperial self, which reduces others to objects of concern, care, or even contempt. They did not begin with the experience of the self as an object to be understood and controlled. They did not begin with the experience of the self that makes God an object of our thoughts. Rather, they began with an experience of the self that was weak (as Nouwen did) or false (as Merton described it). They began with a sense of self grounded in a mystery beyond their control. They began with a sense of self able to transcend itself and to be in communion with others and with God.

The Search for God in a Postmodern Culture

The culture of modernity is still with us just as the classical/medieval world view still exists within us, although in fragmentary forms. However, the modern world view itself is now in crisis, and its basic assumptions are being questioned. We are living through one of those in-between times in history, still in such a preliminary stage that it can only be characterized as being different from what went before it. The intellectual critique of modernity and the challenges posed by the events of the twentieth century have been extended so that there is now a widespread suspicion about the ability of human beings to "fix" the world. There is an increasing rejection of the universal claims made by Western reason.

Modernity assumed that what human beings held in common was reason. Those who were not reasonable should be educated and civilized; those who could not be educated could not be considered human. Today, people from other cultures are claiming their differences as significant and of value. They are resisting the homogenizing process of Western reason, the imperial claims of Western reason, and totalitarian tendencies. The affirmation of the distinct differences in human experience is significant in reflecting on the search for God in the contemporary world. It is no longer so easy to speak about solidarity in suffering. I have faced this difficulty in very real ways as I have lived side by side, in community, in the same house, with refugees from all over the world. I have learned that it is impossible to compare sufferings. Each person has a suffering and pain that cannot be measured or compared to another's. Indeed, it is a grave injustice to measure someone's suffering as being more or less than another. It is a mystery to me why a diplomat who found an easy way out of his country as it was disintegrating, who was able to bring his family with him, seems so much more depressed than a young woman who lost most of her family in the Rwandan genocide.

I have come to accept that there are sufferings I will never understand. In the middle of the night I have driven a frantic mother and her vomiting daughter to the hospital emergency room. I thought of many possible reasons for the severe stomach upset. What I did not consider was the possibility that the day before the mother had gone to the food bank, as she always did at the end of the month, and had picked up a jar of peanut butter, as it was always one of the staples at the food bank. I did not consider that the peanut butter was rancid, that poverty means the ever present possibility that even the little food you have may be tainted.

I also know I will never understand torture. I have no sense what it means to be completely powerless because another human being has absolute power over your life. I cannot imagine what it means to live with the realization that another human being can not only kill your body but your spirit as well. Would it be possible to trust in human solidarity again?

My experience at Romero House has given me some personal insight into the reality of the "difference" that the postmodern culture claims. Human beings have very different weaknesses, vulnerabilities, sufferings. It forces one to rethink the basis for human relationships.

The Justice of God and the Power of Human Beings

I have been reflecting on how Henri Nouwen's search for God led him to articulate a correlation between the experience of human weakness with the experience of God's mercy and how this has been very liberating given the dominant values of modernity. In closing, I would like to present the complementary possibility of finding God in the summons to exercise human power.

This possibility has been expressed philosophically in a compelling way by the French thinker Emmanuel Levinas. His insights coincide with much of my daily experience at Romero House, leading me to the following expression of my reflections:

> There is a knock at the door. A face appears and hesitates.
> And then says, "Please help me."
>> Then you are faced. You are addressed. You are
>> summoned.
> The face is that of someone different from yourself.
> He looks you in the eyes. You want to turn away.
> This is the stranger. You have nothing in common with
>> him.
>> You could close him off and out but you do not. . . .
> Who is he?
> You barely know who you are. You invite him in. You
>> begin to talk.
> "You must help me," he says, again.
>> YOU. There is no one else. This YOU must do.
> You begin to discover who you are as you respond to this
>> "different one."
> This other.
> You know how difficult it will be to get his wife and
>>> children to this country. You know the system, how it
>>> is designed not to work,
>> how it stalls and files lives away. You weaken.
> Perhaps he senses this. "You must be strong for us."
> And you do become strong.
>> You are summoned and commanded to be strong.
>> You cannot afford to be weak. There is a price to be
>>> paid for weakness . . .
> at times such as this.
> They summon up your strength; you summon up their
>> strength.
> We can count on each other.
> We will become a guarantee for each other,
> because life cannot be taken for granted.
> Your life becomes significant, weighty, consequential.

At the heart of the question of the basis for human relationships is the reality of our experience of power. For many people in the world today, power is experienced as a coercive, dominating, and controlling reality. It is the kind of power that people of faith have long rejected. Henri Nouwen rejected the ways in which knowledge can be used as a way to dominate and control and discriminate against others. However, the cry of so many disinherited and uprooted people throughout the world summons us to consider another type of power, a more creative form of power, a power to give life, to bring about justice, to redeem the world.

Everything depends on whether we see power as a thing that some have and others do not. This notion of power inevitably leads to a win/lose situation that divides the world into the powerful and the weak. However, if we understand power as an energy that arises from the interactions among people, then power grows as the quality of those relationships becomes more authentic. The energy of this power also becomes more creative as we are related to the creative power of God—who desires that the world be healed and redeemed.

When human beings begin to act with strength and power they will begin to experience that their actions have consequences, for the better and for the worse. It is within this experience that they can imagine a just God who treats us as responsible human beings, who weighs our actions and the consequences of them. This is an inherently dignifying realization. To imagine the justice of God is to recognize that, even in our failures, we can realize the consequential nature of our lives.

In conclusion, I am left with further questions:

If there is a correlation between our human experience and our image of God, are we all summoned to accept both our weakness and strength so that our image of God becomes more whole?

Or is it possible that each person might have a particular vocation, a unique way of bearing witness to either the mercy or the justice of God?

Or is it possible that we may reflect an emphasis on the mercy or the justice of God at different stages of our lives?

Or is it possible that the circumstances of our lives, the culture and the time in which we live will summon us to bearing witness to either the mercy or the justice of God?

These are questions worthy of our thought.

Note

[1] I owe this insight to Rabbi Emil Fackenheim, a contemporary Jewish theologian and my teacher.

2

The Work of Henri Nouwen as a Meeting Place for Eastern and Western Christians

Rev. Gregory Jensen

The themes Henri Nouwen articulates in *The Wounded Healer*, as well as the other two works contained in ministry and spirituality *(Creative Ministry* and *Reaching Out)* elucidate for the reader an intriguing view of the kenotic spirituality so beloved by Eastern Christians. If the fathers of the church offer us a theological anthropology of kenosis, Nouwen's work, though not without its own limitations, complements their theological vision by offering his reader a view of kenosis that is more experiential, more psychological in orientation.

The juxtaposition of two different but complementary views of kenosis is extremely helpful, because "dogma presupposes experience, and only in the experience of vision and faith does dogma reach its fullness and come to life."[1] Though it is not without its challenges, seeing myself and my tradition through the eyes of another allows me to see things about myself—or my tradition—that I would not otherwise come to know. Nouwen, for example, has helped me see the connection between "sentimentality and violence," two seemingly "quite different forms of behavior . . . anchored in the human illusion of immortality."[2] I have come to appreciate how, both personally and communally, it is tempting to ratify the "illusion that our lives belong to us." When we give in to this temptation, or when we are in the grip of this illusion, "human relationships become subject to violence and destruction. . . . We treat other people . . . as property to be defended or conquered [but] not as gifts to be received."[3]

When I read Nouwen's work, I realize how prone I am not only to sentimentalizing the forms of Eastern Christianity, but to do so in a manner that causes me to undervalue, if not outright reject, the insights into the spiritual life to be found in Western Christian authors. So, for example, rather than asking whether or not what Nouwen has to say is true, I am put off by his language, which I find often dated and overly personal for my tastes.[4] Some of his phrasing, for example, strikes me as clumsy and bordering on the Gnostic—in fact, sometimes his language is so distracting I have trouble grasping his teaching or seeing the man in the words.

Yet, I cannot help wondering if his language is really any more dated and off-putting for me than the classical texts of Eastern Orthodox spirituality such as the *Philokalia*,[5] or St. John Climacus's *The Ladder of Divine Ascent*,[6] or *The Arena* by the nineteenth-century Russian Orthodox bishop St. Ignatius Brianchaninov[7] might be for a Roman Catholic or Protestant (and truthfully, not a few Orthodox Christians)? I think that it is quite possibly Nouwen's very use of what I see as dated language and examples that makes his work most important for the continuing dialogue between Christians of the Western and Eastern traditions.

Albeit in a Western and psychological key, Nouwen's vision of ministry is fundamentally compatible with the kenotic spirituality that is the heart of Eastern Orthodox pastoral ministry. This convergence is important for Orthodox Christians as we strive to be faithful to our own tradition in the midst of a cultural situation that is in many ways increasingly hostile to Christianity (whether Eastern or Western) and which rightly, if not wholly, can be described as a culture of death. Whether we are Eastern or Western Christians, it is a challenge to represent a tradition that grounds itself in history and symbol in a culture that sees little value in either.[8]

This convergence between Nouwen and Eastern Christianity is of value not only for the Orthodox. Turning for a moment to his conclusion to *Creative Ministry*, Nouwen was keenly aware that Roman Catholic and Protestant ministers might "have to look beyond the institutional church to grasp fully the implications" of the biblical call to a kenotic ministry. He points to the growing interest and "great reverence by thousands of young people" for "words such as 'concentration,' 'meditation,' and 'contemplation.'" But while there is a growing interest in prayer, spirituality, and mysticism, the Christian community and its ministers are often on the "periphery" and unable "to offer the rich mystical tradition as a source of rebirth of a faltering civilization."[9]

Orthodox Christians—individually and communally—are certainly no less prone to the crippling consequences of "self-consciousness, fear of rejection, and preoccupation with church quarrels" that prevent Christians "from being free to experience the transcendent Spirit of God, [who] can renew our hearts and minds as well."[10] Like our Catholic and Protestant sisters and brothers in Christ, we too suffer from "the many obvious mistakes, failures, and unintelligible experiments" that "blind us to the fact that . . . [there is in each human heart] a deep desire for new insight, new understanding, and most of all, new life."[11] If Nouwen is right, if Catholic and Protestant Christians have lost touch with the mystical tradition that the East has maintained, it must also be admitted (as the late Fr. Alexander Schmemann never tired of pointing out) that Orthodox Christians have lost touched with the practical and anthropological implications of that very same tradition.[12]

The late Pope John Paul II was correct in his assertion that the church must learn to breathe again with "both lungs," one Eastern, that is, mystical, ascetical, and liturgical, the other Western, that is, anthropological, rational, and analytical. Granted, such a sweeping formulation is not without its theological limitations, but if the sober and careful—to say nothing of prayerful and humble—study of church history teaches us anything, it is that the doctrinal disagreements and quarrels that plague Christians are not the source of our estrangement but are rather symptoms of our estrangement.[13] Before they are anything else, divisions between Christians reflect the division at the center of the human heart. To paraphrase the prophet Amos, we can only walk together if we agree to do so, but this agreement is only possible to the degree that we have allowed divine grace to heal the brokenness of our own hearts.

So with all of this in mind, I invite you to join me in examining the work of Henri Nouwen to see if we can bring about at least a small reconciliation of Western and Eastern Christianity.

Kenosis:
The Wounded Healer

In the spirituality of the Eastern Christian Church, trinitarian theology, Christology, and soteriology form a "seamless garment" (Jn 19:23); God the Son, the Second Person of the Holy Trinity, through an act of divine self-emptying (kenosis) takes on our flesh, our fallen condition with all of its corruption and limitations, and becomes our "great high priest" who can "sympathize with our weaknesses," since he "has been tempted in all things as we are, yet without sin" (Heb 4:14–15).[14]

This point cannot be stated too forcefully: God comes in Jesus Christ to know our life not from above, as our Creator, but from within, as our brother—as one of us. In Jesus Christ, God knows what it means to be human, not simply as God but as a member of the human community.

It is this kenosis of the Son, and the whole of the divine asceticism of the incarnation, that makes our deification, our growth not simply in individual virtue but in personal holiness, possible.[15] As Vladimir Lossky has written: "The descent of the divine person of Christ makes human persons capable of an ascent in the Holy Spirit." It is this "necessary . . . [and] voluntary humiliation," this "redemptive *kenosis* of the Son of God" that makes it possible for fallen humans to "accomplish their vocation of *theosis*, the deification of created beings by uncreated grace."[16] In other words, God the Son empties himself in the incarnation so that the human race can in him be glorified. To borrow an image from Hasidic spirituality, God in Christ becomes small so that in Christ humanity can become great—but our greatness in turn is only possible when, in obedience to the example of Christ, we become small on behalf of others.[17]

Our deification—precisely because it is personal and not natural (that is, because we are called to become gods by grace, not gods by nature)—requires not simply faith in Jesus Christ but also an ascetical effort (for example, prayers, fasting, and a commitment to the works of social justice, peace, and mercy).[18] Faith and asceticism are essential; however, they are insufficient in and of themselves. In the Eastern Christian view of the spiritual life we must live an active sacramental life that both nourishes and perfects our faith and asceticism.[19]

Paraphrasing St. Paul, Nouwen reminds us that only Jesus Christ "was obedient to God and creation unto death, even death on the Cross." He continues, "It was on the Cross that Jesus became the celebrant of life in the full sense because it was there that death was conquered and life regained in the total act of obedience."[20]

One of the first, if not the first, of Nouwen's works that I read was *The Wounded Healer.* Reading this as an insecure and often depressed undergraduate I came to have an appreciation for those aspects of my personality that burdened me with shame and doubt. The worst thing about shame, I think, is that it paralyzes us in exactly those areas where movement is most needed and where, if St. Paul is to be trusted, the strength and grace of Christ "is made perfect," in human—in my—weakness. But how few of us are able (again with St. Paul) to say, "I will boast all the more gladly of my weaknesses, so that the power of Christ may dwell in me" (2 Cor 12:9)?

It is in the image of the minister as a wounded healer that Nouwen and the Christian East most clearly converge.[21] Wisely, Nouwen resists the temptation to "split the archetype," as our Jungian friends might say; the minister, the priest, is not wounded *or* a healer, not broken *or* whole, not foolish *or* wise, but both together. No one with any experience of pastoral work—whether as a cleric or a layperson, whether publicly in the pulpit as a preacher or in the more private spheres of marriage or the monastery—can fail to resonate with Nouwen's description of the personal and professional loneliness that seems so much a part of the minister's life.[22]

In response to this sense of loneliness we are called by Christ not to "spiritual exhibitionism," but rather to "a constant willingness to see [our] own pain and suffering as rising from the depths of the universal condition." While Nouwen's discussion of how our personal pain and suffering can be transformed into a source of healing for both self and others through "concentration" and "community" is worthwhile in its own right, it is not germane to our current discussion of his work as a meeting place for Eastern and Western Christians.[23]

What is important for us is that Nouwen's observations are a fine psychological and pastoral application of the paschal mystery: "Christ is risen from the dead! By death, he has conquered death! And to those in the tombs he is bestowing life!" A Christian is able to be a wounded healer not simply for human reasons of psychology or sociology, but for reasons of Christology. Christ is himself the icon of the wounded healer, of that man of sorrows who bore our wounds and by whose stripes we are healed (see Is 53).[24]

Diakonia:
The Service of Mercy and Forgiveness

Nouwen's observation about the professional challenges of ministry are just as applicable to the personal lives of any who wish, with St. Ignatius of Antioch, not to "merely be called a Christian, but really found to be one" ("The Letter to the Romans," no. 3). Nouwen writes: "The painful irony is that ministers, who want to touch the center of people's lives, find themselves on the periphery, often pleading in vain for admission." Sometimes despite our best efforts as ministers and priests we "never seem to be where the action is, where the plans are made and the strategies discussed." Sadly, we "always seem to arrive at the wrong place at the wrong times with the wrong people, outside the walls of the city when the feast is over."[25] Ministers of the gospel—and by this I mean anyone who with any seriousness accepts the challenges of the gospel—experience not simply a psychological or social loneliness but in Christ are called to bear witness to the cosmic and ontological loneliness that is the human lot since the time of Adam's transgression:

> Adam sat opposite Paradise and, lamenting his nakedness, he wept, "Woe is me! By evil deceit was I persuaded and robbed, and exiled far from glory. Woe is me! Once naked in my simplicity, now I am in want. But, Paradise, no longer shall I enjoy your delight; no more shall I look upon the Lord my God and Maker, for I shall return to the earth whence I was taken. Merciful and compassionate Lord, I cry to you, 'Have mercy on me who am fallen.'"[26]

Like Adam shut outside the gates of Paradise loneliness is not the whole of our lot—there is also the promise, and, more important, the gift of mercy that comes to us by divine grace and the exercise of our own freedom: "Open the gates of repentance to me, O Giver of Life, for my spirit rises early in the morning to your holy temple, bearing a temple of the body all defiled. But as you are full of pity, cleanse it by your compassionate mercy."[27]

While not denying the importance of professional competence and even expertise in areas such as "teaching, preaching, individual pastoral care, organizing and celebrating,"[28] Nouwen asks us to consider "what is there beyond professionalism" and whether or not "ministry [is] just another specialty in the helping professions?"[29] He answers his own questions by reminding us "ministry and spirituality never can be separated." Why? Because ministry is "a way of life, which is for others to see and understand so that liberation can become a possibility." He continues by observing that prayer "is not a preparation for work or an indispensable condition for effective ministry." Rather, prayer "is life; prayer and ministry . . . can never be divorced. . . . [If] they are, the minister becomes a fixer-upper . . . the priesthood nothing more than another way to soften the pains of daily life . . . [and our] professionalism a form of clerical manipulation."[30] The service that we offer then, while not divorced from an array of professional skills, is fundamentally of a different order than that which is found in the world.

As Christians, Georges Florovsky notes, we are "not just moved by . . . other people's suffering." Viewed theologically, that is christocentrically, human "misery is the continued agony of Christ, suffering still in the person of his members." It is the presence of "the humiliated" yet "glorified" Christ to which the Christian church is called to respond. And we are called to respond not with "elaborate schemes for an ideal society," much less as "an authoritarian institution" but "as a hospital for the sick" and a "spiritual home" for the "humble and meek."[31]

Unlike "the Enlightenment's infatuation with the individual," Christians have always understood that it is the church, the community of faith gathered in the name of Jesus Christ by the power of the Holy Spirit to the glory of God the Father, that "is the most significant ethical unit." In the final analysis, "All Christian ethics are social ethics because all our ethics presuppose a social, communal, political starting point–the church." The central ethical challenge facing Christians today is the same ethical challenge that the Christian community has always faced: how is it that through the church's "teaching, support, sacrifice, [and] worship" we are able to transform, by God's grace and our own efforts, "utterly ordinary people" into women and men of "extraordinary, even heroic" Christian virtue? How, in other words, can our communities sustain lives of Christian virtue so that we can "be better people than we could have been if left to our own devices?"[32]

With this in mind, then, what existentially, practically, is this community life that we, as ministers of the gospel, invite people to join by the witness of our shared life?

Koinonia:
The Hospitable Community

Just prior to the recitation of the Creed in the Divine Liturgy there is a brief but important dialogue between the deacon and the congregation. Turning to the gathered assembly the deacon sings, "Let us love one another, so that with one mind we may confess . . . " and the people respond in song, "the Trinity, One in substance and undivided." This formal and dogmatically rich liturgical dialogue reminds us that our love for one another is an essential part of our profession of faith as Christians. It is this mutual love that is at the heart of the church's evangelical witness to the world.[33] Jesus, having come "and fulfilled the divine plan for us. . . [on] the night He was delivered up, or rather when He gave Himself up for the life of the world" (*Anaphora*, Liturgy of St. John Chrysostom), washed the feet of his disciples. Later that same evening Jesus identifies our loving service for one another as not only the content of Christian obedience and sacrifice but also the source of that joy which is so often lacking in Christians (see Jn 15:10–13).

As Orthodox liturgical theologian Fr. Alexander Schmemann points out, it "is only as joy that the Church was victorious in the world, and it lost the world when it lost that joy, and ceased to be a credible witness to it." He continues by lamenting that of "all the accusations against Christians, the most terrible one was uttered by Nietzsche when he said that Christians have no joy."[34]

The love that is the source of Christian joy is different from love as understood by the world because "in this world Christ was rejected."[35] Christians are called to have for one another and the world the same love that is at the heart of the Holy Trinity. Our love is to be a divine love, a love that is not our own, but that we can only receive because it comes to us as a gift–freely given and without cost (though not without responsibility)–"from above" (Jn 6:3).[36] While we "cannot force God into a relationship" with us and "no discipline, effort, or ascetical practice can make God come" and dwell within us, it is also true that there is no intimacy with God "without a continuous and arduous effort."[37] To love in a divine fashion requires from us the ascetical effort that is at the heart of kenosis. Why? Because it is only through asceticism that we can hope "to unmask our illusion of immortality, fully accept death as our human destiny, and reach beyond the limits of our existence to our God, out of whose intimacy we are born."[38]

Christian love is not simply an imitation of the love of the Father, Son, and Holy Spirit. In fact, if we try merely to imitate God we end up "asking for more than a human response" from ourselves and others and "make [others] into idols and ourselves into devils."[39] Christian love is not so much an imitation as it is a shared participation in the divine life itself. It is this participation in the communal life of the Holy Trinity that is the foundation, means, and goal of the Christian community's life. Just as iron when placed in fire takes on all the qualities of fire (heat, light, and movement) while remaining iron, so the human person, in Christ, takes on all the qualities of divinity (holiness, wisdom, and eternal life) while remaining human (contingency, circumscription, and changeable).

In *Reaching Out* Nouwen describes for us this kenotic communal life as being characterized by a spirit of "hospitality," or the "creation of a free space where the stranger can enter and become a friend instead of an enemy." At the heart of a healthy community is the offer of hospitality, of *koinonia*, of the space and freedom people need so that "change can take place." The hospitable community offers a sense of "freedom not disturbed by dividing lines." To be hospitable in a full sense for Nouwen requires from us both the ability and the willingness "to open a wide spectrum of options for choice and commitment," the fruit of which is "the liberation of fearful hearts" that are then able "to find their God and their way." The "paradox of hospitality is that it wants to create emptiness, not fearful emptiness, but friendly emptiness where strangers can enter and discover themselves as free."[40]

St. Tikhon, the nineteenth-century Russian Orthodox bishop of Alaska, reminds us that the forgiveness that Nouwen places at the heart of our shared life is "extremely difficult" to practice. Ironically, it is our very sinfulness that

both cries out for forgiveness and causes us to withhold forgiveness and reject divine mercy.

St. Tikhon is aware of this conflict, and so he offers us the advice given by
another great saint of the church of Russia, John of Kronstadt. St. John tells
us that if we wish truly to forgive our neighbor, if we truly wish to be able to
create the liberating empty space that is necessary for the salvation of others,
then we must first "picture the multitude" of our own sins. Again quoting St.
John, St. Tikhon tells his listeners to "imagine how tolerant" Christ is "of
them" even "while you are unwilling to forgive your neighbor even the small-
est offense." He then tells his listeners to moan and "bewail your foolishness,
and that obstruction within you will vanish like smoke," and you will begin
to "think more clearly, your heart will grow calm, and through this you will
learn goodness, as if not you yourself had heard the reproaches and indigni-
ties, but some other person entirely, or a shadow of yourself."[41] Key to the
saint's advice is the realization that we are not able to reach out to others
unless we first turn inward and acknowledge our own personal and communal sinfulness. It is only then that we can turn outward toward Christ in
repentance and toward our neighbor with mercy and forgiveness.

Sadly, the hospitality that Nouwen describes is often more an aspiration
then a reality because, as St. Tikhon said, "we do not like to acknowledge our
transgressions." While it "would seem natural and easy for a person to know
his own self, his own soul and his shortcomings . . . [this] is actually not so."
We find self-knowledge and repentance to be distasteful, and in their place
we often give ourselves over to the examination of "various things with curiosity."[42] Our desire to serve others and even to create a community where
others are welcome can reflect both our generosity of spirit as well as a darker
motivation: our refusal to engage in the painful but critical work of self-knowledge and self-reflection. The trade-off I make is this: I say to God, Let me
study both friends and strangers in order to create a place for them, for their
self-discovery and realization, but just do not ask me to confront my own
sinfulness in the process. Too often the generosity I show to others is merely
one part of a complicated process that allows me to remain indifferent to my
own sinfulness, to my own need not only for healing but also for repentance
and acceptance of forgiveness.

Nouwen, I think, would agree with St. Tikhon's observation that the sign
that we have refused to repent of our own sins and have instead fled to the
creation of a place for others is that, "when faced with solitude without extraneous preoccupation even for a short while, we immediately become bored
and attempt to seek amusement." Too easily the creation of a hospitable
community can become a dodge that allows us to indulge our love of observing "the sins of others." Unwilling as we are to consider "the beam in our
own eye," we are quick to "take notice of the mote in our brother's eye (Matt.
7:3)."[43] Or, as Nouwen himself observes:

Empty space tends to create fear. As long as our minds, hearts, and
hands are occupied we can avoid confronting painful questions, to which

we never give attention and which we do not want to surface. . . . From a distance, it appears we try and keep each other filled with words and actions, without tolerance for a moment of silence. . . . But by filling up every empty corner and occupying every empty time . . . hospitality becomes more oppressing than revealing.[44]

But this now raises a question: How has this happened? How have Christians, Eastern and Western, forgotten who we are?

Martyria:
The Witness of Nouwen's Work
and the Meeting of East and West

A critical reading of what I have written might—rightly, I think—argue that I have found the convergence between the work of Henri Nouwen and the spirituality of the Orthodox Church that I was seeking out, that I have assumed my conclusion in my premise. That criticism is a fair one—I have found the convergence, the *syndesmos* that I sought—but is this not the way of faith? Faith is not the object of understanding, but its precondition—faith is not that which we see, but that by way of which we see. I suggest that it is the absence of a willingness to see the convergence of East and West that is at least a significant part of the continued divisions we suffer.

Writing about the division within what he calls "the Churches of the Catholic tradition—Roman, Orthodox and non-Chalcedonian," Lawrence Cross asserts that these communities all "fundamentally conceive of God, the economy of salvation and God's operation in the world" in mutually compatible ways. Sadly, because "historical circumstances" have denied Christians in these various traditions "the opportunity to appreciate each other's faith," instead of mutual understanding we have among these churches "mutual ignorance, strangeness and positive misunderstanding [and in some cases not just] a lack of will for reunion [but] an implacable hatred."[45]

As an Orthodox Christian teaching in a Roman Catholic university, I know firsthand both sides of the existential division that Lawrence Cross, himself a deacon in the Melkite Greek Catholic Church in Australia, describes. In the service of keeping this essay positive, I will defer from even a brief recitation of the ways in which this mutual estrangement makes itself manifest. Suffice it to say that, together with Cross, I would say that both the East and the West "have suffered from the absence of the other." As a consequence of the estrangement both "sides limp, as it were. The East lacks something of Western pragmatism, while the West lacks something of [the East's] holistic response to the Christian mystery."[46]

The divisions between Roman Catholic, Eastern Orthodox, and Oriental Orthodox Christians are themselves much older, and in some ways more bitter and tragic, than the more recent division between Roman Catholics and Protestants. While I do not have any way to prove this, I cannot help but think that, had the East and the West not divided, the later schisms of the Reformation might have been avoided.[47]

While I certainly would not wish to minimize the theological differences between the East and the West, I agree with Meyendorff that the "real causes of the schism are to be found in human failure." Because the schism that we suffer is "caused by sins against love, only love can repair and restore the Christian world to visible unity." This means that our attempts at reconciliation cannot "be a matter for the conference table or at the level of the hierarchy alone." No, if "love is not to be abstract, it must arise among the people and be both broad and specific."[48]

The genius of Henri Nouwen is that he understood this imperative to transcend an abstract commitment to Christian love. Nouwen understood that "hostilities [for one another] can be converted into hospitality" and that this conversion, this *metanoia,* is essential because ours is a fallen world, "a world full of strangers, estranged from their own past, culture, and country, from their neighbors, friends, and family, from their deepest self and their God." As they have at all times and in all places, people are on "a painful search for a hospitable place where life can be lived without fear and where community can be found." As Orthodox, Roman Catholic, and Protestant Christians we especially have an obligation "to offer an open and hospitable space where strangers can cast off their strangeness and become our fellow human beings."[49]

Together with this very human desire to find one's place in the world, there is a new challenge. Whether we are Eastern or Western Christians, whether we call ourselves Orthodox, Catholic, or Protestant (and for that matter, whether we are Christian or not), all of us, as Cross says, "are now faced with intellectual, moral and spiritual challenges and issues in a wider world and at a level of complexity not even dreamed of one hundred years ago."[50] In any event, I am convinced that Eastern and Western Christians "must begin to think and to act, as much as possible, as those who already belong together, those whose role is nothing less than the new ordering of the cosmos."[51]

It is easy for Christians to forget, or worse, to become indifferent to, the fact that our divisions are for us and for the world "a long hard winter." The divisions among Christians are the fruit not simply of disagreements between traditions but reflect the fundamental lack of unity in each human heart. It is this division in the human heart that is the source "of great wickedness" and that causes each of us to "[spew] out savagery." But human sinfulness never has the last word. If we are willing to look inward at our own divided hearts, we will see there "Christ, and him crucified" (1 Cor 2:2), on a cross of our own making, offering us mercy and the promise that, if we accept the challenge to reconcile with him and each other, there will blossom "forth for us the first of seasons, the spring of the graces of God, in which we [can gather] together to make a thank-offering to God, a harvest of good works; or, to express it rather in the words of the psalm [73:17–18]: summer and spring, you have made them, remember this."[52]

So what might it look like for Christians—Eastern or Western, Protestant, Catholic, or Orthodox—to breathe with both lungs and take up the challenges inherent in reconciliation? While this question must be answered both doctrinally and ecclesiologically, it must also be answered existentially. To do this, allow me to give Nouwen the last word—a word that any Orthodox Christian could affirm.

Commenting on the hesychastic tradition, on the constant verbal and mental repetition of the Jesus Prayer ("Lord Jesus Christ, Son of God, have mercy on me, a sinner"), Nouwen writes about the wandering Christian who is the narrator of *The Way of the Pilgrim*:

> The prayer of the heart gives the pilgrim an immense joy and an unspeakable experience of God's presence. Wherever he goes and with whomever he speaks from here on, he cannot resist speaking about God who dwells in him. Although he never tries to convert people or change their behavior but always looks for silence and solitude, he nevertheless finds that the people he meets respond deeply to him and his words and rediscovers God in their own lives. Thus the pilgrim, who by his confession of sin and unceasing supplication for mercy recognizes his distance from God, finds himself traveling through the world in God's most intimate company and inviting other to share in it.[53]

When we live this way—as pilgrims—"When our hearts belong to God . . . when God has become the Ruler of our hearts, our basic alienation is overcome." It is only

> when God has become our shepherd, our refuge, our fortress, [that] we can reach out to God in the midst of a broken world and feel at home while still on the way. When God dwells in us, we can enter a wordless dialogue with God while still waiting on the day that we will be led into the house where a place has been prepared for us (Jn 14:2). Then we can wait while we have already arrived and ask while we have already received. Then, indeed, we can comfort each other.[54]

Amen. Amen. Amen. Let it be so.

Notes

[1] Georges Florovsky, "Methodology: Revelation, Philosophy, and Theology," in *Creation and Redemption*, trans. Richard Haugh (Belmont, MA: Norland, 1976), 35.

[2] Henri Nouwen, *Ministry and Spirituality* (New York: Continuum, 2002), 251–52. (This edition combines the texts of three books by Henri Nouwen: *Creative Ministry, The Wounded Healer*, and *Reaching Out.*)

[3] Ibid., 253.

[4] On this and related points, see Susan Muto, *A Practical Guide to Spiritual Reading* (Denville, NJ: Dimension Books, 1976).

[5] *St. Nikodimos of the Holy Mountain and St. Makarios of Corinth,* vol. 4 of *The Philokalia,* trans. and ed. G. E. H. Palmer, Philip Sherrard, and Kallistos Ware (London: Faber and Faber, 1979–99).

[6] St. John Climacus, *The Ladder of Divine Ascent,* trans. Colm Luibheid and Norman Russell (New York: Paulist Press, 1982).

[7] Ignatius Brianchaninov, *The Arena: An Offering to Contemporary Monasticism,* trans. Archimandrite Lazarus Moore (Jordanville, NY: Holy Trinity Monastery, 1982).

[8] Mary Douglas, *Natural Symbols: Explorations in Cosmology* (New York: Pantheon Books, 1973), 1. Douglas reflects on one of the "gravest problems of our day," the "lack of commitment to common symbols." She observes: "If this were all, there would be little to say. If it were a matter of our fragmentation into small groups, each committed to its proper symbolic forms, the case would be simple to understand. But more mysterious is a wide-spread, explicit rejection of rituals as such. Ritual has become a bad word signifying empty conformity. We are witnessing a revolt against formalism, even against form."

[9] Nouwen, *Ministry and Spirituality,* 95.

[10] Ibid., 96.

[11] Ibid.

[12] Alexander Schmemann, *For the Life of the World: Sacraments and Orthodoxy* (Crestwood, NY: St. Vladimir's Seminary Press, 1973), 117–34.

[13] Lawrence Cross, *Eastern Christianity: The Byzantine Tradition,* rev. ed., ed. Jack Figel (Fairfax, VA: Eastern Christian Publications, 1999), 14–26.

[14] In the brief analysis in this section it is important to bear in mind that–as I hope will become clear–a spirituality that focuses on self-emptying is not necessarily the same thing as a way of life based on a lack of healthy love of self or others. Rather, true kenosis, grounded as it is in both the incarnation and the life of the Holy Trinity, is a way of life that is dynamically open in gratitude to the world of persons, events, and things that make up the empirical form of our life. Further, we must not be deceived or confused by the seemingly negative language of self-emptying; true kenosis leads not only to the ennobling of the other, but also, as we see in the example of Christ, to the realization of our own vocation. And if this last point is true, and if, as I contend, kenosis is a central theme in Nouwen's work, then his work might very well serve to help Eastern and Western Christians find one another in Christ.

[15] Christos Yannaras, *The Freedom of Morality,* trans. Elizabeth Briere (Crestwood, NY: St. Vladimir's Seminary Press, 1984), 49–64.

[16] Vladimir Lossky, *In the Image and Likeness of God* (London: Mowbrays, 1974), 97–98. Lossky concludes by saying: "Thus the redeeming work of Christ–or rather, more generally speaking, the Incarnation of the Word–is seen to be directly related to the ultimate goal of creatures: to know union with God. If this union has been accomplished in the divine person of the Son, who is God become man, it is necessary that each human person, in turn, should become god by grace, or 'a partaker of the divine nature,' according to St. Peter's expression (II Peter 1:4)."

[17] Mordechai Rotenberg tells the following story about the social nature of making one's self small: "Through your actions and humbleness you should cause the Almighty also to contract himself and reveal himself to you in smallness. As in the case of the father who sees his son playing with nuts, and then due to his love he plays with him, although for the father this seems a childish act of 'smallness,' nonetheless out of love for his son and so that he should receive pleasure from his son, he contracts his mind and remains in 'smallness' so that the little one will be able to bear him, for if he would have been unable to bear his father, then the father would not

have derived pleasure from him" (Mordechai Rotenberg, *Dialog with Deviance: The Hasidic Ethic and the Theory of Social Contraction* [Philadelphia: Institute for the Study of Human Issues, 1983], 82).

[18] Adrian van Kaam, *Formation of the Human Heart* (New York: Crossroad, 1986).

[19] John Zizioulas, *Being as Communion: Studies in Personhood and the Church* (Crestwood, NY: St. Vladimir's Seminary Press, 1985), 78–82, 114–22.

[20] Nouwen, *Ministry and Spirituality*, 91.

[21] Cf. John Chryssavgis, *Soul Mending: The Art of Spiritual Direction* (Brookline, MA: Holy Cross Orthodox Press, 2000), 35. Chryssavgis writes: "This concept of woundedness or brokenness may, to some, sound negative or discouraging. Yet the idea of the priest as a 'wounded healer,' as a person who—before all else and beyond all else—is aware of his own personal weakness as being the very occasion of divine strength through him, deepens and broadens the notion of the authority of ministry as service (diakonia)."

[22] Nouwen, *Ministry and Spirituality*, 158–61.

[23] See ibid., 161–66. See also Chryssavgis, *Soul Mending*, 35: "The human experience of brokenness is universal. Moreover, from an Orthodox Christian ascetical perspective, the awareness of one's imperfection and brokenness can, paradoxically, become a source not only of personal blessing but also of ordained vocation."

[24] This is more than good pastoral psychology—it also reflects the apophatic character of the gospel and the Christian life. This apophaticism is perfected in the Eucharist. See, for example, the discussion of the theological import of the symbol in Schmemann, *For the Life of the World*, 135–51, where he discusses the Eucharist as the visible symbol of "the invisible as invisible."

[25] Nouwen, *Ministry and Spirituality*, 160.

[26] Vespers for Cheesefare Sunday, http://www.anastasis.org.uk/ChSunV.htm.

[27] Verses at Psalm 50 (51) after the resurrection Gospel on the Sundays of the Great Fast, http://www.anastasis.org.uk/ProdigalE.htm.

[28] Nouwen, *Ministry and Spirituality*, 93.

[29] Ibid., 20.

[30] Ibid., 21.

[31] Georges Florovsky, "The Social Problem in the Eastern Orthodox Church," in *Christianity and Culture*, vol. 2 in the *Collected Works of Georges Florovsky* (Belmont, MA: Nordland, 1974), 135–36.

[32] Stanley Hauerwas and William H. Willimon, *Resident Aliens: Life in the Christian Colony* (Nashville, TN: Abingdon Press, 1990), 81.

[33] Schmemann, *For the Life of the World*, 23–25.

[34] Ibid., 24.

[35] Ibid., 23.

[36] Zizioulas makes a distinction between the hypostasis of biological existence (life as constituted by the laws of biology) and the hypostasis of ecclesial existence (life as constituted eschatologically, that is, "from above," in and through the sacraments) that is most helpful here (*Being as Communion*, 49–65).

[37] Nouwen, *Ministry and Spirituality*, 256.

[38] Ibid.

[39] Ibid.

[40] Nouwen, *Ministry and Spirituality*, 221–22. Nouwen's more psychological language, while it can illumine for us the human face of Christian spirituality, can also inadvertently obscure the theological underpinnings of Christian spirituality. His discussion of hospitality is a good illustration of this difficulty. Focusing on the individual, as he tends to do, I think he misses the fact that his discussion of hospitality

and the community is more than a broadly empirical problem; it is in fact the fundamental problem of sin. As a sinner I view the world—and those in the world—with hostility and suspicion; as a sinner I see the other as my enemy.

41 St. Tikhon, on http://www.holy-trinity.org/spirituality/sttikhon-cheesefare.html.

42 Ibid.

43 Ibid.

44 Nouwen, *Ministry and Spirituality*, 222.

45 Cross, *Eastern Christianity*, 123.

46 Ibid., 129.

47 See John Meyendorff, *The Orthodox Church: Its Past and Its Role in the World Today* (Crestwood, NY: St. Vladimir's Seminary Press, 1996), 35. Meyendorff argues this point when he writes: "While the Eastern Church claimed—and still claims today—to be the only true Church of Christ, it saw its cultural and its geographical field of vision restricted: historically, it became identified with the Byzantine world. The Church of the West, as viewed by the Orthodox Church, lost the doctrinal and ecclesiological balance of primitive Christianity and the lack of balance was ultimately responsible for provoking the reaction of the sixteenth century, the Protestant Reformation."

48 Ibid., 130.

49 Nouwen, *Ministry and Spirituality*, 217.

50 Cross, *Eastern Christianity,* 126.

51 Ibid., 123.

52 Synodikon of Orthodox, http://www.anastasis.org.uk/synodikon.htm. In context, the winter season referred to is the iconoclastic period when Christians were forbidden to venerate, and in many cases even possess, icons. "Spring and summer" refer to the time when icons were restored to the church. In a similar fashion, the division among Christians is a period of great wickedness—if Christians are (as Jesus in the scriptures tells us) the "light of the world," the "salt of the earth," and the "yeast in the dough," how tragically we let down the world by our lack of unity.

53 Nouwen, *Ministry and Spirituality*, 270.

54 Ibid., 272–73.

3

Suffering and Healing

Henri Nouwen and Korean Protestants

KangHack Lee

One of the most significant trends in Korean Protestant churches in the last decade has been the rising interest in the Catholic spiritual writer Henri Nouwen. Among his forty-six books translated into Korean, thirty-two books have been published by companies established by Korean Protestants, including Tyrannus and EunSung. Many Protestant churches and campus mission groups are using Nouwen's books as supportive materials for their spiritual meetings.[1] Many pastors experience Nouwen's books as transformative and inspirational and refer to them often in their sermons. Many seminarians tell me that they have been motivated to study Christian spirituality by reading Nouwen's writings. Many of them wanted to meet and talk with Nouwen when he was alive and now want to visit a L'Arche community in order to experience his spirituality. Considering the strong evangelical or fundamentalistic view of dogma in Korean evangelical Protestant churches and their hesitation to cooperate and dialogue with the Roman Catholic Church, these current phenomena in Korean Protestant churches are significant.[2]

My concern in this essay is how Nouwen's writings appeal to Korean evangelical Protestants' suffering in their relationship with God, themselves, and others. I want to explore this question by using the perspectives of narrative psychology, cultural studies, theology, and spirituality. I believe the theme of suffering and healing in Nouwen's works is the most relevant issue for Korean evangelical Protestants. For them, to read his writings is to experience transformation in their hearts and in their relationships. Relationship is a central word for dealing with the issues of suffering and healing. Following Nouwen and one of his biographers, Deirdre LaNoue, I have divided this essay into three sections: the relationship with God, the relationship with self, and the relationship with others. Nouwen wrote about these three aspects of

22

spiritual life in *Reaching Out*, and LaNoue uses Nouwen's categorization on the three relationships in order to structure her book, *The Spiritual Legacy of Henri Nouwen*. Inner suffering of human beings comes primarily from broken relationships with God, self, and others, so healing comes from recovering these relationships. I explore what makes these relationships difficult for Korean evangelical Protestants and how Nouwen's writings transform them.

Relationship with God

The image of God as a strict father can hinder Korean evangelical Protestants' intimate relationship with God. The most common and influential image of God for Korean evangelical Protestants is Father, because the scripture literally introduces God as Father. In worship, God is frequently referred to as Father in words of praise. According to the object-relations theory, a person's God-images are intimately related to his or her relationship with significant people, usually parents.[3] When the church emphasizes God's image as Father, its members tend to understand God in terms of their images of their own fathers. Therefore, Koreans' relationship with God is greatly affected by their relationship with their father. Traditionally, under the influence of Confucianism, most Korean fathers as the heads of families have been very strict with their children. Korean psychologist Soo-Young Kwon observes that family dynamics in a traditional Korean Confucian culture thwarted the development of emotional relations between a father and his children.[4] Many Korean fathers do not say to their children, "I am proud of you," but frequently judge or scold them. They are not accustomed to expressing their feelings of affection for their children. Confucian proverbs show the image of a strict father: "A strict father produces a filial son" and "Save whip, spoil children." In Confucian culture children are expected to obey every word of their father. They usually feel anxiety and fear when approaching their father. Because the influence of Confucianism in the relationships of Koreans is so prevalent, this fearful relationship with father has not disappeared in contemporary Korean society, including in Christian communities.

The God image as a strict father, influenced by Confucianism, tends to hinder Korean Christians from having an intimate relationship with God. The relationship with the pastor seems to reflect the relationship with God. Koreans had been traditionally taught to consider a king and a teacher as their father, so they serve a teacher at school and a king in government as they serve their father at home. Likewise, a pastor at church has been consciously or unconsciously considered as a father. The typical leadership style in many Korean churches is patriarchal and hierarchical. It seems to resemble the image of God as a strict father or a powerful king. Many Korean pastors, mostly male, feel ashamed when they show their feelings in public because vulnerability means they are weak. In some denominations, senior pastors discourage young pastors from having close relationships with their lay members because they think it will lead to lack of pastoral authority. This hierarchically driven distance affects prayer, too. Contemplative prayer in silence, which draws on an intimate relationship with God, is very hard to practice for Korean Protestants. The image of God as a strict father can generate fear and anxiety for those who do not consider themselves to have obeyed all the words of God. Fear hinders them from having intimate relationships with God. As Nouwen indicates, "Fear creates suspicion, distance, defensiveness, and insecurity."[5]

Why do Korean evangelical Protestants like to read Nouwen's writings? In light of the issue above, Nouwen's writings help them to overcome the narrow theology in Korean evangelical churches that presents God as a demanding father. Nouwen emphasizes that the broken relationship with God is one of the main sources of human suffering, so healing should start from recovering the relationship with God. Even though he argues in *The Wounded Healer* that we are facing a generation without fathers and a shift from a guilt culture of disobedience to a shame culture of nonconformity,[6] we can still meet the strong shadow existence of the distant father in Korea. While Nouwen emphasizes God as a father for a generation without fathers in the North America, his father image helps Korean Christians to correct their image of God as a stern father. The most dominate image of God in Nouwen's writings is a generous father or an intimate friend who offers unconditional love. In *The Return of the Prodigal Son* Nouwen states that under God's unconditional love, his children have freedom to stay home, to leave home, or to return home without fear: "The Father is always looking for me with outstretched arms to receive me back and whisper again in my ear: 'You are my Beloved, on you my favor rests.'"[7] In *Jesus: A Gospel* Nouwen focuses on Jesus as a friend who invites us into his home and into his relationship with God: "By making his home in us he allows us to make our home in him. By entering into the intimacy of our innermost self he offers us the opportunity to enter into his own intimacy with God."[8] The image of God as a generous father and the image of Jesus as an intimate friend liberate Korean Protestants from the fear and anxiety dominating their relationship with God. It helps them rid themselves of paternalistic images that reduce prayer to incessant requests for the petitioners themselves and their acquaintances. Now, prayer as "a loving intimacy with God"[9] can be possible. The acceptance of Nouwen's writings by many Korean evangelical Protestants suggests a shift in the image of God from a strict father based on Confucianism to the generous and intimate father upon whom Nouwen focused.

As I mentioned above, pastors play an important role in Korean Protestants' relationship with God. They can help or hinder the relationship. The leadership style of pastors in Nouwen's writings is quite different from that of many influential Korean pastors. For Nouwen, pastors are "wounded healers" and "living reminders," not strict fathers. This understanding of the pastor's role has greatly affected Korean male pastors and laypeople. A pastor as a wounded healer can make his own wounds available as "a source of healing."[10] In order to be "a source of healing" and "a sign of hope," he should first discover and admit his weakness and his wounds. This is a challenging task for Korean pastors and laypeople because laypeople want pastors to be strong and regard pastors' transparent sharing of their wounds as evidence of failure. However, recently Korean Protestants have been persuaded by Nouwen's writings that the vulnerability of pastors can be shared and be a source of healing. A pastor is a living reminder who makes "connections between the human story and the divine story."[11] Nouwen states that "healing means revealing that our human wounds are most intimately connected with the suffering of God himself."[12] A pastor as "a living memory of Jesus Christ" has the task of revealing "the connections between our small sufferings and the great story of God's suffering in Jesus Christ." Pastors' stories of their woundedness and healing, especially in the Korean context, can lead to their relationship with people becoming more personal and help church members' relationship with God become more intimate.

Relationship with Self

The culturally constructed Korean self can prevent Koreans from viewing their truth. The Korean self is known as relational and collective. As to Korean collectivism, Sang-Chin Choi, a Korean psychologist, suggests a term, *we-ness*. The Korean "we," *woori*, is infused with affective, emotional forces, when compared to the Western "we." "Once the other persons are recognized within the boundary of we-ness, the participants tended to incur instant, and often ungrounded 'sameness' ideas about the persons, or to expect social interdependence and emotional support."[13] In this context a person's behavior greatly relies on what others might think of him or her: "'What would they think about me' is a matter of concern, not 'This is what I think.'"[14] Many Koreans tend to receive social recognition by compromising with the group to which they belong rather than arguing their own thoughts. The relational aspects of the Korean self seem to be greatly affected by Confucianism, which emphasizes order and harmony in the five relationships of society: authority and servant, father and son, husband and wife, elder and younger, and friends. S. Steve Kang's observation of second-generation Korean Americans' relationship with their parents suggests how deeply rooted the influence of Confucianism is for Koreans. He reports that filial piety and respect for elders, which are two of the central Confucian virtues, are internalized as obligations even in many second-generation Korean Americans and frequently cause conflicts in family when the children do not live up to the expectations of parents.[15] In order to avoid having a bad reputation in the community, one is expected to observe every detail of the Confucian virtues in the five relationships.[16] Korean men tend to focus on their fame and reputation in society. They are interested in being respected or publicly accepted by age, position, or achievements. If they are not, they feel helplessness and anger.

   Low self-esteem is another face of the culturally influenced Korean self. According to psychological research, Koreans are likely to endorse negative statements about themselves.[17] Korean parents also are less likely to report that their children have fulfilled their hopes. One of the critical reasons for low self-esteem is rooted in the Confucian virtues. Korean women especially have suffered from low self-esteem reinforced by the Confucian virtues, for example, *Hyun Mo Yang Cho* (Ideal) and *Nam Jon Yu Bi* (Virtue).[18] *Hyun Mo Yang Cho* was the ideal woman image in her limited roles as a submissive wife and a sacrificial mother. The *Nam Jon Yu Bi* belief assumed a woman's inherent inferiority and incompetence and confined her to lifetime sacrificial service roles: as a daughter to her father, as a wife to her husband, and as a mother to her son. The long history of education and social practices of these Confucian virtues have influenced Korean women to have low self-esteem. Kelly H. Chong states that one of the major sources of psychic injury for Korean women is "the problem of emotional deprivation in marriage, especially the felt absence of conjugal love, intimacy, and spousal respect that over time seems to contribute to a decline in the sense of self-worth and self-esteem in many women."[19] Many Korean children also have experienced low self-esteem due to the prejudiced and disrespectful Confucian thoughts about children.[20]
   Adding to the negative aspects of the culturally influenced Korean self, the theological emphasis on human beings as sinners in Korean evangelical churches leads many Korean Christians to pay attention only to their faults and imperfections. One of Calvin's dogmas, the total depravity of human beings, has deeply pervaded sermons and Bible studies in Korean Presbyterian churches, the largest denomination in Korean Christianity. For most Koreans, to sin or to disobey in spiritual life reminds them of trespassing Confucian virtues. Many Korean women who come to church as a break from domestic struggles are taught that God is not pleased with them if they do not obey their husbands because obeying is God's will.[21] The overemphasis on the responsibility to respond well to social expectations in the culturally constructed Korean self and the low self-esteem evoked by Confucianism and the Christian fundamentalist theology are representative examples of the destructive self-image many Koreans have of themselves.
   For Koreans who suffer from the negative aspects of the culturally constructed self and low self-esteem, Nouwen's understanding of the human being as God's beloved is transformative. Nouwen believed that human beings are the beloved sons and daughters of God: "The spiritual life requires a constant claiming of our true identity. Our true identity is that we are God's children, the beloved sons and daughters of our heavenly Father."[22] "You are my son, the beloved" (Mk 1:10) was the declaration of Jesus' true identity. Jesus revealed that we, broken human beings, are invited to the same identity with which Jesus lived. We do not have to prove this, just as Jesus did not have to prove himself in the desert. One's relationship with self has to be based on the unconditional love of God, not on the fulfillment of the expectations of others. The spiritual life, for Nouwen, is a journey from the false

self to the true self, that is to say, from "the social compulsions" resulting in anger and greed to the freedom of the beloved through the transforming grace of solitude.[23]

Regarding the journey to the true self, Nouwen's transparency in his writings is instrumental in inviting Korean Protestants into his life stories and helping them to reflect on their own life stories. His life stories, which show his honesty, remove the barriers that prevent Korean readers from opening their hearts and accepting their realities. His narratives shine on the shadowed areas of the readers' heart that they have forgotten or do not want to explore. Therefore, reading his narratives is like a session of narrative therapy.[24] According to Michael White, an Australian narrative psychologist, the dominant problem-saturated story of a person's life and relationships can be transformed into a new story with a new meaning and new possibility through externalizing the old story, separating from the story, identifying unique outcomes, and rewriting an alternative story using those unique outcomes.[25] For Korean readers, Nouwen's transparency can help them to externalize their weak and painful life stories and separate them from their false selves. Nouwen's assertion of their true identity as God's beloved children can assist them in identifying their true identity in their experiences and in rewriting their life stories from the perspective of being God's beloved child.

Relationship with Others

Even though Koreans seem to exhibit strong emotional support and intimacy with people inside of *woori*, the "we" group, they are divided by various causes, political, economical, and regional. Behind these divisions lie historical tragedies such as thirty-six years of Japanese colonialism, the Korean War, and the more than thirty years of military dictatorship. *Han* is the Korean term that designates a deep feeling of suffering generated by undeserved persecution and oppression: "*Han* is a sense of unresolved resentment against injustice suffered, a sense of helplessness . . . a feeling of total abandonment, a feeling of acute pain of sorrow in one's guts and bowels . . . and an obstinate urge to take 'revenge' and to right the wrong all these constitute."[26] Korean comfort women who were trafficked and forced to serve as sex slaves for Japanese armies in the era of Japanese colonization have lived with *han*.[27] There are around twenty million separated families who are bearing *han* and have been yearning to reunite with other family members who live on the other side of the demilitarized zone (DMZ) since the Korean War (1950–53). Furthermore, many people lost parents or children in the movement for democracy under the period of military dictatorship and live with *han*. There are also numerous people who individually received undeserved treatment in society for various reasons and bear *han*. *Hanpuri*–the healing of *han*–is one of the crucial issues with which Korean Christian ministers or practitioners in other religions deal.[28] For Koreans, *hanpuri* is crucial to

recovering relationship with others. In the era of globalization and capital-
ism, contemporary Koreans, as people in other countries under similar situations, suffer alienation and yearn for intimate relationships with others. *Han*,
accumulated from tragedies in history, and the alienation and competition
that have resulted from industrialization and globalization, have made it difficult for Koreans to experience deep relationships with others.

Meanwhile, Korean Protestant churches, which have been growing quickly
and have large memberships and buildings, do not satisfy their members'
thirst for in-depth relationships. In a Gallup survey, 87.9 percent of the re-
spondents blamed church splits for this dissatisfaction; 84.7 percent the fights
among members over the church budget and finances; 79.6 percent the low
quality of the pastors; and, 79.6 percent the church's pursuit of expansion
instead of the search for truth.[29] Recently Korean evangelical Protestant
churches have been blamed for their overemphasis on evangelization, understood as the quantitative growth of membership, and for their disregard
for the poor and the marginalized in society. Several "mega-churches" in
Korea, mostly evangelical, have been criticized for their similarities with *jaebeol*
(Korean conglomerates) in their success-oriented vision and their competitive style of evangelization and management.

Nouwen's writings respond to the questions of those who have criticized
the self-centeredness of the programs practiced in many Korean evangelical
churches and who want to improve the relationship with others in churches
and in society. Nouwen's thoughts on compassion and social justice are very
helpful to Korean Protestants. Nouwen believed that to love others is based
on God's love: "Laying our hearts totally open to God leads to a love of
ourselves that enables us to give whole-hearted love to our fellow human
beings."[30] The relationship with God is strongly tied to the relationship with
others: "Intimacy with God and solidarity with all people are two aspects of
dwelling in the present moment that can never be separated."[31] According to
Nouwen, God's love is a compassionate love. A Christian is called to the
compassionate life to reveal "the gentle presence of a compassionate God in
the midst of our broken world."[32] Compassion is a call to suffer with and not
to be competitive: "Compassion—which means, literally, 'to suffer with'—is
the way to the truth that we are most ourselves, not when we differ from
others, but when we are the same."[33] The spiritual core of compassion is
"solidarity through real participation in human agonies and ecstasies."[34] Therefore, compassion organically develops into the movement for social justice.
Through his life narratives Nouwen showed how compassion led him away
from the prestigious campus of Harvard University with its highly competitive atmosphere to the Daybreak community of L'Arche to live with people
with mental disabilities.[35] Furthermore, he showed how compassion made
him deeply concerned for the suffering of people caused by the injustice in
Latin America[36] and by the war in Vietnam.[37] Nouwen balanced contemplation and action. For him, prayer and social justice were intimately related.

Many Korean Protestants who are deeply concerned about solving the conflicts between church members who emphasize evangelization and others who

focus on social justice as the church's primary mission have been touched and inspired by Nouwen's life and writings on compassion. Compassionate Christians can deliver new hope to the broken society of Korea. Compassion can heal the *han* of many Koreans who have undeservedly suffered from the structuralized evil power in society, because confrontation, if it is humble and includes self-confrontation, can be an authentic expression of compassion.[38] Compassion can also help Koreans to rebuild regional and political relationships between North and South Koreans and between GyungsangDo, in the southeast area, and JeollaDo Koreans, in the southwest area. In order to help Korean Protestants to understand how intimately connected social justice and prayer are, it is to be hoped that Nouwen's other books on social justice, such as *¡Gracias! A Latin American Journal* and *The Road to Peace: Writings on Peace and Justice,* can be translated soon and added to the list of Nouwen's forty-six books available in Korean.

Conclusion

I have paid attention to some aspects of the sufferings of Koreans and Korean evangelical Protestants and have explored how Nouwen's writings can help them to overcome those sufferings in terms of three relationships: the Korean relationship with God, with self, and with others. First, many Korean Christians have suffered from the image of God as a strict father because the image reminds them of their own father, who has been influenced by the Confucian norms of human relations. The image of God as a generous father or an intimate friend shown in Nouwen's writings can liberate Korean Protestants from the fear that has hindered them from having an intimate relationship with God. Second, the negative aspects of the socioculturally influenced Korean self, one's over-dependence on others' evaluations, and low self-esteem, reinforced by Confucianism and the fundamentalist Christian theology, have thwarted many Korean evangelical Protestants from viewing their truth. Nouwen's emphasis on the truth of the human being as God's beloved has encouraged Korean Protestants to accept and love themselves as they are. Third, and finally, Koreans' *han,* caused by historical tragedies, as well as alienation and competition resulting from industrialization and globalization, have made it difficult for Koreans to have an intimate relationship with others. However, Nouwen's thoughts on compassion, based on the love of God, have inspired many Korean Protestants to find the courage to embrace other people and to confront the destructive powers in their society.

Notes

[1] For some examples, Saegil Church has a small group that meets to share insights from Nouwen's books. Inter-Varsity Press in Korea (IVP), established by a campus

mission group (IVF), has published many of Nouwen's books and uses them for materials in small groups of students. Achim (Morning) Institute for Spiritual Direction has also published several of Nouwen's books and has contributed to the introduction of Henri Nouwen into Korean Protestant churches.

[2] I use Timothy S. Lee's broad definition of Korean evangelicalism. He understands *evangelicalism* as "a species of Protestantism characterized by a literalist bent in biblical interpretation, a soteriology that values the individual over society, fervent advocacy of evangelism, and a piety that emphasizes conversion experience and personal relationship between God and believer" (Timothy S. Lee, "Beleaguered Success: Korean Evangelicalism in the Last Decade of the Twentieth Century," in *Christianity in Korea*, ed. Robert E. Buswell, Jr., and Timothy S. Lee [Honolulu: University of Hawaii Press, 2006], 331).

[3] Ana-Maria Rizzuto, "Object Relations and the Formation of the Image of God," *British Journal of Medical Psychology* 47 (1974): 83–99.

[4] Soo-Young Kwon, "God Representations: A Psychological and Cultural Model" (PhD dissertation, Graduate Theological Union, 2003), 24–25.

[5] Henri Nouwen, *Bread for the Journey: A Daybook of Wisdom and Faith* (San Francisco: HarperSanFrancisco, 1997), February 29.

[6] Henri Nouwen, *The Wounded Healer: Ministry in Contemporary Society* (Garden City, NY: Doubleday, 1972), 30–33.

[7] Henri Nouwen, *The Return of the Prodigal Son: A Story of Homecoming* (New York: Doubleday Image Books, 1992), 78.

[8] Henri Nouwen, *Jesus: A Gospel*, ed. Michael O'Laughlin (Maryknoll, NY: Orbis Books, 2001), 35.

[9] Henri Nouwen, *Reaching Out: The Three Movements of the Spiritual Life* (Garden City, NY: Image Books, 1986), 122.

[10] Nouwen, *The Wounded Healer*, 90–98.

[11] Henri Nouwen, *The Living Reminder: Service and Prayer in Memory of Jesus Christ* (New York: The Seabury Press, 1977), 24.

[12] Ibid., 24–25.

[13] Sang-Chin Choi and Soo-Hyang Choi, "We-ness: A Korean Discourse of Collectivism," in *Psychology of the Korean People: Collectivism and Individualism*, ed. Gene Yoon and Sang-Chin Choi (Seoul: Dong-A Publishing and Printing Co., 1994), 80.

[14] Tae-Rim Yoon, "The Koreans, Their Culture and Personality," in Yoon and Choi, *Psychology of the Korean People*, 21.

[15] S. Steve Kang, *Unveiling the Socioculturally Constructed Multivoiced Self: Themes of Self Construction and Self Integration in the Narratives of Second-Generation Korean American Young Adults* (Lanham, MD: University Press of America, 2002), 130–45.

[16] UiChol Kim, "Asian Collectivism: An Indigenous Perspective," in *Asian Perspectives on Psychology*, eds Henry S. R. Kao and Durgananc Sinha (Thousand Oaks, CA: Sage Publications, 1997), 147–63.

[17] Hazel Rose Markus, Patricia R. Mullally, and Shinobu Kitayama, "Selfways: Diversity in Modes of Cultural Participation," in *The Conceptual Self in Context*, ed. U. Neisser and D. Jopling (New York: Cambridge University Press, 1997), 37.

[18] El-Hannah Kim, "The Social Reality of Korean American Women: toward crashing with the Confucian ideology," in *Korean American Women: From Tradition to Modern Feminism*, ed. Young I. Song and Ailee Moon (Westport, CT: Praeger, 1998), 27–28.

[19] Kelly H. Chong, "In Search of Healing: Evangelical Conversion of Women in Contemporary South Korea," in Buswell and Lee, *Christianity in Korea*, 359.

[20] El-Hannah Kim, "The Social Reality of Korean American Women," 28.

[21] Chong, "In Search of Healing," 363.

[22] Henri Nouwen, *Here and Now: Living in the Spirit* (New York: Crossroad, 1994), 163.

[23] Henri Nouwen, *The Way of the Heart: Desert Spirituality and Contemporary Ministry* (New York: The Seabury Press, 1981), 23.

[24] Jay M. Uomoto, "Human Suffering, Psychotherapy and Soul Care: The Spirituality of Henri J. M. Nouwen at the Nexus," *Journal of Psychology and Christianity* 14, no. 4 (1995): 351.

[25] Michael White and David Epston, *Narrative Means to Therapeutic Ends* (New York: W. W. Norton, 1990).

[26] Hyun Kyung Chung, *Struggle to Be the Sun Again* (Maryknoll, NY: Orbis Books), 30.

[27] Yani Yoo, "Han-Laden Women: Korean 'Comfort Women' and Women in Judges 19–21," *Semeia* 78 (1997): 37–46.

[28] Soo-Young Kwon, "How Do Korean Rituals Heal?: Healing of Han as Cognitive Property," *The Journal of Pastoral Theology* 14, no. 1 (Spring 2004): 31–45; Chang-Sug Shin, ed., *Han eui hakjaejuk yunku* [The Academic Study of *Han*] (Seoul: Cheolhak koa hyunsil sa, 2004).

[29] Byong-suh Kim, "Modernization and Korean Protestant Religiosity," in Buswell and Lee, *Christianity in Korea,* 327, citing *Han'guk kaellŏp [Gallup Korea], Han'gugin ŭi chonggyo wa chonggyo ŭsik [Koreans' religions and religious consciousness]* (Seoul: Han'guk kaellŏp, 1998): 148.

[30] Henri Nouwen, *Letters to Marc about Jesus: Living a Spiritual Life in a Material World* (New York: HarperSanFrancisco, 1998), 75.

[31] Nouwen, *Here and Now,* 25.

[32] Henri Nouwen, Donald P. MacNeill, and Douglas A. Morrison. *Compassion: A Reflection on the Christian Life* (New York: Doubleday Image Books, 1982), 32.

[33] Nouwen, *Here and Now,* 117.

[34] Henri Nouwen, "Coping with the Seven O'Clock News: Compassion in a Callous World," *Sojourners* 6, no. 10 (September 1977): 16.

[35] Henri Nouwen, *The Road to Daybreak: A Spiritual Journey* (New York: Doubleday, 1988); *Adam: God's Beloved* (Maryknoll, NY: Orbis Books, 1997).

[36] Henri Nouwen, *¡Gracias! A Latin American Journal* (Maryknoll, NY: Orbis Books, 1983); *The Road to Peace: Writings on Peace and Justice* (Maryknoll, NY: Orbis Books, 1998); "The Suffering Christ," *The Other Side* 147 (December 1983): 16–19.

[37] Henri Nouwen, "Resisting the Forces of Death" and "'No' to the Vietnam War," in *Liberating Faith: Religious Voices for Justice, Peace, and Ecological Wisdom,* ed. Roger S. Gottlieb (New York: Rowman and Littlefield, 2003), 467–75.

[38] Henri Nouwen, "Not without Confrontation: The Second of a Series on Compassion," *Sojourners* 6, no. 10 (October 1977): 9.

4

What a Friend We Have in Henri

Reflections on the Influence of Henri Nouwen on Protestant Evangelicals

Paul Johansen

I miss Henri Nouwen. For some, his legacy consists of his many books, for others his role as a bridge between Catholics and Protestants, for others his distinguished career at Ivy League universities. For me, though, a single image captures him best: the energetic priest, hair in disarray, using his restless hands as if to fashion a homily out of thin air, celebrating an eloquent birthday Eucharist for an unresponsive child-man so damaged that many parents would have had him aborted. A better symbol of the Incarnation, I can hardly imagine.

—PHILLIP YANCEY,
"KNOWLEDGE OF THE JOURNEY"

What a friend we have in Jesus,
all our sins and griefs to bear.
What a privilege to carry
everything to God in prayer.
Oh, what peace we often forfeit,
Oh, what needless pain we bear,
all because we do not carry
everything to God in prayer. . . .
Can we find a friend so faithful,
who will all our sorrows share? . . .
Precious Savior, still our refuge;
take it to the Lord in prayer.

—GOSPEL HYMN
BY JOSEPH M. SCRIVEN (1820–86)
AND CHARLES C. CONVERSE (1832–1918)

If my capacity for giving and receiving love is to increase, I have to drink regularly from the fountain of the love of God. . . . Another source for me are the writings of Henri Nouwen. I have bought nearly everything he has written. I read his books over and over. He helps me drink from the fountain of God's love.

—BILL HYBELS,
THE PASTOR'S GUIDE TO SPIRITUAL FORMATION

Introduction

One of the most unlikely, undocumented, and underrated successes of Henri Nouwen's legacy is the profound influence he has had on many leaders, pastors, and members of the Protestant evangelical tradition in North America. In addition to establishing and describing the nature and extent of Nouwen's significant place in recent evangelical spiritual culture, this essay reflects on and offers explanations of why a spiritual thinker who worked from a vantage point so clearly outside that of Protestant evangelical spiritual culture was able to articulate a new and often surprising perspective on Christian spirituality, the Christian message and what it means to be Christian in ways which became convincing and profoundly influential within a movement that already carries a reputation for possessing its own distinctive take on the Christian faith. The essay strives to tell the story of this startlingly unusual but wonderful relationship, assuming throughout that it constitutes a powerful chapter in the ongoing saga of the work of the Spirit in Christian spiritual convergence and that it holds true promise for revealing further insight into Nouwen himself, evangelicals as a unique spiritual culture in whose hearts important themes and aspects of Nouwen's journey and ministry found a home, and the place of spirituality in the ongoing character of ecumenical development.

In 1991 Henri Nouwen was invited to be the convocation speaker at Tyndale Seminary (then Ontario Theological Seminary), the largest Protestant evangelical seminary in Canada. The invitation, extended by the faculty and supported by its dean, Dr. Ian Rennie, an evangelical Presbyterian scholar, pastor, and churchman held in high regard by evangelicals across the country, gave rise to a significant controversy and debate among the school's board and constituency, primarily due to that community's historic suspicion of the Roman Catholic tradition. In reprimanding the faculty for their action in a letter, the board argued: "By having Nouwen as an OTS graduation speaker we have provided a platform to one who is part of a system that is not in keeping with our mainstream evangelical posture of scripture alone—

grace alone—and salvation through Christ alone. Our conduct, be it unthink-
ing, has in any case been unwise."[1] Ian Rennie responded to this criticism by
pointing to the spiritual legitimacy of Nouwen's ministry:

> It seemed natural to invite Dr. Nouwen. . . . He has spoken at OTS
> chapel, and when he finished, the sense of God's presence was so real
> that no one wanted to move. . . . We believe that there are many changes
> going on throughout the church of Jesus Christ today, and while we
> seek to resist those movements and emphases that demean our Lord,
> we rejoice to find believers everywhere who share a common life in
> Jesus Christ.[2]

Nouwen did speak at the graduation that year, but the episode raised to
the surface the historic tension within the evangelical culture regarding Roman Catholicism, revealing both the residual existence of an anti-Catholic
predisposition and also pointing to the winds of change in the direction of
spiritual convergence. Though far from marking the beginning of his relationship with evangelicals, the Tyndale invitation and subsequent acceptance
were nevertheless a significant indication of the already pervasive and growing influence of Nouwen's work on key constituencies within the broader
evangelical culture.

The ongoing story of Christian spiritual convergence across traditions with
respect to evangelicals is particularly interesting in this present period of the
church's history because breakthroughs and roadblocks continue to exist simultaneously. Twenty-five years after the Tyndale episode, Wheaton College in Illinois, the flagship of the evangelical liberal arts education movement in America and the alma mater of evangelist Billy Graham, dismissed
a professor who converted to Roman Catholicism, even though he was willing to sign Wheaton's classic Protestant evangelical statement of faith.[3] The
combination of the terminated professor's Catholic confession and his evangelical willingness is in itself an indication that unique changes are already
afoot. These episodes reveal the environment in which the story of Henri
Nouwen's relationship with evangelicals takes place, and together they point
to the complexity of evangelicalism as a theological reality in a way that
makes reflecting on this friendship an important and fascinating study.

In terms of beliefs and practices, evangelicals are classically defined by
British evangelical historian David Bebbington's widely accepted fourfold
pattern. According to Bebbington, evangelicals are Protestant Christians who
bundle conversionism, biblicism, cross centeredness, and activism together
in their faith and practice. Timothy Larsen has recently developed an updated five-point working definition of evangelical commitment that fleshes
out the Bebbington quadrilateral and specifically adds the significance of the
Holy Spirit to our understanding of what constitutes the evangelical mix.[4]
Further, Larsen reminds us that an intimate personal friendship with Jesus,
which comes about through his atoning death on the cross and is practiced
through believing that "God hears their prayers, cares about their daily needs

and trials and desires to receive their love and worship and use them to fulfill divine purposes" is central to the evangelical way. Activism as evangelism is yet another central evangelical distinctive, according to Larsen.[5]

Beyond basic categories of belief and practice, evangelicalism is a trans-denominational, trans-organizational, transnational movement. As such, evangelicalism manifests itself as a culture of broad, overlapping networks and loosely interconnecting organizational realities that includes churches, denominations, schools, conferences, NGOs, mission agencies, publishing houses, political-action groups, evangelistic ministries, businesses, summer camps, and individuals. These are becoming increasingly difficult to catego-rize socially, politically, economically, and theologically, despite their his-toric connections. While unifying impulses exist in the form of key leaders, projects, movements, and organizations, evangelicals constitute a fluid real-ity that continues as a powerful and pervasive expression of Christian com-mitment, enterprise, and influence in the world today.

In terms of corporate personality, evangelicals are popularly believed by those outside the culture to be opinionated, confident, passionate, aggres-sive, visionary, entrepreneurial, theologically concerned yet pragmatic people who know how to raise funds, network, communicate, mobilize, organize, and market effectively and creatively. Evangelical spirituality is typically rooted in personal Bible reading, prayer, church attendance, evangelization, and charity work. World Vision, Inter Varsity Christian Fellowship, Zondervan Publishing, Willow Creek Community Church, Wheaton College, Evangeli-cal Fellowship of Canada, Focus on the Family, and Billy Graham are among a long list of well-known evangelical "brands." At first glance it is not at all obvious or predictable that a contemplative Catholic priest would take an influential place in the midst of such a culture.

Establishing Nouwen's Presence among Evangelicals

Surprisingly, the task of establishing Henri Nouwen's influential presence among evangelicals and within their spiritual culture is as easy as it is amaz-ing. Several years ago, during a time when she was looking for a compelling new project, a process that would eventually lead her to produce a wonder-ful and powerfully defining documentary on Nouwen, Canadian film pro-ducer Karen Pascal, an evangelical herself, recounted to me how she was asking people in her circles whom they were reading. Henri Nouwen's name kept coming up. While Pascal admitted she knew very little about Nouwen at the time, she has subsequently become deeply moved by his story and now sits on the Canadian board of the Henri Nouwen Society, along with other members who also have solid evangelical stories. Pascal's experience is an example of how a quick glance at evangelical culture reveals the wide-spread presence and influence of the famed Catholic spiritual writer.

At the level of popular piety and practice Nouwen's books are prevalent in evangelical bookstores, even competing in number in some instances with

C. S. Lewis, the recognized patron saint of North American evangelicals. A ministry colleague of mine, who reads widely within the evangelical sphere, commented recently that she has not read a book on Christian living and devotion in the last two years that did not reference Nouwen in some way. Wheaton College's website contains the curriculum vitae of June Arnold, health professions coordinator at the college. The personal section concludes with this line: "When she [June] feels the need for spiritual nurture, her favorite author is Henri Nouwen." Standard evangelical publications including *Christianity Today* magazine and *Leadership Journal* have included articles by Nouwen and about Nouwen.[6]

Various popular authors who write for evangelical audiences in the areas of Christian living, ministry advice, or spiritual growth frequently quote Nouwen, refer to his ministry, or credit him in their articles and books for being a key source of insight and inspiration. The list includes such significant evangelicals as Phillip Yancey (author and speaker), Richard Foster (author and professor of spirituality), Brian Stiller (president of Tyndale College and Seminary; former president of the Evangelical Fellowship of Canada), Bill Hybels (senior pastor, Willow Creek Community Church), and the late Mike Yaconelli (co-founder of Youth Specialties, the largest, most influential youth-worker resource business in North America). To say that Nouwen has made his mark on the spiritual map of evangelicals is an understatement; it is widely recognized that he has taken his place alongside the classic devotional giants of the tradition such as Oswald Chambers, A. W. Tozer, and C. S. Lewis as a key source of devotional reading and reflection. It is very common to find Nouwen listed on evangelicals' recommended reading lists and to hear that his books are among those read and reread by individuals in the tradition who are serious about deepening and widening their faith.

It is widely known that Nouwen's speaking schedule found him preaching and teaching at various conferences, denominational events, prayer breakfasts, retreats, renewal meetings, and church services that were either organized by or heavily subscribed to by evangelicals. Nouwen was once the guest preacher at California televangelist Robert Shuller's famed Crystal Cathedral in a service that was broadcast on television to thousands of viewers.[7] It is obvious, based on this impressive ministry record, that evangelicals became very zealous to hear this passionate witness, regardless of his background, because they saw his involvement as a serious source of spiritual growth for their constituencies. It is interesting to note that Nouwen's presence at these events is devoid of the type of controversy that arose in the Tyndale episode of 1991.

A further amazing chapter in the story of Nouwen's deepening presence and influence among evangelicals is the way his work now finds a home among the evangelical professional academic teaching ranks, namely, those given the task of training the movement's pastors, leaders, and scholars. Nouwen's material is conspicuously present on the reading lists and course syllabi of the spiritual formation and pastoral ministry courses of many key evangelical seminaries and graduate schools, including Tyndale (Toronto),

Wheaton (Chicago), Regent College (Vancouver), Fuller (Los Angeles), North Park (Chicago), Briercrest (Saskatchewan, Canada), and ACTS (British Columbia). Professors at evangelical schools are now publishing major works and offering courses devoted to aspects of Nouwen's spirituality.

Perhaps not surprisingly, Nouwen's presence among evangelical professors transcends course content and makes its way to faculty biographies, a sure sign that Nouwen is not simply being seen as an academic resource. Blayne Banting, an associate professor of pastoral ministry at Briercrest Seminary, has the following profoundly personal Nouwen quotation from *In the Name of Jesus* posted in his brief faculty biography on the Briercrest website:

> The question is not: How many people take you seriously? How much are we going to accomplish? Can you show some results? But: Are you in love with Jesus? . . . Do you know the incarnational God?

Similarly, Scottie May, a professor of Christian formation at Wheaton, in describing her professional and personal journey, writes in her biography on the Wheaton website, "My spiritual formation has been significantly shaped by the contemporary writings of Henri Nouwen, Brennan Manning, and Dallas Willard." That Nouwen is mentioned here is significant enough, but that he is mentioned alongside Dallas Willard, a major force in defining evangelical spirituality in recent years, is crucial for making our point and telling our story about the depth and breadth of the Nouwen's influence on the spiritual training of evangelical pastors, missionaries, and leaders.

There is also a compelling witness to the fact that Nouwen's work has made significant inroads into the minds and hearts of a whole class of influential younger professional leaders of evangelical ministries. In the Canadian context alone John McAuley of Muskoka Woods Sports Resort (youth ministry), Glen Soderholm of Moveable Feast Resources (worship renewal), Tim Huff of Youth Unlimited (innercity at-risk street work), and Steve Bell of Signpost Music (songwriter and performer) have all been profoundly influenced by Nouwen's spirit in ways that have affected their thinking, their spirituality, and their ministry.

Alongside popular piety and professional leadership, a final category completes the impressive description of Nouwen's presence on the spiritual radar of evangelicals; it may be the most powerful expression of all and is rooted in Henri Nouwen's unique capacity for friendship. Specifically, many evangelicals had the privilege of meeting and knowing Nouwen personally, and still others visited with him for retreat and spiritual direction at his home and base for ministry, the L'Arche Daybreak community in Richmond Hill, Ontario. Others encountered Nouwen earlier, while he was teaching at Yale and Harvard. The witness of each one is that these encounters rendered them deeply moved and unalterably affected. James Beverly captures the relational tendency in Nouwen's ministry by simply noting, "Before his death Nouwen developed closeness with many evangelicals."[8]

Three prominent North American evangelicals, each with widespread influence, who were fortunate enough to have the blessing of such interactions were Phillip Yancey, Brian Stiller, and Mike Yaconelli. Each one was radically impressed by what he learned, and each one subsequently reflected on, adopted, and promoted key aspects of Nouwen's unique counter-intuitive, prophetically powerful spirituality among his respective audiences. Yancey writes beautifully and unforgettably about Nouwen in his classic article "The Holy Inefficiency of Henri Nouwen," first published in *Christianity Today*, mainstream evangelicalism's leading publication. Various Nouwen references and insights are to be found throughout the body of his widely read work.

Stiller interviewed Nouwen at L'Arche Daybreak on two separate occasions for his nationally televised program *Cross Currents,* which for many years was popular among Canadian evangelicals. Stiller has also been quite willing to rely on Nouwen's work in his own writing and speaking. In one notable instance Stiller quoted Nouwen in an open letter that he wrote to three prominent Canadian evangelical politicians challenging them on their responsibilities as people of faith in the public sphere. What is doubly fascinating about this episode is that Stiller had heard Nouwen deliver the content upon which Stiller was drawing at a National Prayer Breakfast in the nation's capital, an event for which the evangelical leader and the Catholic priest had both been guest speakers.[9]

The story of youth-ministry guru Mike Yaconelli's profoundly personal encounter with Nouwen at a crisis point in his life in 1991 and the resulting radical conversion in faith, practice, and prayer which that encounter, and further exposure to Nouwen's writings evoked, is a deeply moving and provocative story well deserving of its own separate treatment. In many ways Yaconelli's experience is emblematic of everything this essay wishes to communicate. Yaconelli transported Nouwen's spirituality directly into his own ministry of publishing, leading, writing, and speaking. In doing so he began taking the "Nouwen way" to a network of thousands of youth workers and youth organizations across North America. *In the Name of Jesus* was Yaconelli's favorite book and the spirituality of ministry that Yaconelli encountered there caused him to attempt to shape evangelical youth workers into a movement of ministers who were as committed to the interior life of loving Jesus as they were to their exterior ministry. Yaconelli's books, interviews, and articles from 1991 onward constitute a wonderful example of a Nouwen disciple at work.[10]

Yancey, Stiller, and Yaconelli, three influential figures among North American evangelicals and their leaders, who took various opportunities to communicate widely and often about Nouwen's counter-intuitive, incarnational spirituality of God's love, are perhaps the best examples, though not the only ones, that the resistance to Nouwen and Catholicism among large constituencies within the evangelical movement, as emblemized by the Tyndale episode of 1991, was effectively over for vast numbers of evangelicals even before Nouwen's death in 1996. A few short years after that time Nouwen has become a major influence in shaping evangelical thinking about the spiritual life at various levels among average evangelical readers and key evangelical figures. It is no exaggeration to say that Nouwen is one of the key spiritual figures on the evangelical landscape today. Apparently, Ian Rennie was speaking profoundly and prophetically when he suggested that evangelicals could find in Nouwen one with whom they shared a common life in Jesus Christ.

Explaining Henri's Friendship with Evangelicals

Despite the surprise that it may invoke from people not familiar with the unique story of Nouwen's ministry, as well as among Nouwen insiders, who themselves may not realize the extent to which his influence carries on outside of more predictable constituencies, Nouwen's extensive presence and profound influence within the evangelical movement are not a difficult story to tell or a tough case to make. What is more challenging than the description of Nouwen's presence, however, is attempting to offer explanations for this relationship, which, all things considered historically, theologically, and culturally, represents an unlikely alliance. Nevertheless, it is precisely here where great promise lies for a further understanding of the significance of the spiritual-ecclesial development represented by Nouwen among the evangelicals

Friendship typically requires common interests or mutual attractions. The spiritual friendship between the Catholic priest and a great and growing number of Protestant evangelicals, who are coming to rely on Nouwen as a credible and even indispensable source for improving and deepening their own friendship with God, can, at this point in time, perhaps best be explained by referring to three commonalities or touch points that seem implicit in the relationship.

First, Nouwen's acceptance by evangelicals can be explained by asserting that in some profound sense Nouwen was evangelical. To make such a claim does not require an accompanying rejection of prior common interpretations of Nouwen as a contemplative; rather, such a designation contributes to a richer, more complete descriptive framing of Nouwen's unique identity, ministry, and way. Nor does this designation of Nouwen as evangelical detract in any way from the understanding of Nouwen as a Roman Catholic, implying somehow that the priest was becoming more of a Protestant. Rather, this observation is raised in the spirit of recognizing the presence of "evangelicals" in all three of the historic Christian traditions.

In adopting this description of evangelical as a legitimate contribution to understanding Nouwen, keeping Bebbington's classic definition in mind is crucial. Jesus in his life, death, and resurrection was the one in whom the priest's theology was rooted, the one on whom his biblical reflection and writing focused, and the one to whom Nouwen circled back with an overriding, passionate conviction and resolve over and over again, represented by key publications that are unapologetically christocentric and crucicentric.

Furthermore, this focus, for Nouwen, was far more than mere theological observation. On the contrary, it was a relational, prayerful, personal, and passionate reality that led Nouwen on a journey of constant life change, conversion, and deeper growth into Jesus as the revelation of God's love. Nouwen did not stop there, for this passionate relationship with Jesus, from his perspective, meant without a doubt that the believer as disciple is called to evangelize actively, to announce this good news of God's love. This is what Nouwen did wherever he went. This is how Nouwen wrote. This emphasis did not go unnoticed by his evangelical followers.

What seems to have happened is that as well-meaning evangelicals became familiar with Nouwen's work, they began to discern a comprehensive compatibility with him that enabled them to overcome their inherited reservations regarding his tradition of origin, which might have initially prevented them from becoming spiritual friends, and instead allowed them to appreciate and embrace what Nouwen was saying.

It is important to make the point that Nouwen was clearly developing his own sense of compatibility with evangelicals as his contacts with them and opportunities to speak and minister with them grew. On the wall of the Museum of Evangelism, located in the Billy Graham Center at Wheaton College, the following quotation by the great evangelist is inscribed on the wall:

> The human heart is the same the world over. Only Christ can meet the deepest needs of our world and our hearts. Christ alone can bring lasting peace—peace with God, peace among men and nations, and peace within our hearts.

Nouwen would have readily concurred and it is quite easy to detect his emphasis and hear his voice in this quotation. This kind of passionate, Christ-centered view of the gospel has the capacity to make friends in Christ.

A second possible explanation for the attraction of evangelicals to the Catholic Henri Nouwen has to do with his simplicity. This comprehensive characteristic in his writing has connected with evangelicals in three distinct ways, namely, devotional simplicity, thematic simplicity, and incarnational simplicity.

While, historically, the evangelical movement does include sophisticated traditions of theology, we are primarily dealing with a popular spirituality that has always been characterized by straightforward communication in service of a broad appeal that has been accompanied by devotional simplicity, clarity, and personal practicality. Nouwen's widely appreciated simplicity and clarity employed in the service of passionate personal reflection on essential gospel texts seem to have been perfectly crafted for reception by a tradition often characterized as "cutting its teeth" devotionally on such tools as three-point sermons, condensed versions of the gospel message, and short daily devotional readings. It is reasonable to conclude that Nouwen's simple style exceeded the expectations of style and substance of many who were raised within the simplicities of traditional evangelical devotional culture.

As a theological writer Nouwen focused his attention on exploring and explicating universal Christian themes, and this thematic simplicity provides a further way to speak of his evangelical success. In the tradition of C. S. Lewis's classic apologetic, *Mere Christianity*, an evangelical favorite that treats the heart of the Christian faith in a way completely devoid of the particularism and the sectarianism of Lewis's native Belfast, Nouwen seems to have produced "mere spirituality." Clearly, the lack of emphasis on Roman Catholic specificity in Nouwen's writing, with its quietness on such topics as Mary, transubstantiation, purgatory, and ecclesiastical structures, all topics that have historically provided barriers to a Protestant evangelical embrace of the Catholic tradition, is important for this story. Nouwen is now perceived by many evangelicals simply as a Christian just like them, one who is always trying to get to the heart of the matter in his faith.

While evangelicals do not owe Nouwen for their entire introduction to spirituality, it is true that Nouwen has provided a piece of their spiritual progress by making the spiritual life more available, visible, and tangible to a tradition that has been decidedly deficient in the area of historic spirituality. To state it in perhaps a more controversial way, Nouwen seems to have become the saint for evangelicals in this crucial area, in the very way that saints provide us with examples of embodied faithfulness through the practice of incarnational simplicity and clarity.

Phillip Yancey tells a story that exemplifies the impact of Nouwen's incarnational way among evangelicals:

> Once when I was dining with a group of writers, the conversation turned to letters we get from readers. Richard Foster and Eugene Peterson mentioned an intense young man who had sought spiritual direction from both of them. They had responded graciously, answering questions by mail and recommending books on spirituality. But Foster then learned that the same inquirer had also contacted Henri Nouwen. "You won't believe what Nouwen did," he said. "He invited this stranger to live with his community for a month so he could give him spiritual direction."[11]

As writers accustomed to protect their time and space for the sake of their writing, the group was amazed by Nouwen's practice of dropping the professional structures of the writer's life for a more personal approach.

Nouwen was at the core a spiritual practitioner first and a spiritual writer second. While others are writing about the spiritual life, examining it and explaining it, Nouwen was doing it for people to see, so that the writing itself is but the descriptive result of his real attempt to live such a life. By way of comparison, Richard Foster's classic on the spiritual disciplines, *The Celebration of Discipline*, may have done more than any other book to recover crucial lost resources for evangelical readers. This excellent book identifies the disciplines, describes them, and attempts to provide practical applications for their use, yet in the end it remains a kind of catalogue, which, although illustrated from time to time with Foster's personal experiences, fails to paint a convincing embodied portrayal of the writer's life.

By radical contrast, Nouwen's writing allows the reader to develop a clear picture of his struggle in the spiritual life because everything reads somehow like passionate autobiography; Nouwen teaches not by telling but by showing through a kind of incarnational writing that overcomes abstractions. For instance, journaling is a key practice being adopted by people who are committed to deepening their prayer and contemplation. While many resources teach how to journal, Nouwen wrote and published his journals, leaving a resource for people to access that embodies journaling as well as confession, community, prayer, spiritual direction, struggle, and the disciplines and the rhythm of worship. One cannot help but think that people from a tradition with limited exposure to practicing the contemplative way required this kind of embodied witness and responded positively when it was offered.

The final way to speak about Henri Nouwen's influence on evangelicals is by referring to the prophetic. While Nouwen was a priest and a pastor to so many, for evangelicals he was a prophet who was able to put his finger on the essential challenges confronting the evangelical psyche and spirit, both on the surface and deep within. This happened in two ways.

First, it seems that Nouwen worked within areas that were close to essential commitments and convictions within the evangelical tradition. This enabled him to take evangelicals in directions and to depths within those foundations that evangelicals were somehow not able to access on their own. For instance, while evangelicals have been tempted to shape and pass on the message of Jesus in ways that are appealing and attractive for mass consumption by tapping into Jesus as the source of personal fulfillment in this life and the next, in doing so they have risked not developing an understanding of Jesus for the deepest human realities. For Nouwen, Jesus' suffering and brokenness become the occasion for human beings in all their brokenness, sinfulness, inefficiency, and imperfection to embrace the struggling Savior in ways that speak to the great integrity of the gospel. Victorious images of success and successful people so close to the pattern of an evangelical culture nurtured in its American captivity are called into question by a message that presents the suffering love of Jesus as the model for our own suffering.

Likewise, while evangelicals are proud of their commitment to pray, many in the tradition are finding that they actually come to a place where they do not know how to pray. Nouwen addresses that failure, affirms the struggle, and points to a more ancient and authentic way. To those evangelicals weary of their addiction to bigness and busyness as the way of doing church, ministry, and fellowship, Nouwen offers the freedom of community and the possibility of living true friendship, modestly and truthfully. While evangelicals are spreading the news that "God loves you and has a wonderful plan for your life," many of both leadership and rank-and-file are realizing they have not experienced the love of God for themselves.

The following profoundly personal account of Henri's ministry, written in a personal email to me by Glen Soderholm, an evangelical, Presbyterian minister, is as illuminating as it is moving:

> Henri was invited to speak at a gathering of Presbyterian folk. . . . He stood up beside a flip chart and began to speak about identity. He spoke in a halting manner with a thick Dutch accent, but as he continued I sensed that his hesitation wasn't a speech pathology; rather, it seemed as if he was waiting for the Holy Spirit to download the right word to use. He would begin a sentence, hesitate, and then the word came—and what words they were! He spoke about the ways in which the world tries to form our identity out of what we have accomplished and by what others think about us. He would turn and draw simple circles on the flip chart to emphasize his points. As he spoke, I was so tuned in that I became oblivious to the other three hundred people gathered in the sanctuary; it was just me and Henri and the Holy Spirit. I recall earlier moments in my life when I was privy to a fresh encounter with the holy, but this was an epiphany of the first order. As he continued, he spoke of Jesus' own life as the life of the beloved Son of the Father. What he wanted us to know was that we too had been given this identity as the beloved children of God; it seemed to me that he believed this to be true more than anything else in the world. . . . I remember my eyes welling up over and over again as my spirit received this staggering gift, which had been hinted at through the years, but which now found its way to the core of who I was. It both shattered and restored me as the rhythms of grace flowed around.

Soderholm concluded his reflection:

> I was finishing seminary that semester, and this word was the best gift I could ever have received as a graduation present. It became the paradigm out of which my parish ministry would develop.

If Nouwen was prophetically effective in helping evangelicals to grow more vulnerable and mature in areas already close to their theological tradition, he also had a prophetic ability to tap into and critique the dominant evangelical ministry mindset. The book *In the Name of Jesus* has become a favorite of evangelicals and is now a mainstay in the culture of training evangelicals for leadership and ministry. In connecting the three temptations of Jesus to three classic contemporary ministry temptations, Nouwen brilliantly succeeds in critiquing the very heart and soul of evangelical ministry. There are more than a few pastors and leaders from the tradition who have come away deeply convinced by this little book, while at the same time possessing the distinct sense that it was written specifically and prophetically for their tradition more than any other. Nouwen's prophetic genius for evangelical ministry may actually rest in the fact that just as he identifies the ministry temptations to be relevant, and powerful, he also offers responses to these temptations that are not commonly offered as evangelical solutions.

Because Nouwen was so interested in exploring the spirituality of ministry he became an expert in understanding the motivations of ministers, himself included. The temptations he identified and spoke about were examples of Nouwen pulling off his own mask, and, in his struggle for authenticity, he manages to give others permission to pull off their masks too. Increasingly, it is occurring to many evangelicals that much of the evangelical mode of ministry requires masks to cover up our true selves for the sake of success. Nouwen's kind of radical authenticity simply does not come naturally to many trained in the evangelical way. Still, when the message is delivered prophetically, evangelicals have responded. Vernon Grounds, a patriarch of evangelical seminary training, commented recently that many students seem concerned about sensing the presence of God. Grounds says that when students complain about an "unsatisfying spiritual life, I point them to others, such as Henri Nouwen, who struggled with the same thing."

Finally, Nouwen's prophetic role for evangelicals is evident in the long list of practices and insights that were seemingly not accessible to evangelical Christians living and working out of a tradition often characterized by a kind of prideful self-sufficiency; the list is neither short nor insignificant. Nouwen's gifts, which have become prophetically indispensable to evangelicals, include journaling, contemplation, the disciplines of silence and solitude, monasticism, vocational journey, downward mobility, Jesus in the other, spiritual direction, sabbatical, radical honesty, self-reflection, fruitfulness versus success, community, hospitality, the gift of brokenness, and the centrality of the Eucharist.

Evaluating Henri's Friendship with Evangelicals

Henri Nouwen's desire was to share his journey with God with other people so that they could receive help for their own journeys. As startling as it may seem, a significant branch of his fruitfulness has been expanded and has somehow found a home in the warm, receptive hearts of evangelicals. The story of the spiritual friendship between Henri Nouwen and the evangelical movement is one of the most unlikely creative and powerful expressions of the work of the Spirit toward Christian convergence that we have witnessed in recent times. The story as understood to this point has already borne fruit for our ongoing understanding and evolving definition of Nouwen himself, the changing nature of evangelicals as an influential movement, and our emerging understanding of spiritual convergence.

In conclusion, our story first brings us to the place where, despite the potential for misunderstanding and even disagreement, we must add the description evangelical to our emerging and expanding composite understanding of Nouwen's theology, spirituality, and ministry. This is not so much a cultural or denominational designation but a general one that in emphasis and spirit connects Nouwen with many of the key evangelical instincts and practices.

Second, the adoption of Henri Nouwen as a friend, guide, and resource by evangelicals contributes profoundly to our understanding and appreciation of this evolving, living tradition. Evangelicals have acquired a reputation as aggressive, persuasive, argumentative, judgmental, self-sufficient, and dogmatic. The story that we have been witnessing here must cause us to alter this view at least slightly, as we recognize that in effusively embracing Nouwen's unique ministry, evangelicals are proving themselves to be more vulnerable, teachable, and grateful than they are typically given credit for. Undoubtedly, the continued cultivation of this posture on the part of evangelicals will continue to create new possibilities for convergence. Additionally, we might conclude that the continued combination of evangelical conviction and contemplative spirituality promises to be a tremendous force for good in the church and in the world.

Finally, our story invites us to make several observations on the current and possible future nature of ecumenicity and Christian convergence. While we may safely claim that no Protestant evangelical has embraced Nouwen because of technical theological doctrines or through dialoguing intensely and coming to formal, official equitable agreements on issues or barriers that previously they have not agreed with, evangelicals *have* embraced Nouwen's spirituality, his personal life, and his reflective writing ministry as a gift. This friendship suggests an emerging shape and style of ecumenical proximity that is informal, unofficial, organic, relationally based, and can be prophetically received without necessarily giving anything of equal value in return. It is driven powerfully by a deep desire to grow in spiritual depth and practice. Further, the story of Henri Nouwen and evangelicals is a profound example of the powerful priority of spirituality in ecumenical development over other traditional considerations.

Evangelicals root their faith in having a personal relationship with Jesus, but in recent times they have been depending and relying on their friend and brother, Catholic spiritual writer Henri Nouwen, to help them develop a new depth in this relationship, a depth apparently not available to them in their own tradition and their own resources. As a result, many evangelical pastors, leaders, professors, and laypeople can speak about what a friend they have in Henri. In light of this new relationship and given the nature of evangelical passion, it is quite likely that evangelicals will be among the most effective people for carrying Nouwen's legacy beyond this generation.

Notes

[1] In Timothy Larsen and John Vickery, *For Christ in Canada: A History of Tyndale Seminary: 1976–2001* (Toronto: Tyndale University College and Seminary, 2004), 59.

[2] Ian Rennie, quoted in ibid., 60.

[3] Daniel Golden, "A Test of Faith," *Wall Street Journal* (January 7, 2006), A1.

[4] Timothy Larsen, "Defining and Locating Evangelicalism," in *The Cambridge Companion to Evangelical Theology*, ed. Timothy Larsen and Daniel J. Treier (Cambridge: Cambridge University Press, 2007).

[5] Ibid.

[6] See, e.g., Henri Nouwen, "Moving from Solitude to Community to Ministry," *Leadership Journal* (Summer 1995).

[7] Karen Pascal, *Journey of the Heart: The Life of Henri Nouwen,* one-hour documentary film (Ontario: Windborne Productions, 2003).

[8] James Beverly, "Catholics and Evangelicals," *FaithToday* (September/October 2002).

[9] Brian Stiller, "Open Letter to Stockwell Day, Frank Klees, Preston Manning." Available on the BrianStiller.com website.

[10] See Michael J. Cusick, "A Conversation with Mike Yaconelli," *Mars Hill Review,* no. 2, 67–87; see also Michael Yaconelli, *Dangerous Wonder* (Colorado Springs: NavPress, 1998).

[11] Phillip Yancey, "Knowledge of the Journey," in *Nouwen Then: Reflections on Henri,* ed. Christopher De Vinck (Grand Rapids, MI: Zondervan Publishing House, 1999), 23.

5

Dancing the Grace of God

African American Liturgical Dance in Light of Nouwen's *Turn My Mourning into Dancing*

JoAnn Ford Watson and Emily Pardue

An African American liturgical dance presentation under the direction of Dr. Emily Pardue and the JAIA Sisters Ministries of Detroit, Michigan, with dancers Jazmin Crayton and the Rev. Georgia Thompson, followed the presentation of the following paper. Opportunities to practice the exercises of liturgical dance were also offered participants in this workshop session.

Nouwen loved the visual arts. He was drawn to the arts in painting, theater, drama, circus, clowning, and dance. In the foreword to Nouwen's *Clowning in Rome*, Sue Mosteller writes that "as a child Henri was fascinated by the circus and the fascination never left him. For many years and especially during the last year of his life, he was preparing to write a novel based on the circus related to the spiritual life. It was never written because of his untimely death."[1] In *Turn My Mourning into Dancing*, Nouwen uses the visual arts, circus trapeze acts, and dancing to describe movements of the spiritual life.[2] He uses dancing to describe five movements through the hard times of the spiritual life: (1) from our little selves to a larger world; (2) from holding tight to letting go; (3) from fatalism to hope; (4) from manipulation to love; and (5) from a fearful death to a joyous life.

Nouwen uses dance to illustrate the movement in the spiritual life from suffering and mourning to hope:

47

Mourning makes us poor; it powerfully reminds us of our smallness. But it is precisely here, in that pain or poverty or awkwardness, that the Dancer invites us to rise up and take the first steps. For in our suffering, not apart from it, Jesus enters our sadness, takes us by the hand, pulls us gently up to stand and invites us to dance. We find the way to pray, as the psalmist did, "You have turned my mourning into dancing" (Ps. 30:11), because at the center of our grief we find the grace of God.[3]

Nouwen writes that "ultimately mourning means facing what wounds us in the presence of One who can heal."[4] Individually and collectively, African Americans have traditionally had to face suffering, mourning, and wounds. They can relate to Nouwen's five movements through hard times. Nouwen voices what African Americans have known all along: there is a wound that can only be dealt with through movement. For African Americans and for Nouwen, God is the Dancer who invites us to live through the dance.[5]

Liturgical dance as expressed in the African American tradition exemplifies the spirituality of Nouwen. Paul Rhimes writes, "The seed which trembles to be born, the first breath of life, the groan, the struggle for existence, the reaching beyond the everyday into the realm of the soul, the glimpsing of the Great Divine, the ecstasy and sorrow which is life and then the path back to earth—this is dance."[6] The African American community has learned to reach beyond the everyday into glimpses of the Divine, watching for the Liberator of a people, of a soul. Nouwen's idea of God as the Dancer who invites us to dance is complementary; through meeting the Dancer and dancing we are liberated from all that holds us bound.

The worship of the black church finds its origin in the ancient African cultural and religious traditions. African peoples did not see a separation between the sacred and the secular. Worship put people in touch with feelings, community, and deity. The arts were part of the worship and enabled the connection between the secular and sacred.[7] George Ofori-Atta-Thomas declares:

> The African peoples who were transported to the New World brought with them, their religion and worship heritage. . . . Their system of belief included: God consciousness, the affirmation of a religious universe, prayer, corporate kinship in the vertical dimensions (as the extended family-community relationship), spirit possession, immortality and the unity of reality, i.e., no separation between the sacred and the secular. Therefore worship enhanced the connectedness of the whole being as one in touch with feelings, in the harmony of experience, in all existence. . . . European American Christianity significantly affected the religious folk practices of Africans in America.[8]

Dancing was a part of the social fabric and worship of the African religious heritage that was retained and adapted by African Americans. Steve Evans writes, "Dancing in Africa is an essential part of life. Every important event is observed by dancing, including rites of passage, circumcision, prepa-ration for war, victory, celebrations of life and death, harvesting, hunting, courtship, and ancestral worship and ceremony."[9] Evans quotes Andre Massaki, who explains the role of dance in the African emotional and com-munal life, "Movement in the body to the African is very important. . . . Every emotion of the African can be conveyed by the use of the body. . . . Participation in dance represents an individual's acceptance into the group."[10]

In discussing the role of dancing in African societies, Ofori-Atta-Thomas writes:

> In sharing-dancing, every situation of experience is illustrated and so-cialized in the meanings and moods appropriate to that moment in experience: dancing has been the universal rhythmic accompaniment to singing. Africans danced for joy. They danced for grief. They danced for love. They danced for hate. They danced in time of trouble. They danced to bring prosperity. They danced for the joy of dancing. They danced to pass the time. Above all they danced for religion.[11]

Movement is an essential part of African American worship, whether the worshiper rocks, waves the hand, hums, sings, or dances. There is something that connects the spirit of the worshipers to the Spirit of God, their emotions, and their community. The church body as a whole contributes to the wor-ship service, and dancing is a central part of that contribution.

To understand how liturgical dance functions in the African American community, we must understand the worship experience of African Ameri-cans. Theirs is a diverse worship expression based on the experiences born out of African influence. The African concept of *mbutu*, meaning "I am be-cause we are," unites Africans and African Americans as a people who have experienced its conditions individually and collectively as disenfranchised. The concept of *mbutu* is carried on in African American worship with the experience of God individually and collectively as liberator and protector.[12]

Also coming out of African culture is the expression of African Americans as a celebratory people. Celebration is made through movement. Dance, including rhythmic movement, not only plays a major role in worship, but also is significant in human development. There is a connection between worshiping and how the worshiper feels emotionally, spiritually, and physi-cally. True worship is response to God. In worship, African Americans truly see God's presence. Worship in the black religious experience is the visible acting out of what African Americans believe about God and their relation-ship with God.[13] Celebration is a significant way to show gratitude to God.

To understand the African worship experience one must understand the African view of time. John S. Mbiti, an authority on African concepts of time, writes:

> The African concept of time is two rather than three-dimensional. The former view stresses the past and the present with little emphasis on the

future. The three-dimensional view of time focuses on the past, present, and indefinite future. One's concept of time affects one's orientation toward biblical time. The African views future time in terms of a definite time in the near future of six months to two years. The African does not make rigid distinctions between the past, present, and future, which is common in white thinking. Both past and future are brought into the present in a manner that makes it impossible to keep future reality from its impact on the present in practical ways. This realized eschatology in the biblical record would get more emphasis in African thinking.[14]

This view carries into African American worship. It helps to establish emotional well-being in individuals. They look back into the not-so-distant past while moving toward the future yet keeping in mind the implications for the present. This is somewhat the concept with the mystic *Sankofa* bird of West Africa, which flies forward while looking backward with an egg (symbolizing the future) in its mouth. The literal translation, "It is not taboo to go back and fetch what you forgot."[15] The *Sankofa* teaches people to go back to their roots in order to move forward. People reach back to gather the best of what the past has to teach in order to move into the future.

Dance illustrations from the African American tradition are offered for each of Nouwen's five movements of the spiritual life from suffering to hope in the workshop following this presentation. Part I is entitled "From Our Little Selves to a Larger World."[16] Nouwen focuses on widening our context of grief and pain beyond ourselves. To experience pain with others in the grace of God lightens our burden. It is the image of the dancers lifting their feet, hands, and arms in the dance. It is expressing the pain in the dance and then lifting the pain up in God's grace. Nouwen writes:

> And as we dance, we realize that we don't have to stay on the little spot of our grief, but can step beyond it. We stop centering our lives on ourselves. We pull others along with us and invite them into the larger dance. We learn to make room for others—and the Gracious Other in our midst. And when we become present to God and God's people, we find our lives richer. We come to know that all the world is our dance floor. Our step grows lighter because God has called out others to dance as well.[17]

Nouwen writes that "prayer puts us in touch with the God of the Dance."[18] He emphasizes that when we enlarge our context of pain and offer it in community to God, we give it to God in prayer. In the African American tradition, dance is a form of liturgical prayer employed during worship. The community lifts its pain, struggles, hopes, and joys to God in celebration.[19]

For Nouwen, mourning and dancing are part of the same movement of God's grace. Nouwen encourages us to join in the larger dance.[20] He calls us to live our lives in grace and gratitude in Christ. He invites us to perceive life as God's unique way of molding us into his likeness. Nouwen writes: "Gratitude helps us in this dance only if we cultivate it. . . . If mourning and dancing are part of the same movement of grace, we can be grateful for every moment we have lived. We can claim our unique journey as God's way to mold our hearts to greater conformity to Christ."[21]

Nouwen's first movement from self to the larger world is expressed in the African American tradition and context of people pulled away from all they knew in Africa and placed in a culture foreign to their being. Nouwen writes: "By trying to hide parts of our story from God's eye and our own consciousness, we become judges of our own past."[22] To avoid this judgment of their past, African Americans had to learn to dance "into and through" their adversity, pain, and guilt. This comes from not being who they are and trying to be what they are not. African Americans find themselves in that spot as children of God. As such, they can step into the reality from their little selves to their dignified place in a larger world. And the dance begins.

Nouwen observes, "The mystery of dance is that its movements are discovered in the mourning."[23] No one else understands the depth of the pain of African Americans but God. Dancing with God alone and together as community, African Americans are pulled out of their smaller selves into a larger community as belonging to God—a God who understands them and leads them in dance.

In Part II Nouwen focuses on moving "from holding tight to letting go."[24] Growth in the spiritual life happens when we risk listening to God in the midst of life and let go of life's controls. Nouwen articulates, "Discipline . . . is to leave room in our hearts where we can listen to the Spirit of God in a life-changing way. . . . We find in those risky acts something wonderfully beyond what we could have done on our own, by ourselves, without God."[25]

Nouwen describes this spiritual way of living to be like the trapeze artists at the circus. He recounts going to the circus with his eighty-nine-year-old father and watching five South African trapeze artists perform. There were three fliers and two catchers. Nouwen writes:

They danced in the air! The fliers soared and all that was dangerous until they found themselves caught in the strong hands of their partners. I told my father that I had always wanted to fly like that. That perhaps I had missed my calling! I am constantly moved by the courage of my circus friends. At each performance they trust their flight will end with their hands sliding into the secure grasp of a partner. They also know that only the release of the secure bar allows them to move on with arcing grace to the next. Before they can be caught they must be let go. They must brave the emptiness of space.[26]

Nouwen continues his imagery of the trapeze artists. He points out that when we let go and entrust our life to God, we can be secure in the knowledge that God will catch us if we fall. In reaching out to God in moments of struggle, we can know for certain that God will catch us. Nouwen writes:

> Ever since I paid that visit to the circus with my father, ever since I found myself captivated by the trapeze artists, I have joined their circus group every year for a week or so to travel with them. The leader recently said to me, "Henri, everyone applauds for me because when I do those leaps and backflips; they think I am a hero. But the real hero is the catcher. The only thing I have to do is stretch out my hands and trust, trust that he will be there to pull me back up." We can say no less about the God who encircles our little lives and waits to catch us and hold us—in the hard junctures and the good, in the precarious moments and the times we soar. Someone within us and yet beyond us always makes that possible. Because of that our tight grip on life—its joys and even its sorrows—can loosen. We too can learn again to fly—to dance.[27]

The movement of African American liturgical dance is like the trapeze artists' movement. It offers a place for inner emotions to be expressed. Dancers can stretch and lift their painful emotions to God. They can reach out to receive hope and healing from God as they rise and fall on the divine dance floor of grace. Dance expresses the truth of the inner life through the physical agency of the body.[28] African American liturgical dance offers the experience of placing the liberating and protecting God in the midst of the worshiping community.[29]

Nouwen urges us to let go and see the wonders of God. In his recollection of the trapeze artists, he says, "Before they can be caught, they must let go."[30] Prayer enables us to let go. Dancing enables us to join our hearts in prayer through movement. In the dance we no longer hold tight to what we believe is safe. It is only in the letting go that we can receive. We release the grip of our past and present fears, doubts, and strivings, and we enter into an empty place. We wait and are exhilarated when we are caught by the Dancer. In African American liturgical dance, there is a kariotic moment, an "ah ha" moment in which the dancer soars to God!

In Part III, entitled "From Fatalism to Hope,"[31] Nouwen offers the spiritual movement from the no of discouragement to the yes of hope in God. Nouwen writes, "This no to discouragement and self-despair comes in the context of a yes to life, a yes we say amid even fragile times lived in a world of impatience and violence. For even while we mourn, we do not forget how our life can ultimately join God's larger dance of life and hope."[32]

African American liturgical dance draws upon its African roots to emphasize the wholeness of body and spirit. It encourages the dancers to begin to dance where they are. The dancers are encouraged to continue to dance right on into the hopeful presence and grace of God.[33] This dance in the grace of God is sufficient for all of life's journey. It is dance in the power and activity of God.

For African Americans, the dance moves people away from the fatalistic attitude that "what will happen will happen as it has always happened" to the flicker of hope that it might be different this time. Just maybe the status quo will be changed. African Americans dance out of where they are individually and corporately. They dance with a rhythm, a beat, a sway, and a hum that many do not understand because they have not lived the life of an African American. The dance pulls African Americans away from the sense that "what will be, will be," from a sense of inevitability. The dance twirls them into the excitement of hope for just that moment in time. And hope realized brings a movement created out of God, yet for God.

Nouwen says that we should read life backward. "For by not remembering we allow forgotten memories to become independent forces that have a crippling effect on our functioning and relating and praying."[34] This relates to the West African *Sankofa* bird, mentioned earlier, which teaches us to go back to our roots in order to move forward. The dancer by dancing becomes the vessel that pours out the poison that kills life and, as a consequence, receives hope for life. At that moment of hope nothing matters but being in the Dancer's presence. And when the dance is over, there is the residue of hope for another time, another place, another dance.

In Part IV Nouwen focuses on the movement "from manipulation to love."[35] The compassion and love of God are shared in community when we "enter others' dark moments."[36] Nouwen defines community as sharing together in the belovedness of God. He writes, "Community, then, cannot grow out of loneliness, but comes when the person who begins to recognize his or her belovedness greets the belovedness of the other. The God alive in me greets the God resident in you."[37]

Dancing for God connects the pain of the community together in worship. Dancing offers the dancer more experience of God, lifting the dancer's spirit to God. The dance becomes an expression of the needs of the community before God. When the community dances before God, God joins in the dance. God dances with the community in spirit.[38]

Nouwen writes about the movements of the dance. In the dance God's presence of love is offered in the community. Through dance, pain is released and belovedness in God is lifted up. Compassion is poured out for the community through the dance. Nouwen emphasizes Christ's compassion in the metaphor of the dance, stating: "There is no human suffering that has not in some way been part of God's medium and experience. That is the great and wonderful mystery of God becoming flesh to live among us. God becomes a part of our mourning and invites us to learn to dance—not alone, but with others, sharing in God's own compassion, as we both give it and receive it."[39] Nouwen writes, "To live with compassion means to enter each others' dark moments."[40]

As a community, African Americans know dark moments. They are acclimated to the competitiveness of society, all the time trying to find their own voice. They do not see others; they only see what they can do. Or, as Nouwen says, they see others "as characters in a play."[41] They seek to move from the boundedness and manipulation of society to the heart and love of God through dancing. This becomes possible as baggage is dropped and movement into the heart of God is expressed. Dance emphasizes the relationship with the Dancer who is God. The dancer becomes transparent as the light of God's love shines through the dancer, showing God's love. In the dance, the dancers are moving from manipulating and being manipulated into loving one another. Love is expressed in the African American worshiping community through the dance. Nouwen writes:

> When we become persons we become transparent to each other, and light can shine through us, God can speak through us. When we become persons who transcend the limitations of our individual characters, the God who is love can reveal himself in our midst and bind us into a community. We become transparent. Others lose their opaqueness and reveal to us the loving face of our Lord.[42]

In Part V, "From a Fearful Death to a Joyous Life," Nouwen writes that the end of the dance of life in God, death, is joyous.[43] Nouwen states, "Faith asks us to jump, to surrender and believe that somewhere, somehow, Someone will catch us and bring us home."[44] The goal is eternal joyous life in God. It is the eternal dance in God's heavenly kingdom. Nouwen states: "Confronting our death ultimately allows us better to live. And better to dance with God's joy amid the sorrowing nights and the hopeful mornings."[45] When life is lived in the dance of the grace of God, there is always hope and joy for this life and for eternity.

African Americans are a celebratory people. Celebration is expressed through the movements of liturgical dance. In celebration, black people dance to express life lived fully in the power of God.[46] African American liturgical dance is a beautiful vehicle. It expresses the beauty and depth of the spiritual journey from pain to joy, from death to life eternal in God.

Nouwen says, "Life is a school we are trained to depart."[47] The African Americans' service for those departed is called a home-going service. African Americans understand that the world is not their final destination. The funeral, the home-going service, is a celebration of eternal victory in God. Dancing in this service allows glimpses of glory, of the journey from death to life. The journey becomes one not of fear of death, but one that leads to life. Dying to self in the dance leads the dancer to the movement of new life in God. This is freely expressed in joy on the graceful dance floor with God.

Notes

[1] Henri J. M. Nouwen, *Clowning in Rome: Reflections on Solitude, Celibacy, Prayer, and Contemplation.* rev. ed. (New York: Doubleday, 2000), xiii.

[2] Henri J. M. Nouwen, *Turn My Mourning into Dancing: Finding Hope in Hard Times*, comp. and ed. Timothy Jones (Nashville, TN: Word Publishing, 2001).

[3] Ibid., 13.

[4] Ibid., xv.

[5] Ibid., xvi.

[6] "The Black Tradition in American Dance," a plaque in the Charles H. Wright African American Museum in Detroit.

[7] George Ofori-Atta-Thomas, "'The African Inheritance in the Black Church Worship': The Black Christian Worship Experience: A Consultation," *The Journal of the Interdenominational Theological Center* 14 (Fall/Spring 1986): 44.

[8] Ibid., 45.

[9] Steve Evans, "A Study of a Biblical Medium and a Cultural Worship Form in Africa" (2000). Available on the newway.org website.

[10] Andre Massaki, in ibid.

[11] Ofori-Atta-Thomas, "The African Inheritance in the Black Church Worship," 62.

[12] Emily Pardue, *The Drama of Dance in the Local Church* (Orlando: Xulon, 2005), 64.

[13] John Brandon, "'Worship in the Black Experience': The Black Christian Worship Experience: A Consultation," *The Journal of the Interdenominational Theological Center* 14 (Fall/Spring 1986): 113.

[14] Thomas Hoyt, "'The African American Worship Experience and the Bible': The Black Christian Worship Experience: A Consultation," *The Journal of the Interdenominational Theological Center* 14 (Fall/Spring 1986): 7, summarizing John S. Mbiti, *New Testament Eschatology in an African Background* (London: Oxford University Press, 1971), 23–61.

[15] Cited by The W. E. B. Du Bois Learning Center, *The Meaning of the Symbolism of the Sankofa Bird.* Available on the duboislc.net website.

[16] Nouwen, *Turn My Mourning into Dancing*, 3.

[17] Ibid., 13.

[18] Ibid., 14.

[19] Pardue, *The Drama of Dance*, 66.

[20] Nouwen, *Turn My Mourning into Dancing*, 14.

[21] Ibid., 18.

[22] Ibid., 7.

[23] Ibid., 16.

[24] Ibid., 23.

[25] Ibid., 43.

[26] Ibid., 25.

[27] Ibid., 43.

[28] Pardue, *The Drama of Dance*, 56.

[29] Ibid., 64.

[30] Nouwen, *Turn My Mourning into Dancing*, 45.

[31] Ibid.

[32] Ibid.

[33] Pardue, *The Drama of Dance*, 43.

[34] Nouwen, *Turn My Mourning into Dancing*, 59.

[35] Ibid., 65.

[36] Ibid., 67.

[37] Ibid., 83.

[38] Pardue, *The Drama of Dance*, 14–15.

[39] Nouwen, *Turn My Mourning into Dancing*, 86–90.

[40] Ibid., 67.

41 Ibid.
42 Ibid., 85.
43 Ibid., 91.
44 Ibid., 100.
45 Ibid., 110.
46 Pardue, *The Drama of Dance*, 66.
47 Nouwen, *Turn My Mourning into Dancing*, 96.

6

Henri Nouwen, Thomas Merton, and Donald Nicholl

Pilgrims of Wisdom and Peace

Michael W. Higgins

Spirituality is everywhere these days. That is a strange way of putting it, admittedly, but it does speak rather directly to the problem. What, in fact, is spirituality? Why have so many individuals suddenly become experts in the field, if in fact it is a field? And what is one to make of distinctions that allow religion and spirituality to be defined as antinomies?

In a recent article in the *Toronto Star,* discussing the ambitious Toronto stage production of *The Lord of the Rings,* Brent Carver, the Tony-award-winning actor who plays Gandalf in the production, was quoted as saying that "faith is a word with particular resonance for me but although I define myself as spiritual I am not necessarily religious. No one has a patent on faith. No one has a patent on God. We can all write our own way."[1] But how exactly does one write one's own way when it comes to spirituality?

That gnomic scourge of settled opinion Rex Murphy, the CBC and *Globe and Mail* commentator, has acerbically noted vis-à-vis North American culture that "a culture that offers intellectual hospitability to the chatterings of Dr. Phil and the romps of *Desperate Housewives* does not have the stamina to pursue the idea of faith and its agency."[2] A stern judgment, but one not without validity.

Dom Laurence Freeman, O.S.B., author and disciple of the great Benedictine spiritual figure John Main, does not hesitate when it comes to identifying the fault lines of our contemporary spiritual crisis: "It is puzzling and frustrating to try and understand how the mainline Churches, despite all their determination and resources, still seem unable to connect with the profound spiritual needs of our time. . . . [Young people] dismiss what they find as narrowness of mind, intolerant dogmatism, internal feuding, inter-denominational sectarianism, medieval sexism and . . . lack of spiritual depth."[3]

Freeman is talking about the failure of established religion. But he is not talking about its indispensability. He is talking about the skewering of the gospel message, not its irrelevance. So where can we turn for direction, for enlightenment, for sane commentary, and for an integrated maturity of vision?

Thomas Merton, Donald Nicholl, and Henri Nouwen, twentieth-century spiritual writers and thinkers, were, for significant chunks of time, contemporaries. To some degree they spoke out of similar contexts. To some degree they addressed similar crises.

To get a "read" on the three of them, I have drawn on a particularly intriguing idea put forth by J. S. Porter, Canadian poet and professor, who sees in a particular word a point of entry, a code to be unraveled, a probe to be measured. The word, the right word, is the key that unlocks. Porter's book, *Spirit Book Word,* identifies particular words with particular writers and explores why it is that the word is a signature of and an aperture to their soul and imagination. But Porter had difficulty finding his own word. He writes: "I still hadn't found my word. The word that called me, claimed me, owned me. The word written on my body. The word that branded itself in my forehead the way 'Being' burnt itself into Heidegger, the way 'love' surrounded Carver, or the way 'modernism' scalded Swift. I hadn't found a way to link my trinity: words, books and spirit."[4] He discovers at the end that indeed the word was there staring him in the face. It was "Spiritbookword: the breadth of the word in the book. I jumped up and down like a four year old. Hallelujah! I had found my word. I could now look for spiritbookwords in others."[5] One of those others, Thomas Merton, was given the word "mercy."

Spiritbookwords is a marvelous idea, a conceit or principle that can also work when applied to the three subjects under consideration. Thomas Merton's spiritbookword is *point vierge,* for Donald Nicholl it is *scientia cordis,* and for Henri Nouwen it is "wounded healer." I know, they look more like spiritbookphrases than spiritbookwords, but you get my drift.

Point Vierge

In the late 1960s the stage was set for the final installment, the final quadrant, the fourth Zoa: Urthona, or Wisdom. The meaning of wisdom for Merton was fluid, evolving over time, a mature and ripe dimension of life that cannot be hurried, scheduled, or programmed. He thought about wisdom a great deal in its many configurations. If finally he was to embody wisdom, become Urthona, it was a natural progression of many years' seasoning.

The first extended and major treatment of the theme of wisdom can be found in his lengthy prose-poem "Hagia Sophia" (Holy Wisdom), published in 1962, the product of a correspondence he had with his close friend Victor Hammer. A typographer, bookbinder, and calligrapher, in addition to his teaching duties in lettering, drawing, and painting, Hammer was the consummate artist and craftsman. On one occasion when Merton was visiting

Victor and his wife, Carolyn, Hammer showed his guest a triptych he had been working on. The central panel showed a woman crowning a young boy, and Merton asked aloud who the woman was. Hammer had initially conceived of the woman and the young boy as Madonna and Child but no longer knew who she was. Merton then responded, "I know who she is. I have always known her. She is Hagia Sophia."

In a letter dated May 2, 1959, Hammer invited Merton to come and bless the triptych and explain in greater detail what he meant by Hagia Sophia. This latter request Merton met in a twofold manner: in a letter dated May 14, and in the prose-poem of the same name.

The poem is an eloquent meditation on and celebration of wisdom. It is divided into four sections—"Dawn," "Early Morning," "High Morning," "Sunset"—and is modeled on the monastic "Hours": Lauds, Prime, Terce, Compline. Of dawn, or Lauds, Merton writes:

> There is in all things an inexhaustible sweetness and purity, a silence that is a fount of action and joy. It rises up in wordless gentleness and flows out to me from the unseen roots of all created being, welcoming me tenderly, saluting me with indescribable humility. This is at once my own being, my own nature, and the Gift of my Creator's Thought and Art within me, speaking as Hagia Sophia, speaking as my sister, Wisdom.[6]

It is in the dawn, the moment of pristine innocence, the moment of prelapsarian joy, the sweet point, or *point vierge*, that one may happen on Hagia Sophia. In *Conjectures of a Guilty Bystander*, in a passage about the "first chirps of the waking day birds," Merton observes that they

> speak to Him, not with fluent song, but with an awakening question that is their dawn state, their state at the "point vierge." . . . All wisdom seeks to collect and manifest itself at that blind sweet point. Man's wisdom does not succeed, for we are all fallen into self-mastery and cannot ask permission of anyone. We face our mornings as men of undaunted purpose. . . . For the birds there is not a time that they tell, but the virgin point between darkness and light, between non-being and being. . . . Here is an unspeakable secret: paradise is all around us and we do not understand. It is wide open. The sword is taken away, but we do not know it. . . . "Wisdom," cries the dawn deacon [the bird] but we do not attend.[7]

Merton corresponded with Louis Massignon, the distinguished Islamicist, and it was from him that he first heard the term *point vierge*, which means "the center of the soul, where despair corners the heart of the outsider." It is not only the sweet point but the enlightened awareness at the juncture of despair. Wisdom represents the voice of creation and the voice of unity, the summons to being and the sound of judgment. In the dawn state, the poem says, one can recognize the first morning of the world (when Adam, at the sweet voice of Wisdom woke from nonentity and knew her), and . . . the Last Morning of the world when all the fragments of Adam will return from death at the voice of Hagia Sophia.

In part two of the poem, "Early Morning," the poet records that in our human efforts to awaken to the wisdom that speaks at the *point vierge*, we long to leave the blindness of our fallen state and to rediscover our innocence:

The heavenly lights rejoice in the going forth of one man to make a new world in the morning, because he has come out of the confused primordial dark night into consciousness. He has expressed the clear silence of Sophia in his own heart. He has become eternal.

When one is truly innocent one is truly eternal, finding "the impeccable pure simplicity of One consciousness in all and through all."

In the third part of the poem, "High Morning," Wisdom is spoken of as the divinity in all things and as the power of mercy in us,

the yielding and tender counterpart of the power,
justice and creative dynamism of the Father.

Hagia Sophia is both plenitude and nothingness:
God as all, and God reduced to Nothing:
inexhaustible nothingness.

In "Sunset," the concluding part, Hagia Sophia is directly identified with the Blessed Virgin Mary, whose consent to enflesh divinity guaranteed the offer of salvation to a recalcitrant creation. Mary is traditionally titled *Sedes Sapientiae* (Seat of Wisdom):

God enters into His creation. Through her wise answer, through her obedient understanding, through the sweet yielding consent of Sophia God enters without publicity into the city of rapacious men.

The speaker in the poem tells us at the beginning that he is in a hospital, lying asleep, and that it is the second of July, the feast of the Visitation, "A Feast of Wisdom." Sophia comes to him in his sleep as Philosophy came to Boethius and Beatrice to Dante and Gabriel to Mary, a consolation and a dream, a vision and a longing. In a diary entry of the same day in 1960, Merton wrote of dreaming in a very quiet hospital when he was awakened by the "soft voice of the nurse." He asks:

Who is more little than the helpless man, asleep in bed, having entrusted himself gladly to sleep and to night? Him the gentle voice will awake, all that is sweet in woman will awaken him. Not for conquest and pleasure, but for the far deeper wisdom of love and joy and communion.[8]

This recorded experience forms the context of the poem; the speaker and Merton are one and the same. Merton appreciates the unfathomable riches, the "invisible fecundity" of all things, revealed by Sophia. The sleeper, however—as all who sleep a temporal sleep must—*awakens* to the night having *dreamed* in the light:

> The shadows fall. The stars appear. The birds begin to sleep. Night embraces the silent half of the earth. A vagrant, a destitute wanderer with dusty feet, finds his way down a new road. A homeless God, lost in the night, without papers, without identification, without even a number, a frail expendable exile lies down in desolation under the sweet stars of the world and entrusts Himself to sleep.

As long as the speaker/sleeper/Merton dreams of Wisdom, he comes out of the confused primordial dark night into consciousness, into the light of his dream, the luminosity of Wisdom.

In the tradition of the early church fathers and the Neo-Platonists, Merton writes of Wisdom not as a particular quality but as a unique *manifestation* of the triune God. Wisdom is an image or emanation of the Godhead and not some disembodied divine attribute. Wisdom also assists in the repair of creation in the same way that the Virgin assists Christ in the incarnation. And equally, Wisdom will assist the poet in the task of repairing the word.

Hagia Sophia is Urthona, the *point vierge* of our being, the Virgin/window, and the Jungian anima. As Urthona, dethroned by Urizen, Wisdom seeks the cooperation of Art, or Los in Blake's mythology, in order "to preserve some kind of harmony and order and intelligibility in the created world." As the virgin point of our being, Wisdom, Merton notes, is

> a point of pure truth, a point or spark which belongs entirely to God . . . which is inaccessible to the fantasies of our own mind or the brutalities of our own will. This little point of nothingness and of absolute poverty is the pure glory of God in us. It is so to speak His name written in us. . . . It is like a pure diamond, blazing with the invisible light of heaven. It is in everybody, and if we could see it we would see these billions of points of light coming together in the face and blaze of a sun that would make all the darkness and cruelty of life vanish completely. . . . I have no program for this seeing. It is only given. But the gate of heaven is everywhere.[9]

Scientia Cordis

Donald Nicholl taught history and religious studies in both the United States and the United Kingdom, wrote widely and deeply about personalities and issues, and struggled throughout his life to understand what we mean by *holiness*. But to achieve holiness, one must begin somewhere, and for Nicholl it begins with a call from the Holy Spirit, for every call of the Holy Spirit begins with a revelation of the bankruptcy of one's present, habitual mode of life, its tendency toward the death of one's spirit. That moment of awakening inevitably has to be a moment of anguish, of agony, and of repentance, because it is only from the pain of awakening to the contradiction in one's life that the energy to change arises. Nicholl cites an example of an expression of such anguish by one of the most remarkable priests in England, Austin Smith, who spent twenty-five years serving on the front line, in the slums of Liverpool. In *Vocation for Justice* Fr. Austin related how he was struck by the contrast between the way Christians protested against the celluloid *Last Temptation of Christ* of Scorsese's film yet succumbed daily to the real last temptation against which Jesus had to struggle to the very end. Jesus' last temptation, in Gethsemane, was to feel that

> there was still time and space to carry on [with his campaign for the kingdom] and get somewhere. And yet the message of God was, "It is time to suffer and die." This temptation was, if one may so express it, to keep the show going when the show has really run out of steam. Or, to put it another way, a much more radical way, it is the temptation to keep going when we are really washed up, or, if you prefer it, washed out. We keep going when the very gospel of Jesus is saying to us, "Your day is done." We are seduced by the thought that we still have something to offer. We will not die in our present comfortable state to rise to a new state.[10]

To rise to a new state, to undergo the dramatic process of *metanoia* (conversion), we must cut ourselves off from the old ways in order to answer the call to a "new, dangerous form of existence." Our fear hobbles and diminishes us. Although each person's *metanoia* will follow a different direction, we are all called to discard the false self, "infected by death," for the true self, open to the Spirit of Life.

Throughout his own life Nicholl sought bravely to change, to resist always the blandishments of successful and homogenizing ideologies, to avoid the easy comforts of establishment living, to hear the cries of the poor and abandoned, to forge out of the sufferings and crises of both religious and artistic leaders, as well as out of the anonymous multitudes, a genuinely liberating spirituality.

To that end Nicholl read the Russian mystics and poets, explored the spirituality of resistance that occasionally found expression among German Catholics to the Nazis' tyranny, argued for intelligent and respectful dialogue between Catholicism and the other great religions, and campaigned vigorously in the interests of peace. Nicholl believed that humanity could find a common ground of the spirit by pursuing what he called a *scientia cordis*, science

of the heart. This *scientia cordis* is a genuine science with an appropriate authority, but it is not a positive science,

> because positive science tries to formulate immutable laws about what
> is, psychology too attempts to freeze human beings in terms of laws
> about needs and demands that can be specified—but the aspirations of
> the heart always go beyond what can be specified in such laws; and it is
> these aspirations which keep the heart in motion and prevent it from
> being frozen into immobility.[11]

Because the *scientia cordis* concerns itself with human aspirations, its medium of expression is not some law or formula—characteristic of the positive
sciences—but the narrative, the story—which is more proper to art in form.
Nicholl, then, told stories, plenty of them, because he knew that in matters of
aspiration, the chief motto and mode of disclosure is Newman's *cor ad cor
loquitur* ("heart speaks to heart"), because he knew that along the path of
storytelling "dance and joy and truth can travel." But these stories arose out
of Nicholl's own empathy for the suffering and alienated; they spoke of grace
and heroism dearly bought. There is nothing light and frolicsome about them.
Out of Nicholls's spirituality comes a sweet incandescence, luminous wonders in a darkening landscape.

Wounded Healer

In 1972 *The Wounded Healer* by Dutch psychologist-priest Henri Nouwen
ushered in an era of new attention to the "healer" and added a new phrase to
the lexicon of spiritual terms. Nouwen realized that the loneliness and alienation often experienced by healing professionals, especially those who are
ministers of the spirit, could be a precious gift. As Michael Ford expressed
this insight,

> A deep understanding of their own pains . . . makes it possible for them
> to convert their weakness into strength and to offer their own experi-
> ence as a source of healing to those "who are often lost in the darkness
> of their own misunderstood sufferings."[12]

By the time he died of a heart attack in Hilversum on September 21, 1996,
Nouwen had established an international reputation as a spiritual writer.
Author of more than forty books and a retreat-giver and popular lecturer of
promethean stamina, Nouwen stamped a generation with his holistic approach
to spirituality. Although born in the Netherlands on January 24, 1932, educated in Holland at the famed Catholic University of Nijmegen, and ordained
a priest for the Archdiocese of Utrecht on July 21, 1957, Nouwen in fact lived
most of his life outside the continent of Europe. He traveled widely and

taught in numerous institutions, including stints at the University of Notre Dame, Yale, and Harvard. But he also experimented with nonacademic settings, including monasteries, mission centers, and homes for the disadvantaged. Nouwen embodied in his own life that spirit of restlessness and searching that resonated with the youthful rebels of the 1960s, a spirit that resisted amelioration as he aged.

Nouwen understood, both as a psychologist and as a spiritual director, that an essentialist spirituality, a spirituality of the manuals, a spirituality disembodied or disincarnate, could no longer speak to people. Spiritual traditions, exercises, and formulas that failed to respond to the aching disquiet of the individual, that discounted the deep personal experiences of the searcher, and that did not take account of cultural shifts and adjustments failed dismally to address the needs of the time. It was the *kairos,* the hours of the Lord, and people thirsted for a living spirituality. Nouwen would be their oasis.

This living spirituality was profoundly christocentric, and in a moving passage from *Show Me the Way,* Nouwen recounts a Good Friday liturgy at Trosly, France, motherhouse of the international L'Arche communities, when Père Thomas and Père Gilbert took the huge cross that hangs behind the altar and held it for the ritualistic veneration of the congregation. Nouwen was struck by the sweet juxtaposition of anguish and joy found in the faces of the broken and the whole as they came to kiss the dead body of Christ.

> Imagining the naked, lacerated body of Christ stretched out over our globe, I was filled with horror. But as I opened my eyes I saw Jacques, who bears the marks of suffering in his face, kiss the body with passion and tears in his eyes. I saw Ivan carried on Michael's back. I saw Edith coming in her wheelchair. As they came—walking or limping, seeing or blind, hearing or deaf—I saw the endless procession of humanity gathering around the sacred body of Christ, covering it with their tears and their kisses, and slowly moving away from it comforted and consoled by such great love. . . . With my mind's eye I saw the huge crowds of isolated, agonizing individuals walking away from the cross together, bound by the love they had seen with their own eyes and touched with their own lips. The cross of horror became the cross of hope, the tortured body became the body that gives new life; the gaping wounds became the source of forgiveness, healing, and reconciliation.[13]

This visceral passage, teetering on the sentimental, is in many ways vintage Nouwen. It is graphic, unapologetically emotional, and classically orthodox. Nouwen engages the reader with an explicit appeal to the imagination and to the heart, grounding a theological truism in the direct experience of a people at prayer mediated through the observing, but not detached, eye of the writer.

A psychologist of the heart and the soul, Nouwen wrote not only to guide others but to discover himself, to find himself. In his spiritual enchiridion or handbook, *Making All Things New,* he highlighted the spiritual confusion that afflicts our culture: "One way to express the spiritual crisis of our time is to say that most of us have an address but cannot be found there. We know where we belong, but we keep being pulled away in many directions, as if we were still homeless."[14]

Nouwen appreciated the profound displacement at the heart of contemporary humanity, a rootlessness that he shared to an often disturbing degree. He understood that everything in our culture that defines success or fulfillment is predicated precisely upon those qualities that work against our yearning for wholeness. We need to cultivate what he calls "the discipline of solitude and the discipline of community," because we need to attend to the silent voice of God, to eliminate the extraneous sounds that dominate our lives. But he also knew his own "wound":

> What to do with this inner wound that is so easily touched and starts bleeding again? It is such a familiar wound—this immense need for affection, and this immense fear of rejection—will it ever go away. It is there to stay, but maybe for a good reason. Perhaps it is a gateway to my salvation, a door to glory, and a passage to freedom!
>
> I am aware that this wound of mine is a gift in disguise. These many short but intense experiences of abandonment lead me to the place where I'm learning to let go of fear and surrender my spirit into the hands of the One whose acceptance has no limits. I am deeply grateful to Nathan and to my other friends who know me and are willing to bind my wounds so that, instead of bleeding to death, I can walk on to the full life.[15]

Nouwen understood only too clearly the demands of success. His various professorships at prestigious universities, his highly lucrative and very public writing career, and his popularity on the invitational lecture circuit combined to assure him a level of professional success that was the envy of all, but the costs were great. Nouwen often found himself diminished by his achievements, and he sought protection from his own success. He frequently fled to the anonymity of monastic enclosure, requested and received spiritual direction from the abbot, and then wrote about his experience in his next book. Similarly, he would abandon the security of the academy and work in the *barrios* of Latin America. Naturally, he wrote about this experience as well. But these occasional departures from lecturing, teaching, and writing were, in the end, incapable of settling his wandering spirit.

Nouwen was desperate for that mixture of discipline and community that he passionately wrote about but that consistently eluded him. That is, it escaped him until he happened upon the second largest L'Arche community in the world, Daybreak, north of Toronto. Here he would spend the last decade of his life (1985–96), fall in love, experience a breakdown of immense proportions, be emotionally rejuvenated, and, however briefly, come to terms with his homosexuality. Daybreak defined Nouwen's later years, allowed him to speak *about* the wounded *among* the wounded, and provided him with that still point that released for him a refreshing and yet unnerving spring of self-knowledge.

Nouwen's writings could be quite formulaic and predictable. He cherished patterns of three; he drew heavily upon biblical stories, images, and themes; his anecdotes were autobiographical without being tantalizingly confessional, although the books he wrote during the last half of his Daybreak years betray a taste for candid disclosure not found in his other writings; his tone was honest without being ostentatious; he maintained a syllogistic but not constrictive logic in his writing; and he wrote to reveal and not conceal God's encompassing love.

More than anything, Nouwen was committed to shaping a voice for the wounded—the physically handicapped and mentally challenged, the socially marginalized and politically persecuted, the lonely and sexually oppressed or repressed. He proclaimed for all to hear a spirituality of peacemaking:

> I want to speak to you about prayer in the context of our Christian vocation to be peace-makers; to show you a little bit about how prayer is a way of peace-making. Only then can we speak creatively about resistance as a form of peace-making and only then we can see how prayer and resistance can in turn build community. The three indispensable components, then, of a meaningful spirituality of peace-making are resistance, prayer, and community.[16]

Throughout his life Nouwen sought different settings wherein to embody these three components: lecture room, monastic cell, slum, and group home. He pursued the wounded with frenetic energy and sometimes exasperating zeal. Over time, he came to understand his own wounds and to experience rejection as much as love, abandonment as much as affirmation. The humanizing of the celebrity proved to be liberating.

Two years before his death he wrote, in my opinion, his finest work, *Our Greatest Gift*. There is an unnerving prescience about this work, a work written with the intention of befriending his death. Nouwen allows the reader to hear and share in his vulnerability, his fear, in the face of death. But more important still, he invites the reader to experience that hope that makes of death not a foe but a friend: "Our death may be the end of our success, our productivity, our fame, or our importance among people, but is not the end of our fruitfulness. In fact, the opposite is true: the fruitfulness of our lives shows itself in its fullness only after we have died."[17]

Following a funeral Mass in Utrecht, presided at by Cardinal Adrianus Simonis and with a eulogy by Jean Vanier, Nouwen's body was returned to Toronto for a three-hour Mass of the Resurrection conducted at the Slovak Byzantine Catholic Cathedral of the Transfiguration of Our Lord in the neighboring town of Markham. The fruitfulness of the life of this solitary with a desperate hunger for community, of this pastor with a passion for interiority, has only begun to show itself fully.

Spiritbookwords: *point vierge, scientia cordis,* wounded healer. A remedy or elixir for our time? Perhaps. An invitation to deeper self-knowledge? Most certainly.

Notes

[1] Richard Ouzounian (theater critic), *The Toronto Star,* January 29, 2006.

[2] Rex Murphy, *The Globe and Mail,* April 9, 2005.

[3] Dom Laurence Freeman, O.S.B., as quoted in James Roose-Evans, "Into the Light," *The Tablet* (December 17/24, 2005): 30.

[4] J. S. Porter, *Spirit Book Word: An Inquiry into Literature and Spirituality* (Ottawa: Novalis, 2001), 30.

[5] Ibid., 32.

[6] Thomas Merton, *Hagia Sophia* (Lexington: Stamperia del Santuccio, 1962).

[7] Thomas Merton, *Conjectures of a Guilty Bystander* (New York: Doubleday Image, 1968), 131–32.

[8] Thomas Merton, *Turning toward the World: The Journals of Thomas Merton,* vol. 4, *1960–1963,* ed. Victor Kramer (New York: HarperCollins, 1996), 17.

[9] Merton, *Conjectures of a Guilty Bystander,* 158.

[10] Austin Smith, in Donald Nicholl, "Holiness—A Call to Radical Living," *Grail: An Ecumenical Journal* 5 (December 1989): 68–69.

[11] Donald Nicholl, "Scientia Cordis," in *The Beatitude of Truth: Reflections of a Lifetime* (London: Darton, Longman and Todd, 1997), 161.

[12] Michael Ford, *Wounded Prophet: A Portrait of Henri J. M. Nouwen* (New York: Doubleday, 1999), 46.

[13] Henri J. M. Nouwen, *Show Me the Way: Readings for Each Day of Lent* (New York: Crossroad, 1995), 134.

[14] Henri J. M. Nouwen, *Making All Things New: An Invitation to the Spiritual Life* (San Francisco: HarperSanFrancisco, 1981), 36.

[15] *The Heart of Henri Nouwen: His Words of Blessing,* ed. Rebecca Laird and Michael J. Christensen (New York: Crossroad, 2003), 139–40.

[16] Henri J. M. Nouwen, "A Spirituality of Peace-Making," inaugural Devlin lecture delivered at St. Jerome's University, Waterloo, Ontario, September 12, 1982.

[17] Henri J. M. Nouwen, *Our Greatest Gift: A Meditation on Dying and Caring* (San Francisco: HarperSanFrancisco, 1994), 38.

7

Nouwen, Emerson, and the Emerging of the American Vision

Michael O'Laughlin

During his last, sabbatical year Henri Nouwen went off traveling in many directions. Perhaps he was driven from one place to another by the Holy Spirit, or maybe it was just his own peculiar restlessness. He visited Massachusetts, California, New York, Germany, Chicago, and Ireland, to name only a few destinations, and, of course, he returned to Holland. At one point he found himself addressing an audience at the San Salvador Church in Prague, Czechoslovakia. That talk went pretty well, but afterward he received some negative feedback that really irked him; apparently a group of students in the Czech audience had found his style "too American."

Evidently he had been guilty of too much gesturing and had been too dramatic, and he was told this was not the Czech way of doing things. Later that day Henri struggled with this criticism. Why had they said this? He wrote in his diary, a bit ruefully, that here he was—a Dutchman—living in Canada—so how could he be accused of being too American? They should have said he was "too Henri Nouwen," not "too American."[1] Henri did not like the idea that his speaking style or his spirituality was an American type, rather than something that he created all by himself. He would never have admitted that he was "too American" for a European audience.

However, with sincere apologies to Henri, I think there was an American component to his style. It is a fact that the zany, personal intensity and exuberance that became the Nouwen hallmark did not emerge until he began teaching at the University of Notre Dame in the United States. Admittedly, in Holland he was recognized as being different from other people, but in his graduate student days he is remembered primarily as being overly serious and preoccupied with deep questions. It was only in America, and especially at Notre Dame, that Henri began to loosen up.[2]

It is not so much that he took on an American persona. Rather, he underwent a transformation, almost a chemical reaction, upon being exposed to American life and culture. At the same time, he was becoming more his true self by stepping free of the strictures of home. He was not the first European to live more authentically upon arriving in the United States. As John Updike said with regard to the history of art, "America was where Western Man discovered, not for the first time, that what is, is."[3] America is that land without templates or traditions that forces people from other places to cast aside earlier assumptions and conventions. What emerged in Henri's case was a perspective enriched by, and attuned to, identifiably American values and concerns. There is such a thing as an American perspective, and I believe Henri was transformed by exposure to it.

I have long suspected that much of the attitude that we today regard as American—that spirit that is perennially focused on commerce and improvement, that often seems to be either too tolerant or too conservative, that is both risk-taking and innovative—was actually a Dutch invention. If you read much about Holland in the seventeenth and eighteenth centuries, you will find that that country was much more of a forerunner of what the United States is today than the England of the same period. I have thought this for years, and now I am happy to see that someone has gone a long way to proving my hunch right; the book *The Island at the Center of the World* by Russell Shorto claims that the spirit of America was forged primarily on the Dutch colonial island of Manhattan.[4] If we accept Shorto's thesis that American attitudes have Dutch origins, then the more American one becomes, the more one aligns with this Dutch legacy. Perhaps there was no real conflict for Henri between being true to his Dutch roots and adapting to his American audience, since the Dutch and American spirits are one and the same!

Since today we have the unique opportunity to explore Henri's message in a critical setting, I would like to offer one insight into Henri Nouwen's Americanism: for all his creativity and uniqueness, there was someone in America's past who looks an awful lot like Henri, and he was a formative figure. I am referring to the Sage of Concord, Ralph Waldo Emerson, the premier public intellectual of nineteenth-century America. Emerson was a world-class figure; indeed, he was so important for the formation and expression of American values and intellectual style that he has few equals. He lived in the same era as Abraham Lincoln, and he shared Lincoln's towering intellectual ability, simple humility, and powerful charisma. I am intrigued to discover that one of the greatest of Americans seems to have a great deal in common with our favorite Dutchman. I am going to give a few reasons why I say this, and then ask what it means.

Ralph Waldo Emerson (1803–82) was raised in humble circumstances in Boston, went to Harvard, did rather poorly there, but was nevertheless able to continue the family tradition and obtain work in ministry. However, he underwent a crisis and a life transformation before his career really started. He had recently married a wealthy, much younger woman named Ellen Tucker. Ellen suffered from tuberculosis, and she only lived sixteen months beyond their wedding day. When she died, Emerson was devastated. At the same time he was also undergoing a profound spiritual awakening. This awakening caused him to question his faith and to give credence to some of the idealist and critical ideas emerging from continental Europe.

Thus, Emerson was unhappy and unsettled when he was called to the Second Church in Boston, a prestigious pulpit. Although he took the position, he was never comfortable there. The day of his ordination he referred to as his execution day, and he was too full of doubts to be a good pastor. By reading philosophers such as Schliermacher, he was coming to the conclusion that the kind of received faith that was common among his parishioners had little personal resonance or reality. In his writings from this period we find statements such as "Christianity is validated in each person's life and experience or not at all."[5] As his crisis over the source of true religion deepened, he turned to Joseph de Gerando's *Histoire comparée des systèmes de philosophie,* where he found an enthusiastic endorsement of idealism, the belief that morality and law are so fundamental to the life of humanity that they transcend the Christian and Greco-Roman tradition. Morality and justice are also found, wrote de Gerando, in ancient Chinese and Indian scriptures. If this was true, as Emerson was beginning to see, then all people, not just Christians, had morality and even religion.

Thus, while still very young, Emerson came to hold two positions that would be embraced in a slightly different way more than a century later by Henri Nouwen—that true spirituality is grounded in the individual and his or her experience, and that all people and all religions are part of God's plan and God's love. Emerson's relationship to Christianity would evolve, however, in a way quite different from that of Henri Nouwen. Henri deeply identified with the priesthood and never questioned his call to ministry. Emerson's ministry did not survive his spiritual and personal crisis. Still crushed by his wife's death, Emerson announced he had problems of conscience over the administration of the Eucharist and resigned from his Boston pastorate.

Feeling very much adrift, Emerson left the United States to tour Europe. There he met with many of the leading philosophers of the day and came to the conclusion that he should follow the example of Thomas Carlyle, whom he visited in Britain, and become an essayist. After all, he reasoned, when he had been a preacher he had always found something to say. Thus it was that Ralph Waldo Emerson began a career as a writer and public speaker, which is another Nouwen parallel. In the days before mass communication Emerson rode stage coaches and the railroad, which was then an innovative form of travel, to stand before city and small-town audiences all over the United States. Newspaper critics complained that he made a terrible impression as a speaker, yet those who heard him came away feeling that they had been touched personally. Listening to Ralph Waldo Emerson was uplifting and transformative. He inspired others because he was saying things that many felt but had never been able to put into words. As Nouwen would later do, Emerson became known for touching people and changing lives.

At the heart of Emerson's message was a call to authenticity and self-reliance. He wanted people to stand on their own feet and not be mere followers and imitators. He questioned the value of classical and European models, and he recommended that everyone seek first to know his or her own mind. Along with his close personal friend Henry David Thoreau, he advocated embracing the vast beauty of the American continent as the starting point for a new spiritual perspective. Across the continent, in California, nature enthusiast John Muir became an Emerson devotee, and when Emerson reached California, Muir was his host and guide as they explored the high Sierras. Emerson's essay "Nature" launched the Transcendental movement and became one of the fundamental texts of American nature writing. It would appear that Emerson's immersion in nature gave him what Nouwen learned from art and especially from Vincent van Gogh, a contemplative perspective that laid bare the heart of the world.

Emerson was even more like Nouwen in his understanding that his heart was a mirror on the world. Henri remarked often that by exploring his own psyche and revealing his own struggles, he was touching the experience of others, and that "the most personal was the most universal."[6] In the previous century Emerson had had the same sensation. He exhorted the members of his audience to trust their own feelings as part of his description of the American scholar:

> He . . . learns that in going down into the secrets of his own mind he has descended into the secrets of all minds. . . . The poet, in utter solitude remembering his spontaneous thoughts and recording them, is found to have recorded that which men in crowded cities find true for them also. The orator distrusts at first the fitness of his frank confessions, his want of knowledge of the persons he addresses, until he finds that he is the complement of his hearers;–that they drink his words because he fulfills for them their own nature; the deeper he dives into his privatest, secretest presentiment, to his wonder he finds this is the most acceptable, most public, and universally true.[7]

Both Emerson and Nouwen were able to plumb their own depths and find truth there that everyone could share. Inspired by this discovery, they both asked their audiences to lay aside their books and go inside themselves. Henri was adverse to ministers or scholars taking a purely intellectual or impersonal, professional approach.[8] Emerson in his day had his own heretical thoughts, particularly about impersonal scholarship. He told a Harvard audience:

> Meek young men grow up in libraries, believing it their duty to accept the views which Cicero, which Locke, which Bacon have given; forgetful that Cicero, Locke and Bacon were only young men in libraries when they wrote these books. Hence, instead of Man Thinking, we

have the bookworm. . . . Books are the best of things, well used; abused,
among the worst.[9]

Part of Emerson's caution about book learning was that it too often became a substitute for real living and real thinking. Another concern was that
people who sought knowledge in books gave credence to ancient authorities
instead of marking out their own humble path. In his humility we find another interesting parallel with our modern Dutchman. Emerson shared fully
Nouwen's disregard for grandeur. He found in the ordinary life of gardening
and walking and communing with the villagers of Concord ample amounts
of profound truth. While maintaining contact with the leading thinkers of his
day, Emerson actually preferred the life of the village and the quiet of the
woods beyond. Both Nouwen and Emerson identified first with ordinary
people living ordinary lives.

However, neither of these men who loved ordinary living was actually
ordinary. With their surging native creativity they turned topics upside down
and brought to them a fresh perspective. Both men were promoters of personal experience and of sharing the inspiration to be found in that contemplative moment when the Spirit shines through. What was the Spirit and
what was truth? Here they would no doubt differ. Emerson's views on Jesus
would not have been shared by Henri Nouwen, although he saw Jesus as the
touchstone of world spirituality. The name of Jesus, he said, "is not so much
written, as ploughed into the history of this world."[10] Emerson's house in
Concord was decorated almost exclusively with prints from Italian masters
on gospel themes. On his journeys across the country he never challenged
the faith of his listeners in Jesus.

Yet his own personal views of Jesus were different. He lamented, in a
notorious speech given at Harvard Divinity School, that Jesus, the perfect
knower of the human heart, had been completely misunderstood. Instead of
being alive to the Divine, as Jesus had been, people in Emerson's day were
looking back to a God who was, not a God who is. He thought that making
Jesus the focus of one's faith was wrong; it was tantamount to accepting religion as second hand, when Jesus himself had taught the infinitude of humankind:

> Jesus Christ belonged to the true race of the prophets. He saw with
> open eyes the mystery of the soul. Drawn by its severe harmony, rav-
> ished with its beauty, he lived in it, and had his being there. Alone in all
> history he estimated the greatness of man. One man was true to what is
> in you and me. . . . He said, in this jubilee of sublime emotion, I am
> divine. Through me, God acts; through me, speaks. Would you see
> God, see me; or see thee, when thou also thinkest as I now think.[11]

So God is in everyone, and this is the truth that was grasped by Jesus.
Emerson was purposely saying all the things that were guaranteed to rile
the professors at Harvard University, and this speech at the Divinity School

resulted in him being banned from speaking at Harvard for the next thirty years. Emerson, like Nouwen, had never been comfortable at Harvard; somehow, the place always rubbed him the wrong way. Nevertheless, Nouwen would probably side with Harvard against Emerson with regard to this speech, in which Emerson claimed that historical Christianity had substituted for the doctrine of the soul a "noxious exaggeration about the person of Jesus."[12] Emerson saw Christ as true man, not true God, and as someone who had attained a level of enlightenment available to all. This is pretty liberal stuff, but we must not imagine that Henri had no awareness of this kind of Christian understanding. He once described himself as "one who has been exposed to many styles of theological liberalism,"[13] and Nouwen's own greatest contribution to Christian thinking places all of us in alignment with Christ as God's Beloved. During his lifetime Nouwen moved steadily in Emerson's direction.

It would be a mistake to focus too much at this point on theological differences. Rather, let us take note of a few more parallels: Emerson was, like Nouwen, no scholar, yet he read widely, knew what was being said by whom, and dipped into book after book to reinforce his own points. He was, like Henri, a writer, not a reader. He was a man with a following and a national reputation. Indeed, he, like Nouwen, was being read all over the world. A large number of people waited for the appearance of the next book or essay by Emerson, and therein lies another parallel—Emerson was an essayist, a writer of short studies. Henri may never have categorized himself as an essayist to anyone else, but I can remember him telling me, with regard to his trapeze fascination, that he wanted to write something different than his usual short book. In fact, he said to me, "I don't want to just write another essay." He knew that his books really were essays—and in this he was on the same ground as Emerson.

Finally, there is the man himself. Emerson was very much like Nouwen in his lifestyle and treatment of others. With the death of his first wife Emerson received a steady income, and he used the money to buy a house and raise a family with a second wife in Concord. This was a great change of fortune, for Emerson had been raised in genteel but very real poverty. Because he also traveled six months out of the year giving popular and well-paid lectures, Emerson in middle age was financially comfortable. Like Henri Nouwen, a good deal of his money went to supporting friends and worthy causes. When Thoreau built his retreat on Walden Pond, he was camping on land owned by Emerson, and indeed a whole entourage of Emerson's friends and relations was soon in residence around his house in Concord. There were always guests in the house, many of them important authors and innovators, and Emerson divided his time between writing and entertaining his many interesting guests. Does this sound at all familiar?

Concord was not exactly a rustic village, nor was it a city. Concord was a town near a city, much like Richmond Hill, and Emerson was surrounded there by gardens and orchards and farm animals and nature. In fact, he kept his own large garden. He called the orchard and the woods his study, and he claimed to learn more by walking through the trees than from any other source. Emerson styled the true American scholar someone of character more than intellect, and he claimed that "there is virtue yet in the hoe and the spade, for learned as well as for unlearned hands."[14] In this return to the country and to hands-on living, he mirrored Nouwen's embrace of the L'Arche lifestyle.

In exchanging the values of the learned world—of the cultured principles of Europe and its colonial hegemony—in favor of direct experience and humble immediacy, Emerson was rediscovering one of the primary tenets of the gospel, as Nouwen would learn and would teach us a century later. God scatters the proud in the imagination of their hearts and exalts those of low degree. God's work in this regard is not finished, and the world cries out for justice and renewal. As to politics and social change, again we find Emerson and Nouwen taking similar stands. Both addressed the great issues of their day. For Emerson, these were slavery, women's rights, and war; for Nouwen, AIDS, Latin America, and war. Both supported other, more radical figures emotionally and financially. Emerson supported men like John Brown; Henri, people like Fr. John Dear. Both preferred to let others be the standard-bearers and leaders in the field of social and political justice. Both were men of many parts, of many interests, not single-minded martyrs devoted to one cause.

So, what does it mean, ultimately, that Henri Nouwen had a life with some striking parallels to that of another great public teacher who lived a century or more before he did? I think that many things might be said about these parallels I have mentioned, but let me return to my first point: Ralph Waldo Emerson can be credited with defining or distilling a certain American attitude, one that is self-reliant, humble, egalitarian, alive to nature and insisting upon direct experience. In a different time, for different reasons, Henri Nouwen emphasized personal experience, God's inspiration, and the humble place where God can most readily be found. Although not an American, Nouwen went through what could be called a long American phase. This began with his tutelage to figures such as Anton Boisen, Karl Menninger, and Thomas Merton, and wound down when he left Yale for the mission fields of Latin America. By then he had found a larger America, an America of North and South.[15] Later Canada became the place where he was able to hold everything together—the rich and the poor, the American and the European, the gay and the straight, the Catholic and the Protestant. In the end, he superseded his American phase and became an Everyman going Everywhere.

Henri ended his American phase by going to France, and I am going to end by going to France, too. The French say that wine derives its character from the particular place where the grapes are grown and not just from its variety. In French this is called *terroir,* and it refers to soil, rainfall, sunshine, slope, and many other environmental factors. As one wine expert asserts, "There is no single word in English that means quite the same thing."[16] Henri Nouwen and Ralph Waldo Emerson overlap and harmonize in so many ways perhaps due to their identical *terroir;* they both grew to maturity on the same patch of ground and were both heard and heeded by the same grateful country.

Notes

[1] Henri Nouwen, *Sabbatical Journey: The Diary of His Final Year* (New York: Crossroad, 1998), 92.

[2] On this transformation, see Michael O'Laughlin, *Henri Nouwen: His Life and Vision* (Maryknoll, NY: Orbis Books, 2005), 56. See also the observations of Peter Naus and Fr. Don McNeill, quoted in Michael Ford, *Wounded Prophet: A Portrait of Henri J. M. Nouwen* (London: Dartman, Longman and Todd, 1999), 101, 109.

[3] John Updike, *Still Looking: Essays on American Art* (New York: Knopf, 2005), 35.

[4] Russell Shorto, *The Island at the Center of the World: The Epic Story of Dutch Manhattan and the Forgotten Colony that Shaped America* (New York: Random House, 2005).

[5] Ralph Waldo Emerson, quoted in Robert Richardson, *Emerson: The Mind on Fire* (Berkeley and Los Angeles: University of California Press, 1995), 97.

[6] Henri Nouwen, *Bread for the Journey: A Daybook of Wisdom and Faith* (New York: HarperSanFrancisco, 1997), April 14. See also Michael O'Laughlin, *God's Beloved: A Spiritual Biography of Henri Nouwen* (Maryknoll, NY: Orbis Books, 2004), 84–85.

[7] "The American Scholar," in *The Selected Writings of Ralph Waldo Emerson,* ed. Brooks Atkinson, The Modern Library (New York: Random House, 1950), 56–57.

[8] O'Laughlin, *God's Beloved,* 44–45.

[9] Emerson, "The American Scholar," 49.

[10] Richard W. Fox, *Jesus in America* (New York: HarperSanFrancisco, 2004), 19.

[11] R. W. Emerson, "An Address," in Atkinson, *The Selected Writings of Ralph Waldo Emerson,* 72.

[12] Ibid., 73.

[13] Henri Nouwen, "Foreword," in Gustavo Gutiérrez, *We Drink from Our Own Wells: The Spiritual Journey of a People* (Maryknoll, NY: Orbis Books, 1984), xviii.

[14] Emerson, "American Scholar," 100.

[15] Henri Nouwen, *¡Gracias! A Latin American Journal* (Maryknoll, NY: Orbis Books, 1983), xiii-xiv.

[16] Karen MacNeil, *The Wine Bible* (New York: Workman, 2001), 21.

8

Otherness and Justice in the Thought of Paul Ricoeur and Henri Nouwen

Jeremy Wiebe

This essay brings together the thought of the Christian French philosopher Paul Ricoeur (1913–2005), and Henri Nouwen around the themes of otherness and justice. Although Nouwen's writings are about spirituality and Ricoeur's are mostly philosophical in nature, I focus on the similarities between the two. Both Nouwen and Ricoeur spent many years living in North America, teaching in prominent universities and writing with deep insight about the human condition. Ricoeur was more at home in the university than Nouwen, however, and wrote first as a philosopher, bracketing out his faith from his most explicit writing on philosophical ethics.[1] This was in part due to the climate of philosophy in France, which was marked by a reticence to speak of theological concerns or God. Nouwen eloquently wrote on spirituality, transparently describing his personal faith experiences and struggles to be at peace with God and himself. By bringing together Nouwen's more theological voice and Ricoeur's philosophical voice around the themes of otherness and justice, I hope that an enriching picture will emerge of how we can understand and embrace the call to love the other and pursue justice.

In *Oneself as Another* Ricoeur asks what it means to be human, but more specifically, what it means to be a self that is ethical? To be an ethical self, he notes, is to be self-reflexive—there is a movement between our immediate subjective experiences and the more objective experiences in which we reflect at a distance on our own thoughts, emotions, words, and actions.[2] In asking the question "Who am I?" or "Who should I be?" there is a reflective and partial distance one exercises with oneself. Charles Taylor, Canadian philosopher and friend of Ricoeur's, notes that part of the basic self-reflexive quality that humans possess is to have desires about our desires.[3] Often one is angry or frustrated because one is angry, or one feels shame that one is struggling with shame. We desire to be different than we are and sense that we are not who we should be or who we are meant to be. Coupled with these evaluative desires about our desires, thoughts, and behavior is the capability to act creatively and change as a response.

According to Ricoeur, the identity of a person is marked in part by a sense of sameness or constancy but also by that of change. One of the marks of being a self is that a person is capable of self-determined action and change as an individual. There is an aspect of unity to our identities—one usually keeps the same given name, a fairly constant physical body, similar patterns of behavior and thought. When we describe someone, we usually look for unchanging characteristics that in part define that person. At the same time, we are selves, capable of self-reflection and choice, full of capabilities and creative potential to develop and change, to live and love and share life with others.[4] As individuals we experience this constancy and sameness of being, as well as desires and capabilities to choose new ways of living and being. Ricoeur suggests that in moving back and forth between these experiences, a person experiences both a constancy of identity and also oneself as an "other" about whom one has wishes and desires. Otherness usually describes something or someone different than oneself, but in addition to this usual meaning, Ricoeur wants to draw out how the self can also be other to itself.

Related to the question of the self is the question of the other as it is generally understood—the other person, and the other of society or community. Ricoeur and Nouwen both recognize that our lives and our stories are interwoven with the lives and stories of others around us. In relating to others we quickly come to understand that they are much the same as us, and different from us at the same time. There are common struggles and joys that we share as we journey together in various types of community and relationships, yet each of us has our own uniqueness that we have been given and participate in shaping. The other can be close to us, maybe family or friend or someone in our community, or perhaps it is the stranger or enemy who is the other we are encountering. How we relate to the other depends to a large degree on our experience of our self, and the growth from loneliness to solitude that Nouwen talks about in his 1975 work *Reaching Out*.[5]

Nouwen speaks about the movement, back and forth, between loneliness and solitude of heart. It is the experiencing and living out a life of solitude as described by Henri that "makes real fellowship possible."[6] By moving from loneliness to solitude we come to discover our inner self, the deep questions we have, answers sometimes, and our unfolding vocation. It is out of being present to ourself that we can in turn be present to others, and build loving community. Nouwen writes about the importance of solitude for relationships: "Without the solitude of heart, the intimacy of friendship, marriage and community life cannot be creative."[7] For both Nouwen and Ricoeur, before you get to the question of the other, and how you relate to the other, you must start with yourself. Who am I? Where have I come from? Where am I headed? Who am I becoming? In another sense, however, it seems that for Nouwen and Ricoeur it is out of our relationships to others that we are turned back to ourselves in a fruitfully self-reflexive manner.

Experiencing other people as both the same and different from oneself is a fairly obvious observation. There are those with whom we share similar tastes, interests, desires, and hobbies. And there are those we encounter with whom we seem to have little in common, and whom we perceive as different, perhaps radically "other." One of the delights of human experience is finding common ground with those who seem to be different. Of course there is also much agony in the difference and "pied beauty" we find in other individuals and the communities of which we are a part. Ricoeur talks about not reducing others to being either wholly different or exactly the same as oneself, and in a similar way Nouwen speaks of the uniqueness of each of us as God's beloved, each of us being a gift and giving ourselves as unique gifts. Community can bring us together in solidarity and fellowship but should preserve our unique identities and contributions to the community. Overcoming otherness is not what either Ricoeur or Nouwen advocates, but rather a movement between otherness and sameness that changes the way one sees the other and responds to the other.

The sameness and difference of the other comes into play in an interesting way when we consider questions of social justice and responsibility to the other. By *justice* I mean, broadly, concern and action for the injustice that takes place against the other person and the "other" of society. I will not try to provide a systematic definition for *justice* since neither Ricoeur nor Nouwen does so but will leave the term oriented toward a broad understanding of social justice. Following Plato and Aristotle, Ricoeur reflects on injustice before addressing justice. He suggests that it is out of the cry of injustice that we are first made aware of our deep longings and demands for justice. Why have I been treated unjustly? What kinds of injustice are other people experiencing in the world? What should be done about it? Ricoeur says that the cry of injustice is a basic human experience, and it results from such common experiences as "disproportionate retributions, betrayed promises, [and] unequal share."[8] Whatever the injustice, wrong, or pain caused, there is the cry for justice demanding a response from another.

Ricoeur speaks of injustice and justice using the language of fragility and responsibility. For Ricoeur, the human condition is one marked by deep brokenness and evil, or fragility that expresses itself in countless ways. The fragile are people with natural weaknesses, and those who have suffered as the result of human actions, such as those who are marginalized or in danger of physically perishing. When we come into contact with the fragile, responsibility to the fragile arises—and responsibility arises out of the capability and possibility to act that we possess. In his analysis of fragility and its accompanying responsibility, Ricoeur points out that we are all fragile, whether through weakness or our propensity to act unjustly. Ricoeur draws on Jewish philosopher Emmanuel Levinas's idea of the ethical responsibility that arises when we encounter the face of the other, whoever that fragile other may be.[9] The ethical responsibility to act on behalf of those in need arises from the other who summons me. Where Levinas emphasizes the total alterity of the other, however, Ricoeur speaks of both the alterity of the other and a fundamental sameness between the self and the other.[10] For Ricoeur, it is sameness and difference that summon an ethical response in one person toward another. Also, where Levinas emphasizes the one-directional summons of the fragile person to the other for help, Ricoeur sees the summons as coming both from the other person and from oneself.

Ricoeur says that we are made responsible *for* and *by* the fragile.[11] Being responsible "for" the fragile refers to the burden or charge one feels upon encountering those who are fragile. In this instance, before a fragile person asks for help or justice, one sees his or her need and is moved to compassion and a sense of duty to act on the person's behalf. The fragile person counts on us as the other and trusts that we will provide help and care. Thus we are made responsible "by" the fragile. It is both the feeling of a burden rising up within oneself and the expectation of the other that contribute to a person feeling that he or she has been "made responsible." Those who are fragile are suffering in some form, while others respond to this and show compassion. For Ricoeur, responsibility has a present sense of immediacy to it in the face of the fragile, but it is also concerned with responsibility for the past and future.

In the relationship between the fragile person that suffers and the one who acts to respond to that one's suffering, a certain degree of inequality can arise. Ricoeur suggests that this need not be the case, however; reciprocity between individuals is possible. The other, who cries out for justice and care in his or her suffering, has a claim on us. When we find sympathy and compassion welling up within us, we do not give to another who is lesser than us, because we too are fragile. He writes: "While equality is presupposed in friendship, in the case of the injunction coming from the other, equality is reestablished only through the recognition by the self of the superiority of the other's authority; in the case of sympathy that comes from the self and extends to the other, equality is reestablished only through the shared admission of fragility and, finally, of mortality."[12] In Ricoeur's short article "Responsibility and Fragility," he emphasizes our common humanity and locates our responsibility to others largely in our similarity to others. Regarding responsibility to the other, he writes, "Is it not finally a question of mutual recognition, of recognition whereby the other ceases to be alien and is treated like someone who is similar to me and in accord with fundamental human similarity?"[13]

Ricoeur witnessed the fragility of life through many of his own life experiences. He was orphaned at the age of two, was in prison camps for most of World War II, witnessed a French army captain get killed in front of him, and lost a beloved son to suicide.[14] Amid these and other tragedies of life, his work is marked by a faith that trusts in God and God's goodness at work in humans throughout the world. Regarding the question of evil, both in its natural and human manifestations, Ricoeur suggests that the problem of evil is not something to be solved but rather something to be responded to.[15] Our belief and faith in God remain in spite of the evil, pain, and suffering that we each must face. Hope leads to creative responses; thus, we are not merely suffering people, but also people that act and respond.[16]

Similar to Ricoeur's position on fragility and responsibility, Henri Nouwen talks about our relationship with the other in terms of the movement from hostility to hospitality. Creating a place for the other, who is a stranger, immediately implies otherness and difference. But to understand the other and how we can be hospitable, we need to see and feel the need for hospitality. Nouwen suggests that "to fully appreciate what hospitality can mean, we possibly have to become first a stranger ourselves."[17] We find ourselves moving back and forth between being the host, creating spaces of hospitality for others, and being the stranger, seeking places where we can be welcome and bring our true selves and the gift of ourselves. Nouwen talks about a unity that can emerge between guest and host so that the distinctions between them disappear. In a very profound way there is a deep sameness that emerges through this unity with the other. At the same time Nouwen tells us that the stranger or guest has unique gifts to give, and these will come forth if the host allows the guest the freedom to bring forth his or her gifts.

In *Can You Drink the Cup?* Nouwen talks about our shared life in community being one where we can express and accept the reality of both our joys and sorrows. Each of us needs to face and drink the cup of our own life, whatever that may hold. However, the cup is meant to be drunk in loving community with others.[18] If we are willing to face and share who we are, both our strengths and weaknesses, joys and sorrows, we become gifts to others and to ourselves. The image of having a drink with someone is a sign of "friendship, intimacy, and peace," according to Nouwen, and it reflects something more than simply "being thirsty."[19] Having a drink together suggests an expression of our common humanity that can emerge as we navigate being both hosts and guests.

Similarly to Ricoeur, Nouwen reflects on the somewhat unequal relationships that can form between givers and receivers, hosts and guests. He looks at relationships between parents and children, teachers and students, and healers and patients, and stresses that in each relationship free space must be made for guests to give who they are. It is a space that involves receptivity to the other person, as well as the inevitable confrontation that comes from disclosing our thoughts, ideas, opinions, lifestyle—who we are. Poverty of mind and heart in a host, which is marked by receptivity to the other, makes way for a kind of mutuality in relating to the stranger. Instead of entering in to fix problems, give quick advice, or dictate how the stranger should express his or her gifts, space is made for that person to express those gifts.[20] There are some obvious parallels here between Nouwen and Ricoeur, who also sees a movement back and forth between affirming sameness and difference as we relate to the other. We are unique individuals, and yet we are the same in that we are all searching for solitude and searching for hospitality, and it is in reaching out for God that these movements become possible.

Solitude and hospitality are worthy ideals, but they can only find their fullest fulfillment in reaching out to God and learning to meet God in intimacy through prayer. Nouwen says: "It indeed is our vocation to reach out to God . . . and stretch out our arms to the deep sea and the high heaven in a never-ending prayer. When we move from illusion to prayer, we move from the human shelter to the house of God. It is there that our solitude as well as our hospitality can be sustained."[21] Henri talks about the paradox of learning to pray yet only being able to receive prayer as a gift. With God, we seem to experience both an intimate union and estrangement all in one breath. We experience both presence and absence, the already and the not yet, but are called to create spaces where we can stretch out our arms to God and enter into intimacy with God. God remains wholly other, while at the same time uniting with us, calling us to imitate and to follow. With God, as in other relationships, we experience both intimacy and estrangement. We must reach out to God to find fruitful solitude with ourselves and hospitality with our neighbors.

I have been looking at some of the ways that we encounter and experience otherness in ourselves, with others, and with God. Throughout Nouwen's writings there is an emphasis on response to the other, which in many cases concerns justice and peace. This concern arises out of both the sameness and difference we experience with those who are other. Henri warns of the dangers of overemphasizing our differences through competition and comparison. He writes, "When countries and continents follow this road, violence, war, and even global suicide are real possibilities. But when we are willing to acknowledge and even celebrate our intimate connectedness as human beings we are on the road to peace."[22] Sometimes we are the ones crying out for justice, restoration, wholeness, and compassion. At other times we are the ones hearing the cries of others. We are struck by the common fragility that we all experience, as well as by the inequality in situations that cries out for healing and restoration. We are all invited to share in the task of being wounded healers, taking turns binding one another's wounds.

Ricoeur thinks that at the heart of justice is the notion of equality, broadly speaking. Where there is injustice, there is some type of inequality that is unacceptable and demands to be corrected. In one of Ricoeur's explicitly theological writings on justice, however, he includes a reflection on love and the necessity of the demand for justice to be tempered by love. Ricoeur traces some of the common senses of justice in the world reflected in the ideas of *lex talionis* or "an eye for eye," and the Golden Rule that says, "Do unto others as you would have them do unto you." Jesus radically addresses these common understandings of what is just with the dual command to love one's neighbor as oneself and the radical command to love one's enemies without expecting anything back.[23] Ricoeur reflects that the only way to live out the command to love is on the basis of having first received the gift of love from God. What makes love of the other and the laying down of one's life possible is that we have first received the gift of love.

In a similar way Nouwen says that "we come to the growing awareness that we can love only because we have been loved first, and that we can offer intimacy only because we are born out of the inner intimacy of God himself."[24] Intimacy comes through prayer and contemplation, but it is not a turn inward, away from community and the needs of the world around us.

Echoing the words of Thomas Merton, Nouwen writes, "The movement from loneliness to solitude is not a movement of a growing withdrawal but is instead a movement towards a deeper engagement in the burning issues of our time."[25] In Nouwen's life and writing there is a clear link between contemplation and action, the life of prayer and the life of service and peacework. Without intimacy with God, we do not have either the wisdom or the resources to respond to the other in love, offering ourselves as wounded healers. As Ricoeur notes, God's gift of love to us is not simply a free gift; it carries with it the call and responsibility to love others. The command to love God and others is indeed commanded, yet it comes forth from the love of God.[26]

My intention has been to sketch briefly some of the similarities in Paul Ricoeur's writings on otherness and justice and the writings of Henri Nouwen. What Ricoeur speaks of largely in philosophical language, Nouwen speaks somewhat more plainly in straightforward theological language. When we encounter the other of our self, the other person, society, and God, it is an opportunity to receive and respond, an opportunity for conversion. We are the fragile, or walking wounded, yet we are simultaneously full of capability and creative potential for healing and change. Our encounter with the other calls us to solidarity and the recognition of our similarity, while seeing the great and God-given diversity in our midst. The cries for justice that arise in part because of our otherness and woundedness, become an incredible opportunity to walk in love, both to accept our belovedness and to acknowledge the belovedness of those in our midst. As Nouwen reminds us, the call to be wounded healers is part of our cup that we are meant to accept and drink. The question remains: Can we drink the cup?

Notes

[1] Paul Ricoeur, *Oneself as Another*, trans. Kathleen Blamey (Chicago: The University of Chicago Press, 1992), 24. Some of Ricoeur's most explicitly theological writings can be found in "Evil, a Challenge to Philosophy and Theology," in *Figuring the Sacred: Religion, Narrative, and Imagination*, ed. Mark Wallace (Minneapolis: Augsburg Fortress, 1995).

[2] Ricoeur, *Oneself as Another*, 2–4.

[3] Charles Taylor, *Human Agency and Language,* Philosophical Papers 1 (Cambridge: Cambridge University Press, 1985), 15–16.

[4] Ricoeur, *Oneself as Another*, 118–22.

[5] Henri J. M. Nouwen, *Reaching Out: The Three Movements of the Spiritual Life* (New York: Doubleday, 1975), 49–50.

[6] Ibid., 42.

[7] Ibid., 43.

[8] Paul Ricoeur, *The Just*, trans. David Pellauer (Chicago: University of Chicago Press, 2000), xi.

[9] Emmanuel Levinas, *Ethics and Infinity*, trans. Richard A. Cohen (Pittsburgh: Duquesne University Press, 1985), 89.

[10] Ricoeur, *Oneself as Another*, 190.

[11] Paul Ricoeur, "Responsibility and Fragility: An Ethical Reflection," *The Journal of the Faculty of Religious Studies, McGill University* 21 (1993): 9.

[12] Ricoeur, *Oneself as Another*, 192.

[13] Ricoeur, "Responsibility and Fragility," 10.

[14] Charles Reagan, *Paul Ricoeur: His Life and Work* (Chicago: The University of Chicago Press, 1996).

[15] Ricoeur, "Evil, a Challenge to Philosophy and Theology," 258.

[16] Ricoeur, *Oneself as Another*, 190.

[17] Nouwen, *Reaching Out*, 68.

[18] Henri J. M. Nouwen, *Can You Drink the Cup?* (Notre Dame, IN: Ave Maria Press, 1996), 57.

[19] Ibid., 80.

[20] Nouwen, *Reaching Out*, 103.

[21] Ibid., 121.

[22] Henri J. M. Nouwen, *Peacework: Prayer, Resistance, Community* (Maryknoll, NY: Orbis Books, 2005), 78.

[23] Paul Ricoeur, "Ethical and Theological Considerations on the Golden Rule," in Wallace, *Figuring the Sacred*, 300.

[24] Nouwen, *Reaching Out*, 129.

[25] Ibid., 46.

[26] Paul Ricoeur, "Love and Justice," in Wallace, *Figuring the Sacred*, 319.

9

A Spirituality of Imperfection

Wil Hernandez

As a spiritual icon, Henri Nouwen is still shaping America's religious land-scape through the continuing impact of his life and work even after his death over a decade ago. This study focuses on Nouwen's spiritual formation dy-namics and his lived spirituality. The first part presents an approach to spiri-tuality that is holistic, one that Nouwen modeled in his ministry of soul care and spiritual formation. Nouwen construed the spiritual journey as integra-tive—incorporating spirituality, theology, psychology, and ministry in a seam-less fashion.

This integrated view stems from Nouwen's fundamental understanding of the nature of the spiritual life, which involves cultivating—*inwardly, outwardly,* and *upwardly*—one's relation with *self, others* and *God.* In *Reaching Out* Nouwen laid out this same concept schematically, unraveling the interlocking relation-ships of psychology, ministry, and theology with a spirituality that is. a "full and mutual sharing of one thing in the complete reality of the other."[1] This kind of coinherence is what framed Nouwen's integrated approach to ministry.[2]

The second part of this study explores a brand of spirituality that is decid-edly counter-intuitive and counter-cultural, a *spirituality of imperfection* that Nouwen exemplified in his life. He recognized the spiritual journey to perfec-tion as a journey through imperfection, factoring in the realities of struggle, weakness, and incompleteness.

Overall, this study shows how one imperfect saint, with a rare combination of spiritual, theological, psychological, and ministerial insights, has reoriented Christians—and continues to do so to this day through his writings—to a much more realistic and integrated view of the spiritual life and its formation.

Psychology and Spirituality

Biographer Michael Ford distills Henri Nouwen's instinctive ability to in-tegrate the psychological with the spiritual: "Trained in psychology and steeped

in the riches of Christian spirituality, Nouwen managed to balance his awareness of the dynamics of the human psyche with his openness to the workings of
the Spirit."[3] Nouwen considered the matrix of psychology beneficial in the
understanding of self that he believed is integral to the development of the
spiritual life. But he reckoned self-knowledge always in relation to God. Like
Augustine, Nouwen held that the knowledge of self and the knowledge of
God are inextricably bound together. Illustrating their reciprocal dynamic,
he declared, "We become strangers to ourselves" the more we act as strangers before God.[4] The self, as Nouwen viewed it, ultimately derives its meaning in relation to God in that "we can be most ourselves when most like
God."[5] As he affirmed, "I am hidden in God and I have to find myself in that
relationship."[6]

Nouwen's own grasp of what John Calvin referred to as "double knowledge" goes beyond the theoretical; he had his experience to back it up. In
reading *The Genesee Diary* one can sense Nouwen's evident "growth in self-
knowledge and God-knowledge," which brought about greater integrity to his
journey.[7] Indeed, his experience of the dynamic between psychology and spirituality brings to clearer focus our joint pursuit of wholeness and holiness.

Spirituality and Ministry

Not only is psychology integrated with spirituality, but spirituality itself is
entwined with ministry. The Bible's command to love our neighbor as our self
assumes that we do in fact love our self. We cannot give ourselves to others if
we do not have a self that we fully accept and intimately know. To the degree
that we love ourselves, we are able to love and give of ourselves to others.
Ministry requires precisely that—the "giving of self."[8]

Thus, the love of God and the love of neighbor cannot be separated (cf. 1 Jn
4:20–21). Nouwen unpacks the dynamic of the Great Commandment thus:
"The first commandment receives concreteness and specificity through the
second; the second ... becomes possible through the first."[9] Loving God enables us to truly love others; loving others proves that we truly love God. The
melding of these two corresponds to the marriage between spirituality and
ministry.

Ministry must be fueled by genuine spirituality to be effective. For spirituality to be authentic, it must give birth to actual practice of ministry. Nouwen
embraced the conviction that communion with God results in deep community with others and that true community leads to creative ministry. Spirituality and ministry go hand in hand.

Theology and Spirituality

Theology is the final domain that clinches the coinherence trilogy of spirituality. Like psychology and ministry, theology indivisibly fuses with spirituality.

Henri Nouwen saw no discrepancy between them. He understood the word *theologia* to be "the highest level of prayer," which the desert fathers equated with "a direct intimate communion with God."[10]

With Nouwen, all theology is spiritual and practical. As one academician attested, "He [Nouwen] was a pastoral theologian, somebody who made theology existential enough to become a living theology."[11] For one, he always insisted on "situat[ing] our knowledge of God in the concrete circumstances of our existence."[12] His conviction that our doctrinal life is never to be disengaged from our life of faith is evidenced in his *Letters to Marc,* the book that captures Nouwen's doctrine of the spiritual life wherein his faith was fleshed out by what he had "lived out and lived through."[13] Nouwen by no means exhibited perfect balance in his spiritual life, but his writings show that he strove for integrity in living it out.[14]

Concerning the conjoined status of theology and spirituality, Nouwen considered theological moments as "moments of doxology in which knowing God, loving God, and praising God" are one.[15] In an overlapping fashion, they constitute what a living encounter with God entails.

Journey of Integration and Imperfection

Henri Nouwen's proclivity for integration represented a major step toward wholeness. On a deeper analysis, his commitment to pursuing it spoke more about his heightened awareness of his fractured human condition than about an obsessive drive for perfection. Nouwen's integrative pursuit of the spiritual life never obviated but instead incorporated facets of psychological, ministerial, and theological imperfections. Integration, for him, coexisted with imperfection.

Spirituality does integrate with psychology (the inward movement to the innermost self), but it is a *psychology* of imperfection—wherein the path to increasing wholeness involves the psychological realities of brokenness. Referring to our universal human condition, Nouwen openly admitted, "Our brokenness is so visible and tangible, so concrete and specific."[16] He, of course, spoke as a deeply broken man himself, "broken with psychological wounds, physical limitations, and emotional needs."[17] Yet, Nouwen regarded brokenness as, as Frederick Buechner expresses it, "a way of being human in this world, which is the way to wholeness."[18]

In a way, Nouwen's life mirrored the eucharistic formula invoked during holy communion: "taken or chosen, blessed, broken, and given." It could be said that "his life became spiritual bread and wine, body and blood, for others."[19] We are recipients today of untold blessings flowing out of Nouwen's brokenness. His inward journey of imperfection, marked by authentic self-knowledge, continues to inspire us in our own pursuit of wholeness.

Similarly, spirituality integrates with ministry (the *outward* movement toward others), but it is a ministry of imperfection in which the key to a powerful ministry is unlocked through the exercise of powerlessness. The way of

God, Nouwen asserted, is the way of weakness manifested in Christ's birth and death in voluntary powerlessness.[20] Appealing to Christ's example, Nouwen stressed that the way of the Christian minister "is not the way of upward mobility . . . but the way of downward mobility ending on the cross."[21] The mystery of ministry lies in the reality that "ministers are powerless people who have nothing to boast of except their weakness."[22] Like the apostle Paul, "it is precisely in such 'weakness' that true power, the power of God, becomes effective in [our] ministry."[23]

The path of power is through weakness, but it is one that "claims power, God's power, the all-transforming *power of love*."[24] Again, Paul demonstrated this in his own ministry: "Like the cross of Christ, Paul's weakness is an expression of love . . . (2 Cor 4:15)."[25] Ministry then, as a movement toward others, is a powerful love in action, albeit through weakness.

Lastly, spirituality integrates with theology (the upward movement to God), but it is nonetheless represented by a *theology* of imperfection in which the route toward union with God is paved with suffering as a prelude to glory. Nouwen declared with certainty: "There is no journey to God outside of the journey that Jesus made,"[26]–and that includes the inevitable way of suffering. To Nouwen, it is illusory to think that "reaching out to God will free us from pain and suffering."[27] Without any trace of triumphalism, he accepted our residual fallenness as a factor in the suffering that has now become our inevitable lot.[28] As one whose ceaseless struggle proved to be the bane of his existence, Nouwen knew suffering intimately. By any measure, he suffered well himself.[29]

Nouwen further acknowledged that if "communion with Jesus means becoming like him . . . lead[ing] us to a new realm of being . . . usher[ing] us into the Kingdom,"[30] then suffering is the expected pathway to the kingdom. Communion with God is a communion with and through suffering.

To summarize: The inward, outward, and upward journeys are journeys of imperfection, which Henri Nouwen himself exemplified. Yet, in the midst of his personal encounters with the glaring realities of imperfection associated with the experience of brokenness, weakness, and suffering, Nouwen never stopped giving of himself to others through the avenue of ministry, the ministry of soul care and spiritual formation in particular.

Integrated Approach to Soul Care and Spiritual Formation

Henri Nouwen's ministry style was expressly broad. As a minister he functioned more as a generalist than a specialist, instinctively combining the dynamics of soul care and spiritual formation into a singular thrust and engaging the disciplines of the mind, heart, and body in order to create space for God.[31] Such an integrated mindset and approach account for much of his practical style of ministry.

Indicative of such a holistic approach, Nouwen combined the ministerial tasks of *healing, sustaining,* and *guiding,* which all stand for the same foundational principles of pastoral theology advocated by Seward Hiltner, one of his mentors at Meninger Clinic. Integrating them into his own applied understanding, Nouwen recast these three shepherding functions into the overlapping roles of *pastor* (one who heals the wounds of the past), *priest* (one who sustains life in the present), and *prophet* (one who guides others to the future).[32]

In his ministry of formation Nouwen wore all three hats, so to speak, in ways that seemed almost indistinguishable. It is difficult if not impossible to pigeonhole Nouwen into one exclusive role. Depending on the situation, Nouwen displayed flexibility in his ministry approach. Conversant with a whole gamut of soul care and spiritual formation helps, including spiritual friendship, spiritual guidance, spiritual mentoring, and spiritual direction, Nouwen was able to make productive use of their combined elements with creativity and ease.[33]

Integrated Ministerial Dynamics

Henri Nouwen believed that a real minister is a convener—a task he equated with the exercise of hospitality.[34] In his thinking, all of ministry is to be seen as hospitality: "To help, to serve, to care, to guide, to heal . . . [are] all used to express a reaching out toward our neighbor whereby we perceive life as a gift not to possess but to share."[35]

Soul care is exactly this: a selfless sharing of one's life motivated by a deep caring for another person's life. As Nouwen defines it, care "is the loving attention given to another person."[36] For him, "the care of the soul is paramount, not the cure of the soul, as a necessary first step in deepening one's own spirituality."[37]

It was apparent that Nouwen's focal thrust in ministry was formational. Yet he never claimed it was his job to form others. He looked at spiritual formation as the process of emptying our heart for the Spirit to be released to do its work.[38] As he elaborated: "The point of spiritual formation is to discern where something is happening . . . [where] God is doing something. Our task is to become aware of where and how God is presently acting and to recognize that indeed it is God who is acting."[39]

Spiritual Journey of Imperfection

Henri Nouwen's integrative approach to ministry, based on his clear grasp of the coinherence of spirituality, psychology, ministry, and theology, was both propelled and tempered by his own experience of imperfection. With characteristic honesty, Nouwen confessed: "I am unable to say that I have arrived; I never will in this life."[40] He, in fact, issued this warning: "Those who think they have arrived, have lost their way. Those who think they have reached their goal, have missed it."[41] Evidently, "the spiritual journey for

Nouwen was never about perfection, but about struggling to live in a deep and meaningful relationship with God that would bear fruit in the lives of others."[42]

Henri Nouwen never hesitated to expose his own spiritual inabilities, even if by doing so it would seem, on the surface, to neutralize the power of the gospel that he sought to proclaim. On the contrary, instead of jeopardizing his witness, Nouwen's credibility increases even as he "becomes a mirror for all of us Christians who daily fail to be perfect as [our] heavenly Father is perfect."[43]

At the same time, Nouwen possessed a spiritual wisdom that ensured that imperfection did not become the overriding theme of his life as much as his courage and willingness to confront imperfection in light of the power of the gospel. His transparent life bore out the truth that only in the full awareness of one's limitations does one discover God's ample supply of power and grace. Herein lies the blessed side of a an imperfect existence.[44] As a restless seeker, wounded healer, and faithful struggler, Henri Nouwen emerges as the embodiment of an authentic spirituality lodged in an imperfect personality.

Nouwen is a quintessential example of a restless, wandering soul searching for himself, seeking out others and the world, and deeply longing for God. Through his restless seeking, Nouwen confronted his troubled self, his conflicted relationships with others, and his sometimes wavering relationship with God. To his dismay, he confessed one time, "My own restlessness . . . [has] made me flee solitude as soon as I have found it."[45]

Coming out of his seven-month experience of living as a monk at the Abbey of the Genesee, Nouwen looked back and, with searing honesty, bemoaned, "Somehow I had expected that my restlessness would turn into quietude, my tensions into a peaceful life-style, and my ambiguities and ambivalences into a single-minded commitment to God."[46]

On his fifty-fourth birthday, six months before settling into his newfound home at L'Arche Daybreak, Nouwen reflected upon his life and the restlessness that beset him still: "Very little, if anything has changed with regard to my search for inner unity and peace. I am still the restless, nervous, intense, distracted, and impulse-driven person I was when I set out on this spiritual journey."[47]

Suffice it to say that the lifelong battle to secure peace and quiet for his soul never subsided for Nouwen. Although he could not fully resolve his restlessness, he realized that it always brought him back to God, the Perfect One whom he was ultimately seeking. Thus it could be said that, in the midst of imperfection, Nouwen was, at least, drawing closer to Perfection.

None of us is whole, at least not yet. We are a damaged, broken, and wounded lot. Not only did Nouwen acknowledge this intrinsic condition of all of humanity, but he vividly lived its reality as a "saint with wounds."[48] He often has been identified with a memorable phrase that has become the virtual cornerstone of his spirituality: "wounded healer."

Nouwen wrestled all through his life with a deep wound of loneliness that no earthly relationships could satisfy. He himself characterized it as "this immense need for affection, and this immense fear of rejection," pointing to its fragility in his own life.[49]

Despite the agonizing struggle that came with having to live with his inner wound, Nouwen devoted his energy to bringing healing to other wounded souls: "He guided many through the dark places of doubt and loss of faith. While he was doing this for others he was himself powerfully afflicted by dark thoughts and mental pains. He knew anxiety and depression, from which there was only temporary release."[50]

Nouwen's enduring concept of the wounded healer did not lack its share of critics though. One in particular complained: "Many see the Nouwen minister as a weakling. . . . The wounded-healer pastor may become an inward-looking chaplain of the emotions who forgets his function as a prophet of God and servant of those in need."[51] The fact is that Nouwen, in *The Wounded Healer,* warned against a form of "spiritual exhibitionism" that grossly misuses the wounded healer concept.[52] He actually urged us to "find the freedom to step over our wounds."[53]

In reality, Nouwen's woundedness served as a vast channel through which God's limitless power could be displayed. "It is indeed through our broken, vulnerable, mortal ways of being that the healing power of the eternal God becomes visible to us," Nouwen claimed.[54] Nouwen simply lived out his humanity and his unique calling. The core of his humanity was his being "wounded," and the core of his true calling was his being a "healer."[55] He lived both core truths well.

In restlessness as in woundedness Nouwen embodied imperfection. Struggle proved to be the common thread of his experience. As a genuine seeker, Nouwen was restless. As a true healer, he was deeply wounded. As a real struggler, he was faithful.

At the heart of an authentic spiritual life lies the perennial experience of struggle. As Nouwen paints it, our new life is "a life of joy, but also of sacrifice. It is a glorious life, but also one of suffering. It is a life of peace, but also of struggle."[56] From experience he testified again and again that struggle was the stuff of imperfection he had to live with.

For many, the spiritual life resembles a tug of war. Nouwen was no stranger to this experience of constantly being pulled in opposite directions. His journals sometimes read more like a dizzying record of contradictory statements than a coherent expression of thoughts. They showcase Nouwen's continual struggles to translate his intentions into actions, his ideas into reality, and his endless professions into concrete expressions. He conceded: "There are so many contradictions within me. . . . The distance between insight and practice is huge."[57] Sue Mosteller concluded that Nouwen's "struggle to close the gap between the ideal and the reality is so real, so painful, and so human!"[58]

None of Nouwen's struggles is unfamiliar to any of our own experiences except that, unlike most of us, he freely talked about them openly. Yet, like many of us, he genuinely longed to overcome this lifelong battle. Nouwen posed a revealing question to which he volunteered his own answer: "Can the tension be resolved in an integrated life? . . . Few have accomplished this wholeness. I certainly have not."[59] The presence of tension is further exacerbated by the inevitable presence of darkness looming both inside and outside all of us.

Much as he wanted to dispel it, darkness hovered about like a heavy cloud in Nouwen's life. Even when it seemed like he had finally found the "light" at L'Arche after a long, dark journey, Nouwen had to admit: "Life in community does not keep the darkness away. To the contrary. It seems that the light that attracted me to L'Arche also made me conscious of the darkness in myself. . . . Community life has opened me up to the real spiritual combat: the struggle to keep moving toward the light precisely when the darkness is so real."[60] Despite his awareness that times of darkness are standard ingredients for a life of faith, Nouwen never envisioned going through the worst of them.

It was while serving as pastor of L'Arche that Nouwen encountered the darkest episode of his life. It concerned the breakdown of his friendship with Nathan Ball. From his anguished account, we glimpse Nouwen's version of the "dark night": "Here I was . . . flat on the ground and in total darkness. . . . It was as if all that had given my life meaning was pulled away and I could see nothing in front of me but a bottomless abyss. . . . I felt that God had abandoned me. . . . The anguish completely paralyzed me. . . . All had become darkness."[61] By God's grace, Nouwen came out of his own dark night with a far greater motivation to love more deeply. Because he decided "to choose, in the face of it all, not death but life," Nouwen was able "to look back at that period of life and see it as a time of intense purification that had led gradually to a new inner freedom, a new hope, and a new creativity."[62]

Henri Nouwen openly embraced the reality of struggle as a normative experience of spiritual imperfection. He welcomed spiritual tension and learned to manage its imposing presence. He accepted spiritual darkness and willingly passed through its black corridors without losing his spiritual vision. Through it all, Nouwen never gave up on the struggle but remained faithful.

Faithfulness is the one outstanding trait for which Nouwen is best remembered by people closest to him. In Nathan Ball's recollection, "So often and in so many ways, Henri expressed his desire to be faithful—faithful to God, to his own inner self, to the demands of love, to friendships, and to his chosen vocation as a priest."[63] Determination proved to be key for him in exercising faithfulness.

Drawing upon such determination, Nouwen confronted what most assumed to be the crux of his struggle, which was dealing with his homosexual orientation. Michael Ford's revealing portrait of Nouwen exposed this largely hidden struggle and depicted the priest's sexuality as "a source of deep anxiety and conflict" due to his unbending "commitment to live out his vow of celibacy."[64]

Celibacy was no small issue for Nouwen, who understood well the complications of trying to live a chaste life.[65] Still, he faithfully committed to conduct his "hidden and secret life" with purity of heart, no matter what.[66] For someone whose craving for human love and affection seemed insatiable, the protracted struggle could be punishingly painful. To the best of his closest friends' knowledge, "Nouwen may have struggled, but he made no compromises with his convictions."[67] "Guided by the deep awareness that we are called to be living signs of God's faithful presence among us," Nouwen quietly struggled his way through until the end of his life in a posture of fidelity.[68]

Henri Nouwen freely chose to reveal himself candidly in all of his writings; thus, no more accurate sketch of his spirituality is needed than what he himself so keenly portrayed. It is a spirituality of imperfection that is deep and authentic. Nouwen was of the conviction that even "while we ourselves are overwhelmed by our own weaknesses and limitations, we can still be so transparent that the Spirit of God, the divine counselor, can shine through us and bring light to others."[69] In a way, it was his imperfection that qualified him to minister to others.

In *The Holy Longing*, Ronald Rolheiser wrote a moving dedication to Henri Nouwen that best captures Nouwen's "imperfect" influence upon so many: "By sharing his own struggles, he mentored us all, helping us to pray while not knowing how to pray, to rest while feeling restless, to be at peace while tempted, to feel safe while still anxious, to be surrounded by a cloud of light while still in darkness, and to love while still in doubt."[70]

How can such an imperfect vessel also be a fountain out of which abundant blessings flow? What accounted for the impact of Henri Nouwen's spirituality? Despite what may sound like a platitudinous rhetoric, it must be Jesus, Nouwen's Jesus, that made all the difference: "Nouwen embraced his crosses, carried them, and allowed them to lead him to Jesus."[71] Much as many would have preferred Nouwen's woundedness to feature less prominently in his life, his close friend Robert Jonas cleverly reminds us that "his ever-present, accompanying shadow was there only because of the Light in which he walked."[72] Henri Nouwen did walk with Jesus, his true Love and the true Lover of his wounded soul.

On September 21, 1996, the restless, wounded, and struggling soul of God's beloved at long last found peace, wholeness, and contentment in the arms of his eternal Lover in God's eternal home. The world mourned the death of a saint, so scarred, so wounded, so imperfect that the church to which he belonged might consider him the least likely candidate for beatification, much less canonization. The Christian world, however, lost a real saint, who by his life demonstrated that the journey to perfection is through imperfection.

Henri Nouwen's writings still speak—even more loudly today—and continue to arrest many of our spiritual distortions. They beckon us to listen, but in a rather different mode: counterintuitively and counterculturally. G. K. Chesterton remarked that "the saint needed by each culture is the one who contradicts it the most."[73] Nouwen assumes that role even today.

To a culture that remains highly individualistic, Henri Nouwen inculcates the ideals of community; to the narcissistic tendencies of the majority, he promotes the value of compassionate living; instead of the cherished notion of upward mobility, with its undue emphases on success and productivity, he elevates the path of *downward* mobility, with its themes of self-sacrifice and humility; to a wounded lot seeking recovery and healing, he enhances the value of *care* more than *cure* of souls; and finally, to a professedly "spiritual" generation seeking power and perfection, he introduces a theology of weakness, powerlessness, and imperfection. All in all, Henri Nouwen's spirituality is summed up in a simple but compelling phrase: a spirituality of imperfection.

Notes

[1] Henri J. M. Nouwen, *Reaching Out: Three Movements of the Spiritual Life* (New York: Doubleday, 1975), 13–14.

[2] See Timothy George and Alistair McGrath, eds., *For All the Saints: Evangelical Theology and Christian Spirituality* (Louisville, KY: Westminister John Knox Press, 2003), 3.

[3] Michael Ford, *Wounded Prophet: A Portrait of Henri J. M. Nouwen* (New York: Doubleday, 1999), 15.

[4] Henri J. M. Nouwen, "Spiritual Direction," *Worship* 55 (September 1981): 402.

[5] Henri J. M. Nouwen, *Lifesigns: Intimacy, Fecundity, and Ecstasy in Christian Perspective* (New York: Doubleday, 1986), 26.

[6] James R. and Elizabeth Newby, *Between Peril and Promise* (Nashville, TN: Thomas Nelson, 1984), 40.

[7] See Luci Shaw, *Life Path* (East Sussex, England: Christina Press, 1997), 13. See also Henri J. M. Nouwen, *The Genesee Diary: Report from a Trappist Monastery* (New York: Doubleday, 1976).

[8] Henri J. M. Nouwen, *¡Gracias! A Latin American Journal* (Maryknoll, NY: Orbis Books, 1993), 85; cf. Henri J. M. Nouwen, *Creative Ministry* (New York: Image Books, 1978), 51.

[9] Henri J. M. Nouwen, *The Living Reminder: Service and Prayer in Memory of Jesus Christ* (San Francisco: HarperSanFrancisco, 1977), 32.

[10] Henri J. M. Nouwen, "Theology as Doxology: Reflections on Theological Education," in *Caring for the Commonweal: Education for Religious and Public Life*, ed. Parker J. Palmer, Barbara G. Wheeler, and James W. Fowler (Macon, GA: Mercer University Press, 1990), 96.

[11] James E. Dittes, quoted in Ford, *Wounded Prophet,* 113.

[12] Nouwen, "Theology as Doxology," 94.

[13] Henri J. M. Nouwen, *Letters to Marc about Jesus: Living a Spiritual Life in a Material World* (San Francisco: HarperSanFrancisco, 1988), 6–7.

[14] See, in particular, Henri J. M. Nouwen, *Spiritual Journals: Three Books in One* (New York: Continuum, 1997).

[15] Nouwen, "Theology as Doxology," 109.

[16] Henri J. M. Nouwen, *Life of the Beloved: Spiritual Living in a Secular World* (New York: Crossroad, 1992), 69.

[17] Rebecca Laird and Michael J. Christensen, *The Heart of Henri Nouwen: His Words of Blessing* (New York: Crossroad, 2003), 131.

[18] Frederick Buechner, *The Longing for Home: Recollections and Reflections* (New York: HarperCollins, 1996), 109–10; see Nouwen, *Life of the Beloved,* 75.

[19] Laird and Christensen, *The Heart of Henri Nouwen,* 14.

[20] Henri J. M. Nouwen, *Finding My Way Home: Pathways to Life and the Spirit* (New York: Crossroad, 2001), 33, 35.

[21] Henri J. M. Nouwen, *In the Name of Jesus: Reflections on Christian Leadership* (New York: Crossroad, 1989), 62.

[22] Henri J. M. Nouwen, "The Monk and the Cripple: Toward a Spirituality of Ministry," *America* 142 (March 1980): 207, 205.

[23] Timothy B. Savage, *Power through Weakness: Paul's Understanding of the Christian Ministry in 2 Corinthians* (Cambridge: Cambridge University Press, 1996), 185–86.

[24] Nouwen, *Finding My Way Home*, 42.

[25] Michael J. Gorman, *Cruciformity: Paul's Narrative Spirituality of the Cross* (Grand Rapids, MI: Eerdmans, 2001), 293.

[26] Henri J. M. Nouwen, *The Return of the Prodigal Son: A Story of Homecoming* (New York: Image Books, 1992), 56.

[27] Nouwen, *Reaching Out*, 150.

[28] See Henri J. M. Nouwen, "Living the Spiritual Life: An Interview with Henri Nouwen," by Catherine Walsh, *Saint Anthony Messenger* 93 (April 1986): 11–15.

[29] Michael O'Laughlin described Nouwen as "a man of sorrows walking his own personal *via dolorosa*" (*God's Beloved: A Spiritual Biography of Henri Nouwen* [Maryknoll, NY: Orbis Books, 2004], 7).

[30] Henri J. M. Nouwen, *With Burning Hearts: A Meditation on the Eucharistic Life* (Maryknoll, NY: Orbis Books, 2002), 74.

[31] See Henri J. M. Nouwen, "Prayer and Health Care," *CHAC Review* 17 (Winter 1989): 11–16.

[32] Nouwen, *The Living Reminder*, 75.

[33] See Beth Porter with Susan S. Brown and Philip Coulter, eds., *Befriending Life: Encounters with Henri Nouwen* (New York: Doubleday, 2001); and Christopher de Vinck, ed., *Nouwen Then: Personal Reflections on Henri* (Grand Rapids, MI: Zondervan, 1999).

[34] See Henri J. M. Nouwen, "A Visit with Henri Nouwen," an interview by Todd Brennan, *The Critic* 36 (Summer 1978): 46.

[35] Nouwen, *Reaching Out*, 109.

[36] Henri J. M. Nouwen, *Our Greatest Gift: A Meditation on Death and Dying* (New York: HarperCollins, 1995), 58.

[37] Jay M. Uomoto, "Human Suffering, Psychotherapy, and Soul Care: The Spirituality of Henri J. M. Nouwen at the Nexus," *Journal of Psychology and Christianity* 14 (Winter 1995): 347, 352.

[38] Henri J. M. Nouwen, *From Resentment to Gratitude* (Chicago: Franciscan Herald Press, 1974), 30.

[39] Nouwen, "A Visit with Henri Nouwen," 45.

[40] Nouwen, *The Return of the Prodigal Son*, 17.

[41] Nouwen, *The Genesee Diary,* 133.

[42] Deirdre LaNoue, *The Spiritual Legacy of Henri Nouwen* (New York: Continuum, 2000), 108.

[43] Robert Waldron, *Walking with Henri Nouwen: A Reflective Journey* (Mahwah, NJ: Paulist Press, 2003), 9.

[44] Cf. Wallace Stevens's poetic metaphor: "The imperfect is our paradise" (quoted in Philip Simmons, *Learning to Fall: The Blessings of an Imperfect Life* [New York: Bantam Books, 2002], 32).

[45] Nouwen, *Our Greatest Gift*, 1.

[46] Nouwen, *The Genesee Diary*, 217.

[47] Henri J. M. Nouwen, *The Road to Daybreak: A Spiritual Journey* (New York: Doubleday, 1988), 127.

[48] Ford, *Wounded Prophet*, 8, 44, 50.

[49] Henri J. M. Nouwen, *Sabbatical Journey: The Diary of His Final Year* (New York: Crossroad, 1998), 25.

[50] Vera Phillips and Edwin Robertson, *The Wounded Healer* (London: SPCK, 1984), vii–viii.

[51] John McFarland, "The Minister as Narrator," *The Christian Ministry* 189 (January 1987): 20.

[52] Henri J. M. Nouwen, *The Wounded Healer* (New York: Image Books, 1979), 88.

[53] Henri J. M. Nouwen, *Here and Now: Living in the Spirit* (New York: Crossroad, 1994), 45.

[54] Henri J. M. Nouwen, *A Cry for Mercy: Prayers from the Genesee* (New York: Image Books, 2002), 144.

[55] Nathan Ball, interview with author, tape recording, Richmond Hill, Ontario, April 28, 2004.

[56] Henri J. M. Nouwen, *Heart Speaks to Heart: Three Prayers to Jesus* (Notre Dame, IN: Ave Maria Press, 1989), 43–44.

[57] Nouwen, *Sabbatical Journey*, 13.

[58] Sue Mosteller, "Foreword," in Nouwen, *Sabbatical Journey*, ix.

[59] Nouwen, *Sabbatical Journey*, 39.

[60] Nouwen, *The Return of the Prodigal Son*, 136.

[61] Henri J. M. Nouwen, *The Inner Voice of Love: A Journey through Anguish to Freedom* (New York: Image Books, 1998), xiii–xiv.

[62] Ibid., xvii–xviii, 59–60.

[63] Nathan Ball, "A Covenant of Friendship," in Porter, Brown, and Coulter, *Befriending Life*, 95.

[64] See Robert Durback, "Henri Nouwen: Memories of a Wounded Prophet," *America* 181 (July 3–10, 1999): 16–17.

[65] Nouwen, *The Road to Daybreak*, 169.

[66] Nouwen, *Sabbatical Journey*, 24.

[67] Ibid., 17.

[68] Nouwen, *Here and Now*, 129.

[69] Nouwen, *The Living Reminder*, 68.

[70] Ronald Rolheiser, *The Holy Longing: The Search for a Christian Spirituality* (New York: Doubleday, 1999).

[71] Waldron, *Walking with Henri Nouwen*, 86.

[72] Henri Nouwen and Robert A. Jonas, *Henri Nouwen: Writings Selected with an Introduction by Robert A. Jonas* (Maryknoll, NY: Orbis Books, 1998), xiv.

[73] G. K. Chesterton, cited in Mark S. Burrows, "Gospel Fantasy," *Christian Century* (June 1, 2004): 23.

10

Reflection
on the Biographers' Panel

Peter Naus

Although the Turning the Wheel conference was to commemorate Henri Nouwen's death a decade on and to assess his spiritual legacy, it was not meant to be focused exclusively on him. Recent developments in spirituality, especially those inspired by Nouwen's life and writings, were to be reviewed as well. The conference organizers decided to include a panel of his biographers in the program in the belief that a better understanding of Nouwen as a person might aid in the assessment of his legacy. They also felt there were some unanswered questions about his personality and his life, which is not surprising given the absence, thus far, of an authoritative biography. Furthermore, the organizers hoped that the panel would provide those in attendance with an opportunity to cast new light on Henri Nouwen and his teachings.

Members of the biographers' panel were Jurjen Beumer, Robert Jonas, Deirdre LaNoue, and Michael O'Laughlin. Beumer authored the first biography of Henri, which was published in the Netherlands in 1996 and one year later in the United States under the title *Henri Nouwen: A Restless Seeking for God.* Jonas wrote an extensive biographical sketch of Henri in 1998 as the introduction to his book on Henri: *Henri Nouwen: Writings Selected with an Introduction by Robert A. Jonas.* Deirdre LaNoue did not write a biography, as such, but rather an assessment of the impact of Nouwen's writing on American spirituality. Her book, *The Spiritual Legacy of Henri Nouwen,* appeared in 2000. Michael O'Laughlin completed two books about Henri: *God's Beloved: A Spiritual Biography of Henri Nouwen* and *Henri Nouwen: His Life and Vision,* published in 2004 and 2005, respectively. Unfortunately, the author of one other book-length biography of Henri, Michael Ford, was unable to attend the conference. His book, *A Wounded Prophet: A Portrait of Henri Nouwen,* appeared in 1999. I served as the panel's moderator. Henri and I became friends in the 1950s during our student days in Holland. We also taught together in the psychology department at the University of Notre Dame in 1966–67.

96

The procedure adopted for the discussion was intended to maximize audience participation. To this end, introductions were kept brief, as were the exchanges within the panel. Several issues were raised by either the panelists or the audience, although the issue that became somewhat of a focal point for the discussion was Henri's homosexuality. After one panelist mentioned it, several others followed suit, and there were questions and comments from the audience as well. It was noted that some of Henri's close friends had known about it for a long time but that he had not told everyone close to him and had chosen not to reveal his sexual orientation publicly. Presumably, Henri's main reason for not "coming out" was his fear that doing so would be sensationalized and would detract from his spiritual message. There are indications that Henri continued to agonize about his decision. One person suggested that Henri's suffering illustrates the deep hurt and pain gay people feel in a society that does not accept their sexual orientation.

Henri's decision to keep his sexual orientation to himself illustrates another issue that emerged in the discussion: the measured and guarded nature of Henri's self-disclosure. Henri's confessional style of writing should not be mistaken for an unrestrained baring of his soul. As one panelist pointed out, Henri was always conscious of the possible impact of his confessions and often experienced a certain tension between wanting to be truthful and true to himself and desiring to be respected, perhaps even adored. His was a rather heavily edited confessional style. Another panelist suggested that Henri fashioned an image of himself in his writing that inspired readers but became a straitjacket for himself. Because of the incompleteness of his self-disclosure, our understanding of Henri is at best provisional. One of the panelists observed that trying to penetrate Henri's inner dynamics was like peeling an onion; no sooner had one peeled off one layer of his personality than another would appear. At least one member of the audience expressed some discomfort with attempts to dissect Henri's personality. He referred to the bible story about the blind man who was asked by the Pharisees whether he thought Jesus was a sinner and answered "I don't know if he is a sinner: I only know that I was blind and now I can see" (Jn 9:25–26). Similarly, it does not matter who or what Henri was, what counts is how he affected people.

A third issue drawing a fair amount of attention was the question about the degree of consistency between Henri's teaching and what he lived. In fact, the panelists and I agreed ahead of time to use this question as the starting point for the discussion. One panelist stressed that Henri made his life an integral part of his message. He genuinely tried to model gospel values in his everyday life, but he did not hide either his failures in this regard or his struggles with putting his spiritual insights into practice. There seemed to be a consensus among those who spoke to the issue that Henri was not able fully to live what he preached, but that he was indeed quite open about this and, more important, that this imperfection, if one wants to call it that, was an important reason for the appeal of his writing. As a member of the audience put it, the disjunctions and contradictions in Henri's life created a space in which his spiritual desire was awakened, which in turn kindled a spiritual desire in other people. Moreover, Henri used transparent language that helped his readers to give voice to their own struggles and spiritual desires. People recognized in Henri's brokenness their own and as a result felt connected to him and validated by him. "He knew the map of my heart" is how somebody expressed it in a video biography of him.

The developments in Henri's writing, specifically the development of his core themes, was another question that came up. One panelist suggested that Henri laid out the basic framework of his spirituality, including the core themes, in one of his earliest books, *Reaching Out,* and that much of his subsequent writing was devoted to an elaboration of these themes. Panelists pointed out, however, that Henri's later writing represented a more mature, spiritual treatment of the original insights. An example is *The Return of the Prodigal Son.* One panelist proposed that some themes were present from the beginning, whereas others emerged in reaction to events in his life. He also had a tendency to become absorbed by a particular subject, such as the spirituality of Vincent van Gogh, but then to move on to other subjects with little reference to his previous passionate preoccupation.

Two other subjects were raised. One panelist expressed his reservations about the various compilations of Henri's writings. He feared that when Henri's ideas are lifted out of their proper context, connections Henri intended are severed. He would like to see instead a more concerted effort to engage in "ongoing translation"; that is, a passing on of Henri's ideas in our own way, in our own words, and within an ever-changing context. He suggested, as an example, that someone might write about sexuality in the spirit of Henri. A person in the audience asked the important and intriguing question to what extent biographies of Henri contribute to "myth making and myth breaking." Unfortunately, her question did not receive the attention it deserved.

Did the biographers' panel meet its purposes? As indicated before, the panel was included in the conference program to facilitate the assessment of Henri's legacy, to fill in some gaps in our knowledge of him, to provide conference participants with an opportunity to refine their picture of Henri, and to gain a better understanding of the relationship between Henri as a person and his work. Were there any important questions or issues in this regard that were overlooked? Did the discussion paint a balanced picture of the man and of his legacy?

The answer to the first question is not clear. It is difficult to ascertain whether the discussion indeed aided the assessment of his legacy, if only because there were no attempts to relate specific biographical information to this legacy. I believe our knowledge of Henri improved because panelists elaborated on what they had written and even provided new information and ideas. Although there was a fair amount of opportunity for participants to test their own impressions of Henri against those of the panelists, it is not known whether they indeed adjusted their views. Informal feedback suggested that at least some of the participants heard things about Henri they were not aware of before.

As to the questions of completeness and balance, the answers are much more unequivocal. Some important matters were overlooked, and it might be argued that there was too much focus on Henri's sexual orientation. However, it is not at all obvious that this could have been avoided. Although Michael Ford gave much play to Henri's homosexuality in his biography, this topic has received little publicity since the appearance of the book. Some other biographies of Henri did not mention it, and other publications were more focused on his spiritual writings than on his person. Given that the conference was the first major gathering since Henri's death to reflect on his spiritual legacy, and brought together many of his former close friends and associates as well as all but one of his biographers, it is not surprising that his homosexuality became a subject for discussion. Because of the ambivalent and sometimes hostile attitude toward homosexuality in our society and the myths surrounding it, the suggestion that Henri was gay was bound to capture the attention of the participants. Moreover, it is tempting to believe that knowing someone is gay somehow tells you much more about that person than knowing the person is straight. Yet, the only thing you know for sure is that the person is forced to come to grips with a lack of acceptance, perhaps even rejection, because of sexual orientation. Regrettably, no one asked explicitly whether Henri's homosexuality was at all relevant for understanding him or his spirituality. There is evidence that he struggled with his sexuality and that this contributed to his restlessness and his inner turmoil. But, as I have argued elsewhere (see *Befriending Life*), there may have been more fundamental reasons for his emotional challenges.

Because of the emphasis on Henri's homosexuality, some other important questions about his personality and his work did not come to the fore. For instance, the presence of his biographers offered a unique opportunity to examine in more detail the internal struggles and tensions that caused him much pain and suffering at times, but also seemed to have been a rich source of his spiritual insights and directions. What is true of many creative and inspirational individuals also applies to Henri: he was a great spiritual guide not despite of but because of his own vulnerabilities and imperfections.

Yet, however valuable a description of Henri's "shadow side" is for a more complete grasp of the source of his spirituality and impact on people, it can easily leave us with a one-sided view of his personality. He was a troubled man, but he was also full of life, with a delightful sense of humor and many charming and endearing qualities. This lighter side of him was not mentioned at all in the discussion. It also would have been helpful to reflect on the question of why Henri's writings appeal to such a wide range of readers. Although there were just a few participants from outside North America, it would have been worthwhile to share impressions about the possible differences in the reception of Henri's writing in different countries. There was a hint of these differences when, in one of the more lively exchanges in the panel discussion, one of the panelists questioned another panelist about the rather exalted language he used in his description of Henri. Intriguing in this regard is why Henri's popularity in his country of origin has never come close to that in North America. Is it because his particular spirituality does not resonate with the spiritual questions of his compatriots? Do they resent his hesitancy to associate himself with renewal efforts within the church as an institution? Or are they perhaps uncomfortable with his confessional style of writing?

Given that a major goal of the conference was to assess Henri's legacy ten years after his death and to identify the relevance of his spirituality to our time, we should perhaps have asked the biographers for their views. Would it have been useful if we had asked them to speculate about the themes Henri would be writing on if he were still alive? Is there indeed a need for the "ongoing translation" of Henri's ideas? These are just a few of the questions that could and perhaps should have been put forward. With the advantage of hindsight, maybe I should have used the power of my role as moderator to steer the discussion and ensure a better and more balanced coverage of major topics.

Looking back on the panel discussion there is one final question that needs to be addressed. Was the discussion sufficiently respectful of Henri and of the feelings about him on the part of those in attendance? It is conceivable that some people found the scrutiny of Henri's character and persona a violation of his privacy. Some may even have questioned the value of the in-depth analysis of Henri the person, believing it is only Henri the writer that counts. Other people may have heard things about Henri in the session that were not only new but also shocking to them. That audience perceptions and interpretations of the discussion would vary was to be expected, and it would have been virtually impossible to avoid misunderstanding and upset on the part of some. However, that would not have justified one-sidedness or lack of respect. In my concluding comments at the end of the session I referred to Michael Higgins, one of the main speakers at the conference, who, in one of his newspaper columns remarked that a major responsibility of a biographer is to "honor the soul" of the subject. I suggested that the discussion had lived up to that responsibility, that we indeed honored Henri's soul, but I do not know whether my judgment was shared by the audience. I have been told that Henri worried about how people would talk about him after his death. Would he have been pleased by what he heard if he had been present at the session?

11

Prefer Nothing to Christ

The Influence of the Rule of St. Benedict on Contemporary Seekers of God

Constance Joanna Gefvert, S.S.J.D.

The latter half of the twentieth century evidenced an enormous interest among laypeople in the Benedictine, including Cistercian, tradition. Thomas Merton in the 1950s and 1960s, and Henri Nouwen in the latter part of the century, along with others, had a profound effect on two phenomena: the renewal of monastic life in many areas; and the interest of laypeople in monasticism.

I cannot claim to be a scholar of either Merton or Nouwen—I am rather an admirer and fellow spiritual traveler with them. My own journey from an academic career to an Anglican monastic community whose ethos is Benedictine has been profoundly influenced by both. I read *The Seven-Storey Mountain* as a graduate student in English and felt drawn to Merton's longing for the contemplative life. I read Nouwen's *Genesee Diary* shortly after receiving a tenured university position—and again I felt a strong pull out of the academy into the monastic life. It would be some years after that, however, before I finally took the plunge myself and came to Toronto to join the Anglican Sisters of St. John the Divine. But the seeds were planted years before.

It would not be difficult to identify probably thousands of people who through the influence of Merton and Nouwen either had their career paths interrupted by a call to the monastic life or who felt called to become affiliated members of monastic communities—oblates, associates, tertiaries.

So I speak out of my own experience—not as an objective scholar but as an insider, a lover or *aficionado*.

On June 2, 1974, Henri Nouwen entered the Abbey of the Genesee, a Cistercian community, as a temporary monk. In the introduction to *The Genesee Diary*, the book that chronicles his spiritual journey there, he writes of his motivation:

My desire to live for seven months in a Trappist Monastery, not as a guest but as a monk, did not develop overnight. It was the outcome of many years of restless searching. While teaching, lecturing, and writing about the importance of solitude, inner freedom, and peace of mind, I kept stumbling over my own compulsions and illusions. What was driving me from one book to another, one place to another, one project to another? What made me think and talk about "the reality of the Unseen" with the seriousness of one who had seen all that is real? What was turning my vocation to be a witness to God's love into a tiring job? These questions kept intruding themselves into my few unfilled moments and challenging me to face my restless self.[1]

Henri had great hopes that living under the Rule of St. Benedict for seven months would help him find answers to these questions and to others that presented themselves to the mind of this restless seeker during his time at the Genesee. Not only would he be living under the Rule of St. Benedict, but like his spiritual mentor Thomas Merton, he chose the most challenging of the Benedictine orders–the Trappists or as they are officially known, the Order of Cistercians of the Strict Observance. What drew him to that specific place at that time?

Before attempting to answer that question, I would like to ask a few related questions:

1. Why it is that so many women and men, lay and ordained, of virtually every Christian denomination have found themselves drawn not only to visit but to affiliate themselves with Benedictine communities?
2. Why have so many people chosen to write about their experiences in Benedictine communities?
3. Why, at a time when traditional religious life, including monastic life, seems to be declining in so many places, does there seem to be a compensatory increase in the numbers of oblates, associates, and tertiaries of monastic communities?

Recognizing the danger of oversimplifying, I would nevertheless say that the answer to all three of these questions–as well as to the questions that Nouwen raises in the introduction to *The Genesee Diary*–is basically the same. It is a complex and multifaceted answer, but it is really a single answer: Christians are hungering for a way to reconnect with their humanity, which of course includes their relationship with God, in a world that is dehumanizing, mockingly destructive of Christian experience and encouraging of fragmentation and extreme individualism.

People who are not Christian intuitively seem drawn to know more–hence the popularity of fictional characters like Brother Cadfael in the Middle Ages (in the novels of Ellis Peters) and Sister Fidelma in the eighth-century Celtic church just following the Synod of Whitby (in the novels of Peter Tremayne).

Not only are these novels superb examples of the genre of historical mysteries, but they offer readers a way to reconnect with the values of an explicitly Christian culture in times that seem simpler, more humane, and (in the case of Sr. Fidelma, at least) inclusive of women in positions of authority both civil and ecclesiastical.

Fictional monks notwithstanding, Nouwen is only one of many people in the last thirty years to write of their experience with a Benedictine community, and he is only one of thousands who have intentionally spent time living within or alongside a monastic community. All of these people are bound together by one innocuous-looking little book, written in the sixth century—a book that has influenced more Christians over fifteen centuries than any book except the Bible. That, of course, is the Rule of St. Benedict, whose teachings Nouwen refers to in *The Genesee Diary*. That Rule is at the heart of thousands of communities—traditional Benedictine communities, reformed Benedictine communities like the Cistercians and the Trappists, contemporary and experimental Benedictine communities like the priory in Montreal founded by John Main, and many Anglican, Protestant, and ecumenical Benedictine communities.

Rowan Williams, the Archbishop of Canterbury, in a 2003 address, had this to say about the spirituality of the Rule of St. Benedict:

> The Rule's sketch of holiness and sanity [raises a few issues for us], as Church and culture. It suggests that one of our main problems is that we don't know where to find the stable relations that would allow us room to grow without fear. The Church which ought to embody not only covenant with God but covenant with each other does not always give the feeling of a community where people have unlimited time to grow with each other, nourishing and challenging. We have little incentive to be open with each other if we live in an ecclesial environment where political conflict and various kinds of grievance are the dominant currency. And, believers and unbelievers, we'd like to be peacemakers without the inner work which alone makes peace something more than a pause in battle. We are bad at finding that elusive balance between corrupt and collusive passivity which keeps oppression alive and the litigious obsessiveness that continually asks whether I am being attended to as I deserve. . . . And so we'd better have some communities around that embody the stability that is at the heart of all of this.[2]

Archbishop Williams is asking, on a communal level, the same questions Nouwen asks on a personal level. How can we find the stability and holiness of life that arise from a deep intimacy with God and one another and that give rise to a renewed respect for human life and the survival of our planet?

These are the same questions that Benedict dealt with in the sixth century, and with which many contemporary writers are dealing. In particular, I want

to talk about three of these writers—all of whom wrote after Nouwen published *The Genesee Diary* and all of whom I believe were influenced by it:

- Esther de Waal is an Anglican laywoman who became interested in St.
  Benedict when she was living in Canterbury. Her husband, an Anglican
  priest, was at that time the dean of Canterbury Cathedral, and she became intrigued with the Benedictine history of Canterbury, starting a
  series of week-long retreats in the Cathedral precincts called Benedictine
  Experiences—opportunities for laypeople to experience the balanced
  lifestyle of a Benedictine community, with prayer, community time, rest,
  study, and manual labor, not unlike the lifestyle of St. Augustine's suc-
  cessors at Canterbury in the Middle Ages. The book that was inspired
  by these retreats is called *Seeking God: The Way of St. Benedict;* it was first
  published in 1984 as the Archbishop of Canterbury's Lent book for that
  year.
- W. Paul Jones spent four months in a Trappist monastery at Snowmass,
  Colorado, and like Nouwen was welcomed into the heart of the community. The book chronicling his experiences is called *The Province beyond
  the River.* Jones grew up in the Appalachian mountains, was a Method-
  ist minister who taught at Yale and Princeton seminaries before moving
  to inner-city Kansas City as part of a community dedicated to radical
  social action. There he also taught at St. Paul School of Theology. Eventually he divorced, was ordained a Roman Catholic priest, and became
  a Family Brother of the Trappists. He now lives as a hermit in the Ozark
  mountains, sought out by others on their spiritual journey.
- Kathleen Norris is a Presbyterian laywoman, best known as a poet and
  nonfiction author of books such as *Dakota* and *The Virgin of Bennington.*
  She is a wife and mother who lives in South Dakota and in Honolulu,
  and she is an oblate of Assumption Abbey in North Dakota. She spent
  two years at the Ecumenical Institute at St. John's Abbey in Collegeville,
  Minnesota. Her recent books *The Cloister Walk* and *Amazing Grace* reflect
  on her experience in these two Benedictine communities.

Like Nouwen, all three of these people have influenced thousands of others—lay and ordained—who are part of the extended family of monastic affiliates in communities as different, and similar, as St. John's Collegeville (one
of the most famous) and my own St. John's Convent in Toronto (an Anglican
community). In all of these places, associates and oblates come to share time
with their respective communities, and the communities open their doors in
traditional monastic hospitality, welcoming all kinds of people not only for
formal retreats but even more so, for shorter or longer periods of time in
which to find space, silence, and support for life in a culture that militates
against silence, peace, intimacy with God, and spiritual companionship.

Let me mention a little about these three examples of monastic affiliates,
all of whom have clearly been influenced by Merton, Nouwen, and others
like them. In her introduction to *Seeking God,* Esther de Waal points out:

The world into which St. Benedict was born was a troubled, torn apart, uncertain world. It knew little of safety or of security, and the church was almost as troubled as the secular powers. It was a world without landmarks. It had this in common with the twentieth century: life was an urgent struggle to make sense of what was happening.[3]

She talks of the violence with which the Roman Empire was being torn apart, and the corresponding fracture of the church, which was

not only suffering through wars and political disorders but split theologically. . . . Christians must have looked back with nostalgia to the age of the Fathers and asked themselves if ever again the church could produce a St. Augustine and a City of God to hold out the promise of peace and order and light on a scene which seemed instead to be rapidly descending into chaos. And then on this scene there appeared the man who built an ark to survive the rising storm, an ark not made with hands, into which by two and two human and eternal values might enter, to be kept until the water assuaged, an ark moreover which lasted not only for one troubled century but for fifteen, and which has still the capacity to bring many safe to land.[4]

After fifteen hundred years we find ourselves once again in the midst of cultural disintegration—both civil and ecclesial. People seem to experience monastic life—especially in the Benedictine tradition—as a kind of ark that not only will "survive the rising storm" but that, it is to be hoped, will land on fertile soil that can receive the seeds of a renewed Christianity and a renewed world.

The ark also reminds us—inevitably in Nouwen's context—of the L'Arche movement, of Jean Vanier and his call to the world for a humane inclusiveness of all God's children, of community that is not for the theologically sophisticated or academically trained. While L'Arche is not, strictly speaking, Benedictine, the principles that underlie L'Arche—the recognition of Christ in every person, the centrality of community, the acceptance of legitimate authority while also exercising compassion and sensitivity to individual needs, the absolute necessity of transparency and relating to others out of one's own vulnerability, out of the kenosis of Christ—are central themes in the Rule of St. Benedict. They weave like a beautiful Celtic knot through all the writings of Nouwen. In *The Road to Daybreak* Nouwen writes of his desire

to know Jesus not only in the solitude of prayer, but also in the community of love. Thus the same Lord who reveals himself in the most intimate place of my heart will also reveal himself in the fellowship of the weak. It will not be easy to be faithful in this, since the temptation to search for consolation and comfort in the intimacy of a unique friendship is so great, especially during periods of depression and spiritual fatigue.[5]

The Rule of St. Benedict is an ark with the capacity to renew our world, and the Christian faith is at the heart of all those who write from the perspective of the Benedictine "extended family." W. Paul Jones, after about three months in the monastery, wrote of his discovery that

> the monks in this place are subversives, not so much because of what they say or even think, but what they are. . . . In the midst of a culture of noise, these little white-robed men who like to play with bells choose silence; in a culture of work, they choose contemplation; in a culture of self-realization, they renounce the self; in a culture of achievement, they declare that the winner will be loser and only the loser winner; in a culture whose economy is utterly dependent on consumption, they insist on emptiness; in a culture structured by possession, they insist upon detachment; in a culture intoxicated by facts and education, they insist on ignorance as the basis of wisdom; in a culture of complexity they call us to the simplicity of willing one thing; in a culture intent on a high standard of living they insist on a high standard of life. Achievement versus grace; the exposure of the emptiness of fullness for the fullness of emptiness. . . . The heart of this subversion is in planting within a person the appetite for silence. And once planted, once one tastes silence, and listening, and stopping, and being flooded by a Depth beyond all words, once one lets go so that one's hands are empty for the first time, once you do nothing, say nothing, think nothing, but just let yourself be in the midst of Capital Peak or a columbine field or Snowmass Creek or the mist of a morning valley—if you ever let it happen, it is all over for you. From then on, everything else seems insane.[6]

I believe this is what happened to Nouwen. As a diocesan priest in Holland, as a university professor at Notre Dame, Yale, and Harvard, he lived alone, his only community his parish or the students he taught. He looked to unique relationships or unique friendships to turn his loneliness into community, but each of these, for one reason or another, was not enough. It was not until his time at Genesee that he discovered the tremendous insight of Benedictine monasticism—that God is found in community, and that God is found as we let go of our public persona and accept the need to be vulnerable. Once he discovered that, he was bitten. University life would never be the same, and he would continue a restless search for the community he longed for, a search that took him to South America, as he chronicles it in *¡Gracias!*, and to other places and other roles. It was not until he discovered the radical nature of community in L'Arche that his restless soul found some rest.

At the end of Jones's four months at Snowmass, he—like Henri—talked of how his experiment in monastic living created a hunger for something more:

> Like life, journals don't end—they stop. The real "province on the river's far side" is the craving soul. Whoever is bitten by it will not rest in its

testing of the darkness. My monastic experience brought no certainty, one way or another. It was far worse. It brought an intoxication for the darkness itself, in all its graciously shattering antinomies—the joy of the universally sorrowful, the unspeakable gift just of surviving, being acceptedly unreconciled, longing for the Mystery no longer doubted, as the cold emptiness has somehow persisted as the warm silence.[7]

At the end of *Cloister Walk*, Kathleen Norris reflects on that darkness in the context of Compline, the monastic office of night prayer:

The great desert monk Anthony once said that "the prayer of the monk is not perfect until he no longer realizes himself or the fact that he is praying." Frank O'Hara speaks ". . . of love assuming the consciousness of itself . . ." Between these two poles, it seems to me, we seek to become complete: between shedding our self-consciousness and taking on a new awareness, between the awesome fears that shrink us and the capacity for love that enlarges us beyond measure, between the need for vigilance in the face of danger and the trust that allows us to sleep, Night comes . . . and we turn our lives over to God. We are able to rest, in the words of an old hymn, "on the promises"; we are willing to lean "on the everlasting arms."[8]

The contemporary influence of Benedict's Rule on seekers of God is evident not only in Nouwen and Jones, de Waal and Norris. It is also evident in the birth of new and "new-ish" communities that are either directly Benedictine (follow the Rule of St. Benedict as their community's Rule) or strongly influenced by the Rule of St. Benedict.

This movement goes back to the first half of the nineteenth century, when double revival of religious life occurred in England. First was the reestablishment of orders that had existed before the Reformation and that, for over 250 years, had to survive (if they survived at all) in exile on the Continent. New Benedictine, Cistercian, and Trappist foundations were made in England, Ireland, and Wales. At the same time there occurred a revival of the Catholic tradition in the Church of England. That revival was known as the Oxford movement; one of its leaders was John Henry Newman before he converted to Roman Catholicism.

A major legacy of the Oxford movement was the establishment of religious orders within the Church of England. From there the Anglo-Catholic movement, with its religious orders, quickly spread to other churches in the worldwide Anglican Communion (including the United States and Canada). These new communities were inspired by and adapted the Rules of pre-Reformation communities—Franciscan, Benedictine, Cistercian, Augustinian, and so on. Many of the Anglican Benedictine foundations have survived and thrived to this day. One of the most notable is West Malling Abbey, a community of Anglican Benedictine women near Oxford; another being the Society of the Holy Cross, an Anglican women's Cistercian community in Wales (of which Archbishop Rowan Williams is an associate, similar to a Benedictine oblate). Anglican Benedictine communities were also established in the United States and Canada, for instance, the Order of the Holy Cross, whose motherhouse is in New York State. There are many other Anglican communities throughout the world—like my own, founded in Toronto in 1884—that have their own foundation Rule but are intentionally based on Benedictine values.

Most interesting of all is the way in which ecumenical communities whose inspiration is at least in part Benedictine have grown up over the last fifty years. I would like to highlight a few of them.

The **Iona Community** was founded in 1938 by George McLeod, a Scottish Presbyterian minister who rebuilt the ancient Abbey on Iona (founded in 563 by St. Columba following the Celtic pattern; it became Benedictine by the Middle Ages). Iona is an ecumenical community of about 250 vowed members, as well as 1,500 associate members. It is a dispersed community, throughout the British Isles. Its members come together four times a year, and all spend time on the island of Iona assisting in the ministry of hospitality that, in their Benedictine tradition, is central to the community's charism. Through the music of George Bell and others, the Celtic/Benedictine tradition, with an emphasis on peace, justice, and respect for the earth, has been shared with all denominations of Christians. Iona's publishing arm, Wild Goose Publications, distributes the community's music and books.[9]

The **Taizé Community** was founded in 1949 by Roger Schultz, who remained the Community head until 2005, when he was murdered in the midst of Vespers with his brothers. The 100 or so brothers who are vowed members of Taizé go out in twos and threes to live with people around the world in the poorest conditions and to share Christian community with them. Their ministry of hospitality at Taizé in France is well-known worldwide, particularly the influence they have on young people. As with the Iona Community, the music that has come out of Taizé, especially the contemplative chant music, has spread the Taizé message of peace through the cross of Christ throughout the world.[10]

The **Community of Jesus** was founded in 1958 by two Episcopalian (Anglican) women on Cape Cod and has grown to have a membership of about 350, made up of families as well as a convent of sisters and a house of brothers. Married couples take the three traditional Benedictine vows of obedience, stability, and conversion of life. The sisters and brothers take those vows along with the vows of poverty and celibate chastity. The community is growing, and in addition to the central campus on Cape Cod Bay, where the community has built a convent, a friary, and a large monastic church, various families have bought houses in the neighborhood as they have become available over the past forty years. As with Taizé and Iona, the Community of Jesus has music and other forms of the arts at the heart of its charism. It is a community that bridges traditional categories of conservative and liberal. The Divine Office is sung in Latin, in Gregorian Chant, according to the usage of Solesmes. The Eucharist is celebrated daily according to a contemporary rite based on the Episcopal Church's *Book of Common Prayer* but adapted to its ecumenical context. The community's publishing company, Paraclete Press, publishes the work of many contemporary authors who write about Benedict and Benedictine spirituality and its influence in the world today.[11]

The **World Community for Christian Meditation** (WCCM) is a dispersed community, literally worldwide, headed by the prior, Lawrence Freeman, O.S.B., who followed the leadership of Dom John Main at the Benedictine Priory in Montreal. The WCCM exists to encourage contemplative prayer among laypeople, not for the sake of individual piety alone, but because of the strong belief of John Main and Lawrence Freeman that contemplative prayer is a way into the monastery of the heart and ultimately to the conversion of the world to peace. The WCCM publishes the works of Main, Freeman, and others, and encourages the formation of contemplative prayer groups in local communities.[12]

All four of these communities are dedicated especially to unity—not only unity among Christians, but a spiritual unity among people of goodwill in all religions. They have all been influenced by Thomas Merton's vision of a Christianity that can be open to conversation and shared prayer with people of other faith traditions. They all believe in the critical importance of Christian unity—an extension of local community—for the survival of our planet and human culture.

This brings us back to Nouwen and to his own search for community. Ultimately he found his home at L'Arche Daybreak—not Benedictine, strictly speaking, but certainly influenced by Benedictine values of community, stability, and dedication to human/divine intimacy. Like Nouwen, hundreds of thousands of people worldwide are searching for ways to live out the values of the Rule of St. Benedict. I believe that taken together, the traditional Benedictine communities, the Anglican and Protestant communities, and the ecumenical ones are a force to be reckoned with as contemporary seekers for God find in that tradition encouragement for a new way of being human in our world.

There are many writers today who are making the Rule of St. Benedict accessible for laypeople; Joan Chittister, Noreen Vest, and Brian Taylor are among the best and most insightful. The popularity of their adaptations of and commentaries on the Rule of St. Benedict is evidence of the longing for community, for stability, for conversion of heart that is so much a part of contemporary Christian life and that is at the heart of Benedictine values.

There are others who write specifically about contemplative prayer and centering prayer—especially Cistercians like William Menninger, Basil Pennington, and Thomas Keating. These men, together with Episcopal (Anglican) priest and hermit Cynthia Bourgeault, founded the Contemplative Society on a smaller scale than the WCCM but with similar aims and values.

All of these writers reflect the tremendous longing in the hearts of people everywhere for intimacy, to know themselves as beloved, and out of that relationship to work for the coming of the reign of God. Like Nouwen, and influenced by him and Merton before him, they share with all of us that restless longing at the heart of the spiritual life.

I would like to close with a quotation from the Rule of St. Benedict that reflects the longing and search for meaning that we find at the heart of Nouwen, Jones, de Waal, and Norris. In Chapter 73, "This Rule Only the Beginning of Perfection," Benedict says that he has written his "little rule for beginners" to instill the beginnings of virtue and holiness, and he refers the reader to the fathers of the church, the writings of John Cassian, and the Rule of St. Basil. Then he challenges us:

> Are you hastening toward your heavenly home? Then with Christ's help, keep this little rule that we have written for beginners. After that, you can set out for the loftier summits of the teaching and virtues we mentioned above, and under God's protection you will reach them. Amen.[13]

I believe that Nouwen must have found this ending of the Rule to be most encouraging. God always sets before us something to hope for. Longing for divine union is at the heart of what it means to be human. Working toward peaceful unity is (or should be) at the heart of civil and international life. With Benedict, and with Nouwen, we accept that the spiritual journey will always leave us feeling a bit like unrequited lovers, always drawn deeper and deeper into the journey with God and our fellow human beings.

Notes

[1] Henri J. M. Nouwen, *The Genesee Diary: Report from a Trappist Monastery* (Garden City, NY: Doubleday, 1976), xi.

[2] Archbishop Rowan Williams, "God's Workshop," address at the Trinity Institute, Shaping Holy Lives: Benedictine Spirituality in the Contemporary World, April 29, 2003.

[3] Esther de Waal, *Seeking God: The Way of St. Benedict* (Collegeville, MN: Liturgical Press, 2001), 15.

[4] Ibid., 15.

[5] Henri J. M. Nouwen, *The Road to Daybreak: A Spiritual Journey* (New York: Doubleday, 1988), 226.

[6] W. Paul Jones, *The Province beyond the River* (Nashville, TN: The Upper Room, 1981), vii.

[7] Ibid., 150.

[8] Kathleen Norris, *The Cloister Walk* (New York: Riverhead Books, 1996), 382.

[9] For more information, see "Introduction," in *Iona Worship Book* (Glasgow: Wild Goose Publications, 2001); see also the iona.org.uk website.

[10] For more information, see Roger, Brother of Taizé, *Parable of Community* (London: Mowbray, 1980); see also the taize.fr website.

[11] For more information, see the communityofjesus.org website.

[12] For more information, see the wccm.org website.

[13] Cited in Joan B. Chittister, O.S.B., *The Rule of Benedict: Insights for the Ages* (New York: Crossroad, 1993), 179.

12

Compassion in the Lives of Vincent van Gogh and Henri Nouwen

Carol Berry

Vincent—Henri's Saint

Flying over Los Angeles at night a tapestry of twinkling lights reaches as far as the eye can see. It brings to mind a star-filled sky, the kind you can see on a clear night from a high mountaintop. This tapestry of lights also graphically brings to mind that millions of people live down there.

Almost one quarter (821,004) of the population of Los Angeles flocked to the Los Angeles County Museum of Art in 1999 during the three-month exhibition *Van Gogh's Van Goghs*, and I was among the throng of people who managed to get tickets for a timeslot during the last forty-eight hours of the exhibition.

It was one o'clock in the morning, and the waiting line swelled to hundreds of people from all walks of life—young parents with babies in strollers, frail people in wheelchairs, tough looking teenagers attired in baggy pants, scantily dressed teenage girls. All social classes and ethnicities were represented. What did they know about Vincent that made them wait for hours in the chill desert night outside the small annex of the Los Angeles County Museum of Art to view seventy paintings by an artist whose contemporaries did not think his art worthwhile and who sold but two paintings in his life time?

Had Vincent van Gogh himself waited in line with us, he would not have been surprised. He believed that sooner or later his work would elicit a response in people, as long as he continued to express something real and honest in his art.

Most likely no one in line had attended or even knew of Henri Nouwen's course "The Compassion of Vincent van Gogh," which he gave at Yale

Divinity School in 1979. Nor had they read Vincent's eight hundred soul-revealing letters written to his brother, Theo. Why had they come to see the art of someone who was considered crazy by most, who was disagreeable and a social outcast, who mutilated himself by cutting off part of his ear, who drank excessively and visited brothels, and who, finally, committed suicide?

When I asked some people what made them come to see paintings by Van Gogh, they could not give me clear answers. However, most of them had been moved by images of his sunflowers, of his worn-out work boots, of a starry night; they were now drawn by some irresistible force to see more of what Vincent had to offer them.

As a Dutchman himself, Henri was drawn to Vincent van Gogh's work. But he was likely drawn, too, by an irresistible force like those people I encountered in those early morning hours.

At Yale Divinity School, Henri taught for several years a course called "Compassion." Although he was lecturing in a highly academic setting, he was convinced that what he really needed to instill in future pastors in order to prepare them for a deeply effective ministry was that most fundamental quality—a compassionate heart. Just as Vincent van Gogh, while training to be a lay missionary, had realized over a hundred years before that his oppressed parishioners did not need theologically sound sermons but basic compassionate understanding along with practical support for managing the struggles of daily life.

In 1975, while teaching at Yale Divinity School, Henri had the opportunity to meet the nephew of Vincent van Gogh, Theo's son, also called Vincent van Gogh. Henri asked him why he thought that so many people came to see his uncle's paintings. Mr. van Gogh stated: "Because Vincent offers comfort. He was able to crawl under the skin of nature and people and find there something truthful, something beautiful, something joyful. He was able to draw out the inner secret of what he saw."[1] It is this secret that he was able to express and reveal through the language of his art.[2] His nephew's answer prompted Henri's own in-depth study of Vincent's art and letters. Henri's study, reading the letters and the memoirs of people who had known Vincent, indeed revealed that to offer comfort was precisely what Vincent van Gogh's mission and intention had been. This study became the basis for his course, "The Compassion of Vincent van Gogh," and is what drew me to his class.

Through Henri's lectures and slides we were given a unique opportunity to have a deep and personal encounter with Vincent van Gogh. Henri introduced Vincent to us as a sufferer, a comforter, a seeker, a loving brother, a wounded healer. Henri made us recognize in Vincent a minister who, even today, offers us a glimpse of hope, joy, and strength through the example of his own life's struggles and through his ability to express honestly what he saw and felt.

Henri identified with Vincent and with his search for God, which was intense and real and was expressed through deep yearning, doubting, despairing, hoping, and rejoicing (one of Vincent's and Theo's favorite expressions was "sorrowful, yet always rejoicing"). Through Vincent's words and images Henri discovered and revealed to us how Vincent consciously used all his senses in his search for God.

While working in the damp soil of Holland, inhaling the odors of freshly cut hay and smoke-filled peasant homes, walking for hours along country lanes in England, or living among the homeless and the destitute in Den Haag, Vincent's mind and soul were constantly searching and questioning the presence of God and his own purpose and duty. Then, when he experienced the bright sun of France and delighted in the colors of the changing seasons, where he identified with the gnarled olive trees as well as with the flaming cypresses reaching into the sky, Vincent felt profoundly that, through nature, the presence of God was revealed. This sensuous and earthy longing to find God in all that surrounded him was what Henri affirmed.

It was a longing for a God who would not abandon humanity but rather permeate all creation with the divine presence. It was a God who lived among poor peasants, miners, the lonely and oppressed, and who comforted them and shone his love and light into the darkest corners of their lives. Henri told us:

> I feel close to Vincent because I think that he is a man who really struggled with real spiritual questions and therefore has a lot to say to people who search for God in their lives and want to bring good news to their fellow human beings. The longer I live, the more I try to make sense out of my own struggles, the more I find Vincent to be a real companion. In a strange way I consider him my saint.[3]

"The Compassion of Vincent van Gogh"

Henri used the life of Vincent van Gogh as a powerful case study to introduce his students to the three components of a compassionate life—solidarity, consolation, and comfort.

Solidarity: "The compassionate manifest their human solidarity by crying out with those who suffer" (Henri Nouwen).

Henri presented Vincent to us first as a boy who had often accompanied his minister father on pastoral visits to his parishioners, hard-working farmers in the villages of Brabant in the South of Holland.

Vincent wrote years later, when he had become critical of his father, that he had always felt drawn with great compassion into the homes of the poor and struggling peasants while he believed that his father merely stooped down from his higher position to administer a bit of pastoral care. His father, to the sensitive and observant Vincent, did not lose himself or abandon his position to carry his parishioners' burdens. He did not walk in their shoes. He did not give his life as Christ commanded.

Vincent, the boy, was not free to do that, yet he witnessed the poverty and struggle of the Dutch peasants. Once he had shaken off the shackles of parental control and attachment, he went that further step. He was drawn into the suffering of humankind, becoming one with the men and women whose plight he had seen countless times in the homes of his father's parishioners, and whose sorrow he had seen expressed in the faces of the worn-out women and hungry children.

But first, at age fifteen, he still followed a path dictated by his family connections and expectations. While failing several attempts at training to become an art dealer, a teacher, and a book seller, he began to immerse himself seriously in the study of the Bible and of books such as Thomas à Kempis's *Imitation of Christ.* This intense study, as well as the pressure put upon him to decide upon a means to support himself, led him to the conviction that he would embark yet upon another training—that of becoming a minister. His fervent desire is heard in a letter to Theo in which he writes: "Whoever wants to preach the Gospel must carry it in his own heart first. Oh! May I find it, for it is only the word spoken in earnestness and from the fullness of the heart that can bear fruit."[4]

At first Vincent tried to follow the traditional path demanded by the church, but he failed his theological studies because of his lack of interest in the more esoteric aspects of the discipline. He said to Mendes da Costa, his tutor in Latin and Greek, "Do you seriously believe that such horrors are indispensable to a man who wants to do what I want to do; give peace to poor creatures and reconcile them to their existence here on earth?"[5]

He was also dismissed as a lay missionary-in-training by the Belgian Missionary Society for being overly zealous in his attempt to minister to his parishioners in the poverty-stricken mining district in Belgium, the Borinage. His removal from the Missionary Society's care made him once and for all reject the institutional rules and restrictions of the church.

Free at last, he began to follow his own heart. He no longer tried preaching the word; he now lived it. Staying on in the Borinage, he began to live as one of the miners. He gave his clothes away to the miners and shared his last crust of bread with them. He went into miners' homes and helped their wives do the laundry and take care of the children. He nursed back to health a miner who had been badly burned in a mining accident and given up to die. He ripped up his last shirt to use as bandages. His was a down-to-earth ministry, a ministry where "the rubber hits the road."

Henri must have heavily underlined all those accounts in Vincent's letters and in the memoirs of people who had known Vincent. When Vincent decided to leave the hospitable home of a miner's family to go and live in a hovel of a very needy family, Vincent explained to the miner's wife, who protested his leaving, "Esther, one should do like the good God; from time to time one should go and live among His own."[6] Upon reading this, Henri must have said an emphatic "yes—this is the kind of compassionate ministry for which I am called to prepare my students!"

Solidarity, Henri said, is when you make the choice to be like one of them, when you realize that you share the basic human traits with all humanity, when you are not afraid of defining yourself as being the same and not different.

Later, once Vincent had begun his career as a painter he signed his paintings simply "Vincent," wanting to convey the message to those for whom he painted that he was one of them.

Consolation: "The compassionate manifest their consolation by feeling deeply the wounds of life" (Henri Nouwen).

Henri said that consolation is not the avoiding of pain but the deepening of a pain to a level where it can be shared. Consolation demands that we be "cum solo" with the lonely other and be with that person exactly where he or she is lonely and hurting and nowhere else. Henri felt that in Vincent we see one of the most moving portraits of consolation. It was in the Borinage that Vincent developed his ability to console through feeling deeply the wounds of life suffered by the miners and their families.

Vincent became one with those to whom he ministered. He entered into their experience of desperation, of deprivation, of vulnerability, of hopelessness by living as they did, by denying himself all comfort, and by confronting the mine boss to demand higher wages for the miners. He was often heard weeping at night in his hovel from hunger and cold.

This experience of solidarity and consolation finally liberated Vincent from that which had defined him in the past—the pastor's son, the nephew of the well-known art dealer Cornelius van Gogh. Sharing the most basic struggles for survival with the miners, he finally hit rock bottom. He could not be saved by his former position in life, or by anyone, except by that inner life spark that was his alone. In his most anguished moments of utter loneliness and despair he clung to that spark. It brought him to the discovery of the unique means to fulfill his vocation. For it was among the miners that he began to make "hasty sketches" with the lumps of coal found everywhere he went. During this time he wrote to Theo: "I should like to begin to make rough sketches of some of the many things I meet on my way, but as it would probably keep me from my real work, it is better not to start."[7] He did not yet fully recognize that in order to do this "real work" he had to develop a new way for the message of the gospel that he carried in his heart to bear fruit.

One of the letters Henri emphasized was Letter 133, written to Theo after a long period of silence on Vincent's part. Vincent had been accused by his parents, even by Theo, of being idle, of not having any direction, of being incapable of earning a living, and of being a burden. Vincent remained silent for several months, hurt, offended, not understood, but doing what he needed to do, which was to encounter himself in the deepest recesses of his heart. He was twenty-seven years old.

Vincent had gone deep down, literally into the pit of hell, the mine, and upon emerging from the level of solidarity with the miners, he began to understand that in order to minister, to console, and to comfort, in order to pursue his desire to minister, he would not preach God's word but express it in translation. He was not going to abandon his desire to minister to the poor; on the contrary, he would intensify his consoling and comforting work. Like Rembrandt, whom he admired and whose work moved him deeply, he would use the language of art to spread the message of the gospel. Throughout his stay in the simple huts of the miners, often sharing a room with the children, he would hang on the walls prints of artists whose work spoke to him, comforted him. He realized that he could make pictures too, which could hang on the walls of poor people's homes and bring some joy and comfort into their lives.

In Letter 133 Vincent likened the three years spent in the Borinage to a molting time. Just as birds shed their feathers and then emerge with new plumage, so Vincent too had shed his last shirt among the miners. When he left the Borinage, it was as a man who had a new plan, a vocation to fulfill—and this time, he would train himself.

He had the gospel in his heart, he had seen enough work by artists he admired, he had read enough to know what could reach people through the language of art and he had lived for three years in a place where he came face to face, or heart to heart, with the sufferings of humankind. He wrote, "If I could work quietly for about three years in such a district, always learning and observing, then I should not come back from there without having something to say that was really worth hearing. I say so in all humility and yet with confidence."[8]

In his subsequent years in Holland and Belgium, Vincent's work consisted of struggling through hundreds of practice drawings to develop his new language in order to connect with the depth of the human spirit in a new way. He wrote, "What is drawing—it is working oneself through an invisible iron wall that seems to stand between what one *feels* and what one *can do*."[9]

Vincent had learned to feel a deep solidarity with the poor and the oppressed in the Borinage, and this solidarity became the basis for his effort to express in drawings the toils and trials of the people among whom he lived. For four years he labored (he often referred to his drawing as "laboring") tirelessly to master his heart-to-eye-to-hand coordination. He wanted to be able to make his hands follow what not only his eyes saw but his soul felt. He wanted to capture the essence of the daily struggles of the rural poor—struggles he understood:

> My dear Theo, I want you to understand clearly my conception of art. One must work long and hard to grasp the essence. We must continue to give something real and honest. Painting peasant life is a serious thing, and I should reproach myself if I did not try to make pictures which will rouse serious thoughts in those who think seriously about art and about life. . . . One must paint the peasants as being one of them, as feeling, thinking as they do.[10]

He wanted to be able to uplift the extraordinary sacrifices they made with the ordinary labors of the field. He wanted to bring their plight to light, so that they could receive their true place in the scheme of life and would feel worthwhile and thereby feel blessed and comforted:

I feel that my work lies in the heart of the people, that I must keep close to the ground, that I must grasp life in its depths, and make progress through many cares and troubles. I can't think of any other way . . . but to be there to share the same level of feelings with the lonely other.[11]

He made countless sketches of sowers (sometimes also copying artists he admired and whose subjects were the same people of the soil, such as Millet), of women peeling potatoes, of diggers, of shepherds, and of plowed fields and dark, thatched cottages. He sketched a sick farmer seated near the fireplace with his head in his hands and his elbows on his knees:

Rijksmuseum Vincent van Gogh

"A Digger, Summer 1885, Nuenun."

In this print I have tried to express what seems to me one of the strongest proofs of the existence of "quelque chose là-haut" [something on high] . . . namely the existence of God and eternity—certainly in the infinitely touching expression of such a little old man, which he himself is perhaps unconscious of, when he is sitting quietly in his corner by the fire. At the same time there is something noble, something great, which cannot be destined for the worms.[12]

In The Hague he chose as his models men and women from the soup kitchens and a prostitute called Sien, whose image has been immortalized as the essence of sorrow:

Midlands, Walsall Museum and Art Gallery

"Sorrow, April 1882, Den Haag."

I want to do drawings which touch some people. "Sorrow" is a small beginning; perhaps such little landscapes . . . are also a small beginning. In those there is at least something straight from my own heart. In either figure or landscape I should wish to express, not sentimental melancholy, but serious sorrow. In short, I want to progress so far that people will say of my work, He feels deeply, he feels tenderly—not withstanding my so-called roughness, perhaps even because of it. What am I in most people's eyes? A nonentity, or an eccentric and disagreeable man—

somebody who has no position in society and never will have, in short, the lowest of the low. Very well, even if this were true, then I should want my work to show what is in the heart of such an eccentric, of such a nobody. This is my ambition, which is, in spite of everything, founded less on anger than on love.[13]

Living with his parents in the rural south he shared everyday moments with the potato farmers, drawing their sharp features. And after endless studies of heads and figures he finally painted his first great masterpiece, "The Potato Eaters":

> When one lives with others and is united by a feeling of affection, one is aware of a reason for living and perceives that one is not quite worthless and superfluous, but perhaps good for something; we need each other and make the same journey as traveling companions.[14]

Comfort: "The compassionate offer comfort by pointing beyond the human pains to glimpses of strength and hope" (Henri Nouwen).

Having moved from drawing to painting, having "launched his boat" with the completion of the most expressive of all his work so far, "The Potato Eaters," Vincent left the dark colors of the peat bogs, potato fields, and peasant cottages behind.

He traveled to Paris to be with Theo, his brother, an art dealer, at the absolute right time in the history of art. The palettes of the avant-garde artists, soon to be called Impressionists, were dripping with the vibrant and ever-changing colors of light. The arts of other cultures, especially the prints of Japan, were beginning to influence the way artists used the principles of composition.

Having mastered the expressive quality of line, and having found the courage to begin using the brush to paint, Vincent began experimenting with innovative ways of composing his work. With his ability, gained through tireless discipline and practice, to draw what he saw and felt, he was now prepared to use the expressive energy of color to paint things that comfort (for example, sunflowers), paintings that would reveal more powerfully and clearly the something more, the "quelque chose là-haut" that he saw in the every day, in the ordinary moments of life. In keeping with Goethe's maxim that "color is the language of the soul," Vincent added this new dimension to his art and appealed to even greater depths of the human soul.

After two years in Paris, Vincent, with new tubes of vibrant colors in his suitcase, left for the south of France. He was once again drawn to the rural way of life he had known as a child. But this rural landscape spread out before him in much brighter colors than the peat bogs and potato fields he had left behind. Here in the Provence the sun shone much more brilliantly onto the plowed fields, the orchards, and the lives of the peasants.

It was this light that he began to paint, not as fleeting impressions in nature, but as solid statements and symbols for the warmth and love of the divine Creator. Having struggled with nature Vincent began to understand its secret—that all that was visible pointed to the deeper truth of creation, that all reality was at the same time a symbol of the Eternal.

From this time on Vincent dedicated his life to expressing through his art his deeply felt conviction that God was present in all that surrounded him. He wanted others to perceive this too. He believed that people would be comforted by looking at his paintings and recognize the presence of the Divine in the ordinary stuff of their lives. Vincent wanted to make people understand, for there is comfort in understanding. Henri said that the powerful images of the familiar—the sun, the changing seasons, the cyclical labors of sowing and harvesting—became in Vincent's paintings transcendent messages of the eternal and comforting presence of God. The sun symbolized the light in the darkness. Henri found an example of compassionate ministry in Vincent's search for a meaningful way to connect his art to his mission as a minister of the gospel. He said that Vincent's consoling and comforting work began first with the dark pictures of basic human life—not only to show his solidarity but also to have us, the viewers, recognize ourselves in these paintings, to recognize our sameness in terms of our basic human condition, that is, the struggle for survival, companionship, loneliness, basic needs, basic questions, sickness, death, hard work.

Having established the groundwork, the commonality we all share, Vincent took the Sun and shone it upon all the darkness, the difficulties, the misery, not to negate it all but to suffuse it with that force that binds us all together, that gives us hope, that makes all the struggles worthwhile.

Nothing has changed in the human condition, except that it has been given a purpose: all the human struggles are woven together through an embracing, healing, comforting love. Compassion manifests itself first of all in the consciousness of being part of humanity, in the awareness of the oneness of the human race, in the intimate knowledge that all people, wherever they dwell in time or place, are bound together by the same human condition. Through this inner sense of solidarity and consolation, the even deeper bond with all of creation can be sensed—and that gives us strength.

Conclusion

Vincent often concluded his letters by writing, "with a Firm Handshake, Yours, Vincent." When I picture Henri, my memories of him always include images of the emphatic ways he used his hands. Henri drew us into his talks, roped us in, so to speak, with his expressive gestures. In informal discussions in a class or at home we received a visual translation of his talks through the vigorous gestures or tender caresses expressed by his hands. Giving lectures on a stage with his hands flying all over the place, drawing images in midair, with his whole body often following suit, Henri transmitted the intensity of his emotions to us not just through his words but through his whole being.

When one looks at Vincent's paintings and sees the forceful brush strokes that leave furrows in the textured paint, when one discovers the marks his fingers made when he needed a more tactile and intimate connection with his painting, and when one sees the bits of sand, the flies stuck to his paintings as he painted them in the strong mistral winds of the Provence—one is "roped into" a dialogue with a very real and emphatic artist. If Henri had had a paint brush in his hands and lots of tubes of thick oil paint in the colors Vincent used in the south of France, I imagine Henri's style of painting would have been very much like Vincent's. Vincent's tangible sculpting in paint makes his presence felt today. When reading Henri's books, readers have the feeling that Henri is talking directly to them.

Both Henri and Vincent were real—they were honest about their hurts, needs, shortcomings, sufferings, joys. Through their written and painted messages both make us more conscious, more aware of our own feelings, struggles, and hopes. Both sought to minister out of a sense of their own needs and woundedness. After epileptic seizures started, Vincent painted out of the need to comfort himself—and these paintings are among his most powerful messages of comfort. Henri saw in Vincent the affirmation of his own struggles. We see in both Henri and Vincent the affirmation of ours. We are touched by their honesty, vulnerability, sacrifice, and desire to comfort. Both saw in the ordinary incidents, in the everyday encounters, in the basic moments of life, the something more, the something on high, the reality of creation being manifested in the ordinary. Vincent: in nature, in peasant huts, in a human face. Henri: in Adam, in the trapeze, in the wheel. Both internalized the gospel message and tried to live as authentically as possible, following Christ's example, not imitating it, but wholeheartedly believing in it and seeking to act it out.

We all know that exemplified living speaks louder than the most erudite sermon. Henri's and Vincent's "sermons" are the printed and painted expressions of exemplified living. That is why we respond to them, seek them, use them, delight in them, live by them. Drawing tirelessly all that he looked at deepened in Vincent van Gogh the ability to find in the dirtiest corners a ray of light. Through painting and using the colors of light Vincent was able to connect to that great Source of creative energy and see in creation the symbols of a loving and comforting Divine Presence.

Both Henri and Vincent invite us to live more fully, with greater awareness and honesty. They invite me as a teacher to deepen my students' awareness of our world, to help them connect through looking, through

Rijksmuseum Vincent van Gogh

"At Eternity's Gate, Autumn 1882, Den Haag."

learning to draw in order to see. Henri invites us to let our hearts speak and to extend our hands to one another so that we can connect in solidarity and love. Vincent invites us to look until we see–and understand.

Notes

[1] Henri Nouwen, "Introduction," lecture notes for his course "The Compassion of Vincent van Gogh," Yale Divinity School, 1979, Carol Berry's notes.

[2] Ibid.

[3] Ibid.

[4] Vincent to Theo and Mother (Letter 77), October 13, 1876, in *The Complete Letters of Vincent van Gogh (with reproductions of all the drawings in the correspondence)*, 3 vols. (Boston: Little Brown and Company, 2000), 1:71.

[5] Personal memories of Vincent van Gogh during his stay at Amesterdam, by Dr. M. B. Mendes da Costa (Letter 122a), December 2, 1910, in *Letters,* 1:69.

[6] Reprint from Louis Pierard, *La vie tragique de Vincent van Gogh*, rev. ed. (Paris: Editions Correa and Cie, 1939); Letter 143a, in *Letters,* 1:230.

[7] Vincent to Theo (Letter 126), November 15, 1878, in *Letters,* 1:177.

[8] Ibid., 179.

[9] Vincent to Theo (Letter 237), n.d., in *Letters,* 1:469.

[10] Vincent to Theo (Letter 404), April 30, 1985, in *Letters,* 2:371. Vincent always included Theo ("*We* must continue . . . ") in the making of his art. It was a collaboration between the two brothers, since Theo supported him.

[11] Vincent to Theo (Letter 197), May 11, 1882, in *Letters,* 1:365.

[12] Vincent to Theo (Letter 248), n.d., in *Letters,* 1:495.

[13] Vincent to Theo (Letter 218), n.d., in *Letters,* 1:416.

[14] Vincent to Theo (Letter 132) October 15, 1879, in *Letters,* 1:191.

13

A Rich Harvest

Henri Nouwen's Archival Legacy

Gabrielle Earnshaw and Anna St. Onge

> The fruitfulness of our lives shows itself in its fullness only af-
> ter we have died. We ourselves seldom see or experience our own
> fruitfulness. Often we remain preoccupied with our accomplish-
> ments and have no eye for the fruitfulness of what we live. But
> the beauty of life is that it bears fruit long after life itself has
> come to an end. Jesus said, "In all truth I tell you, unless a wheat
> grain falls into the earth and dies, it remains only a single grain;
> but if it dies it yields a rich harvest" (John 12:23).
> —HENRI NOUWEN, OUR GREATEST GIFT

Henri Nouwen's life was, and continues to be, a great gift for others. The
fruitfulness of his legacy, ten years after his death, can in part be traced directly to the preparations he made in his lifetime for the preservation and
care of his records. This chapter describes the ways in which Nouwen safe-
guarded his records and explores, through a selection of documents housed
in the Nouwen archives, the vast resource of primary and secondary material available for research and study. Particular attention is paid to Nouwen's
voluminous correspondence.

Laying My Life Down for My Friends: The Origins of the
Henri J. M. Nouwen Archives and Research Collection

Officially, the Nouwen archives was founded on September 21, 2000.
However, Nouwen had been consciously building and preserving his archives

for most of his life. He had a natural inclination to document everything, and he never threw anything out. His high school report cards, invoices for photocopying class handouts, and address books falling apart from constant use were kept just as carefully as drafts of his books. It was not long before he had boxes, filing cabinets, and bags filled with records.

Nouwen was also philosophically predisposed to placing value on his records for two reasons. First, he used archival records in his own research. For example, his insights about the compassion of Vincent van Gogh were based on his reading of van Gogh's letters. In addition, he visited the archives of Anton Boisen and Thomas Merton and used documents and research notes for his teaching and writing. Second, Nouwen drew extensively from the life stories and literary legacies of others for his writing about the spiritual life. Examples of this are numerous. He wrote a short biography of Thomas Merton in *Contemplative Critic* and included biographical details about Rembrandt van Rijn in *The Prodigal Son*. He also wrote an unpublished biography of his friend Richard White, took careful notes about the life of Daybreak assistant Lorenzo Sforza-Cesarini for a potential book, and conducted extensive oral history interviews with the circus troupe The Flying Rodleighs for a book he was planning on the spirituality of the trapeze. Nouwen referred frequently to the scriptural passage that asks us to lay down our lives for our friends, and the numerous ways he used biography to explore the spiritual life explain in part the importance he placed on his own documentary record.

While Nouwen may have been a natural collector and a supporter of archives generally, it was the practical issue of storage space and increased demand for copies of his records that led him in the summer of 1975 to make an appointment with Martha Smalley, a librarian at the Yale Divinity School Library, to discuss temporary storage options. Smalley vividly recalls the day that Nouwen arrived like a whirlwind, carrying a bundle of papers under his arms, and breathlessly inquired if she would mind keeping his papers temporarily while he was in Latin America. She agreed to help out in the short term, little realizing that this armful of papers would lead to twenty-four years of annual deposits totaling more than ten linear meters of records. The arrangement with Yale Divinity School was so informal that no deed of gift form was signed and no schedules of transfers were arranged; material would simply arrive when Nouwen ran out of room. This arrangement continued until he died.

An interesting question to consider about his collection at Yale is the type of records Nouwen selected for preservation. What aspects of his life and work did he think would be helpful to future generations of ministers, religious teachers, spiritual seekers, and others? A study of the finding guide from Yale gives us some insight. It lists six types, or series, of records in the Nouwen collection. Series I, *Notes and Manuscripts*, consisted of Nouwen's unpublished and published work. It contained draft manuscripts of many of his books as well as his articles, talks, and sermons. The sermons were brought together in leather-bound books, a good indication of the value he attached to these documents. Series II, *Teaching Materials*, contained his lecture and

2

reading notes. Like his sermons these documents were sent to be bound at the end of the class and sent to the archives. Series III, *Collected Material,* consisted of material he used for his own research and study. It included records he collected about Anton Boisen, the founder of the clinical pastoral education movement in the United States and the subject of many articles by Nouwen, as well as Nouwen's unfinished theology dissertation; Seward Hiltner, who focused on the interface between psychology and theology; and Thomas Merton. Series IV, *Published Works,* consisted of copies of his publications, including books (and their translations), as well as articles by or about him. Series V, *Tapes,* included audio and video cassettes of lectures, retreats, and other events. The sixth and last series, *Personal Papers and Memorabilia,* consisted of promotional posters, awards, degrees, and other miscellaneous material.

In reviewing these series, we see that Nouwen selected records that documented his professional role of teacher and writer. His life as priest was only marginally represented by the sermons, and records of his personal life as a son, brother, friend were missing altogether. Where were the records of his childhood or his seminary papers and reports? Where were his photographs and financial files? Where were the records from his work as pastor at L'Arche Daybreak? We also notice that for the most part the records deposited at Yale were polished and finished products. Where were the records that documented the process of all he was living? Where were the administrative files related to getting a book published? Where were the files that kept track of his hectic

From Abbey to Zeman: A Brief Anatomy of Nouwen's Correspondence

Many theorists in the study of archives regard correspondence as the administrative backbone of an organizational entity. Certainly what became known as the General Files served this role in Nouwen's life. There are approximately sixteen thousand letters contained in the incoming correspondence files ranging from 1964 to 1996. They measure more than four linear meters in extent, including mostly textual records as well as the occasional audio cassette and at least one video letter. Nouwen managed and stored these files throughout his adult life regardless of numerous changes of venue and circumstance. From Notre Dame to L'Arche, Nouwen and his assistants carefully filed fan mail and church bulletins; letters as impersonal as political form letters to the most intimate confessions of a troubled correspondent; and letters from friends and family, politicians and bishops, social activists and housewives, prisoners and foreign missionaries. It is clear that Nouwen placed great value on the correspondence he received; indeed, one could argue that he saw his response to these letters as an extension to his religious ministry and vocation.

Despite the complications of priestly confidentiality, privacy rights, and the often personal nature of many letters, Nouwen's correspondence can provide answers to many of the gaps in his own biographical record. It provides a unique source of evidence for late-twentieth-century spiritual and social history. Researchers at the archives can also catch glimpses of the dozens of dedicated individuals who, as secretaries, teaching assistants, and clerical aides, helped Nouwen in his vocation, as well as the chorus of thoughts, opinions, and advice of regular citizens, housewives, laypeople, students, grassroots activists, nuns, deacons, priests, monks, ministers, and preachers who have left their trace, through correspondence or collaboration, on Nouwen's archival legacy.

speaking schedule? Where was his correspondence with his legendary thousands of friends?

This partial archive at Yale may well have been our only portrait of Henri Nouwen had it not been for the final preparation he made for his literary legacy: the selection of Sue Mosteller, S.S.J., as his literary executor. Mosteller, his very good friend from the L'Arche Daybreak community, was not forewarned about this privileged but onerous gift; however, upon learning of her responsibility to Nouwen's legacy, she began almost immediately to unite the public and private records of her friend. She also began the process of bringing them closer to his Daybreak home, north of Toronto. By 1999, with the kind cooperation of the Yale Divinity School Library, this consolidation was accomplished, and the material from Yale was transferred to the University of St. Michael's College, a Catholic college within the University of Toronto. Then, in June 2000, more than thirty linear meters of material was transferred from L'Arche Daybreak, creating the largest and most comprehensive archival collection on Henri Nouwen in the world.

The records from L'Arche included all that had been missing from the Yale collection: publisher files (consisting of correspondence, drafts, art work, contracts, galleys and proofs); administrative files related to the myriad invitations he accepted to lecture, lead retreats, give homilies, and officiate at weddings and funerals (many containing original handwritten notes); his tax returns, credit card statements, and other financial files; his photograph collection, including hundreds of photos of his friends and their growing families and slides from his extensive travels as a young man; records in Dutch from his student and seminary years in Holland; subject/reference files that he kept on a variety of topics, including Buddhism, celibacy, and nuclear arms; and the administrative records related to his role as pastor for the Daybreak community. Also found in these boxes were files of letters.

Highlights of the Collection

The archives is a treasury of information and inspiration. Here are reproductions and descriptions of four gems.

> The signs of the last days, of the coming of the son of man are always ~~there~~. present
>
> One of the signs, we feel so ✱ terribly deep, is the doubt. We ask: where is Jesus Christ in this world. Even on a small ship as this there are different places of worship. It has become very difficult to recogonize Jesus Christ in this world. Perhaps is that one of the reasons that on a ship with about 1000 people only a few want to give an hour of worship to God.
>
> There are so many different ways of thinking and so many opinions, so many Churches and so many customs, that many people get lost and are not able to recogonize Jesus Christ behind the curtain of human weakness.

Nouwen, "Sermon for Holland-America line," 1962, Item 9a,
Manuscripts-Short, Nouwen Archives.

When Henri served as a chaplain for the Holland-America steamship line in 1962, he was thirty years old and just five years out of the seminary. These are handwritten notes for a sermon written on postcards from the ship. While the archives has drafts of earlier sermons from his seminary days in Holland, this is the earliest English sermon housed in the archives. There are a few spelling mistakes that remind us that, while he wrote most of his books in English, this was not his first language. The format of this sermon on postcards is unique. If one were to study the evolution of his homiletic style using the more than one hundred sermons preserved in the archives, a clear development is discernable. While Nouwen may have started out needing cue cards, by the end of his life he rarely required more than three points on his page when delivering a homily.

GROUP SESSIONS

For me the group meetings were extremely important and revealing.
Although I have the feeling that our group is still in an elementary phase
of development I felt this group experience of essential value for the
training program.

1. Group interaction in ecumenical perspective.

To begin with I feel that in this case I have to see as of primary
importance the experience of a group from the standpoint of a Catholic.

I don't think that I ever had the experience of group work before.
It even seems to me that I come from a tradition in which real group
work never is applied in its full consequences. Here the same experience comes back as I had in supervision. My frame of reference still
was that of teaching and therefore authority. In this frame I tried to
conceive group discussions as a better tool for the authority to get
his message across. I knew better but I don't think I ever lived
better. In the past I was accustomed that you were allowed to discuss
your ideas and feelings freely but that it was then up to the authorities to decide what had to be done.

One of my first discoveries was that most of the ministers came
from a background in which shared responsibility meant shared authority, and in which group interaction and group decisions are a part of
their daily church life. Especially the set-up of the Presbyterian
church shows clearly the striking differences between the Catholic
and Protestant way of approach.

I mention this because I felt that for most of the group members
the proceedings of the group were in line with what they had done before.
Not so for me. This means that really using the group hours was a
difficult thing in the beginning. Or I wanted to get some helpful
information, or I wanted to teach. That a group has different lines

Nouwen, "Evaluation of Six Months Pastoral Training,"
Research and Study Notes, unprocessed, Nouwen Archives.

From 1964 to 1966, Nouwen was a fellow in the program for religion and psychiatry at the Menninger Clinic in Topeka, Kansas. This document is the first page from the second chapter of an assignment to evaluate his first six months of clinical pastoral training. This document (reproduced on page 128) provides, among other things, insight into the influence of Protestantism on his thought and his early reflections on the value of ecumenism. We also see here some reflection on authority, which may have had an impact on the way he would live his life as a priest. The files from his experience at the Menninger are extensive, including papers as well as study and reading notes. They also mark the beginning of his interest in the clinical pastoral movement, particularly in Anton Boisen.

HARVARD UNIVERSITY
THE DIVINITY SCHOOL

45 FRANCIS AVENUE
CAMBRIDGE, MASSACHUSETTS 02138

Dear George -

~~This~~ After some more thinking and praying
and asking advice I have come to the conclusion
that it is better to make this semester my last
semester at A.D.S. It was not a very easy
decision to come to but during the last few
weeks all signs have pointed in the same direction.

I am very grateful to you for your
willingness to discuss this with me at several
occasions. I know how many other things are
at your mind and I have experienced it as a
sign of real friendship that you took the time
to help me think this through -

Henri Nouwen, "Letter to George Rupp, Harvard Divinity School, May 9,
1985," File 4657, General Files, Nouwen Archives

This is a handwritten draft of Nouwen's letter of resignation to George Rupp, dean of Harvard Divinity School, which he submitted on May 9, 1985. The official letter submitted was not very different from what we read here. It shows Nouwen at a very difficult time in his life trying to discern God's will for his priesthood. It would not be long, however, before he would hear a clear vocational call from the unlikely location of Richmond Hill, Ontario, Canada.

In addition to the letter sent to the dean of Harvard Divinity School, Nouwen also drafted a slightly different letter of explanation for his decision to leave Harvard that he sent out to his friends and students. This was not the first time that Nouwen used the letter form to explain major changes in his life. Upon his return from South America in 1982, Nouwen sent out a flurry of letters to friends and colleagues, each communicating his indecision about his future path. The letters included the same facts but were expressed in different ways. The personal tone of much of Henri Nouwen's writing can deceive readers into believing there was only one Henri "Just Me" Nouwen—an individual who poured out his personal spiritual journey onto the published page. It may seem that anything one would want or need to know about Nouwen can be found in his published works. In fact, Nouwen was quite adept at using several public and personal voices for the same purpose to appeal to a wide range of individuals. Creative use of the General Files can reveal the many roles that Nouwen constructed for himself as priest, author, friend, professor, and speaker, as well as his more intimate and personal self that he shared with family and friends.

May 17, 1994

John Dear SJ
Chowan County Jail
P. O. Box 78
Edenton, NC
27932

Dear John:

It is so good to hear from you, and I am grateful for all that you
are sharing with me.   There was a time in which I thought about
prison as a place where I could be quiet, pray, and write, but your
story makes it very clear that all of this is pure fantasy.   I am
deeply aware of the suffering that the noise, and the restlessness
around you creates.   For me that too, that would be the greatest
source of pain.   Hopefully you can gradually find some inner
silence and inner space in the midst of all the clamour and shouts,
it certainly must ask for a generous discipline.

As far as my life is concerned I have been extremely busy. I went
to Edmonton, Vancouver, and Mobile, Alabama to give retreats to
l'Arche communities there, and to help them in their fundraising.
There were always large groups of people who came to the talks, and
mostly I did not have much time for myself.   After most of the
presentations, there were two hours of signing books and talking
with individual people about their struggles and pains. I really
want to be attentive to people's suffering but after a long
time of listening, I often feel very exhausted and sometimes a
little depleted and am in need for a more intimate space, and my
desire for personal friendship always grows in these situations.
I also went to Houston, Forth Worth and to Manhattan and to Rye,
New York with two members of my community to speak about l'Arche
and to offer some reflections on solitude, community and care.
Although   these   retreats   were   very   intense,   and   demanding
spiritually, as well as emotionally, at the same time I felt that
many good things happened and people felt called to a deeper
relationship with God and a deeper knowledge of their call to live
in community. Now I am back in my community for a few days trying
to keep up with the mail and with all the community events.   Next
week I will give a seven day covenant retreat in Toronto.   On the
2nd of June I will receive an honorary degree from the Chicago
Theological Society and then I fly on to Brussels to give two
l'Arche retreats in Belgium and Holland.

Nouwen, "Letter to John Dear from Henri Nouwen, May 17, 1994,"
Accession 2001 43, Nouwen Archives

This letter is part of a donation of letters that John Dear made in December 1998 to the literary executor, Sue Mosteller. At that time Mosteller began a campaign to collect Nouwen's handwritten letters from the thousands of people with whom he had had a correspondence. This letter, written to Dear in prison, shows Nouwen's deep commitment to social justice activists. This letter also offers a firsthand look at how busy Nouwen's life was. In 1994 alone he would publish Here and Now, Our Greatest Gift, *and* With Burning Hearts, *and at his death leave several books to be published posthumously:* Adam, Bread for the Journey, Can You Drink the Cup?, Sabbatical Journey, *and* The Inner Voice of Love.

Conclusion

The Nouwen archives has responded to more than 580 research requests from people in more than fourteen different countries since it opened in 2000. It is clear that the fruitfulness of Nouwen's legacy continues to reveal itself through the use of his archival records, whose care and preservation he prepared before his death. The rich variety of themes being researched by scholars attests to Nouwen's continued vitality as an influential thinker and teacher. Use of the archives by religious educators reveals his continued vitality as a spiritual leader. Questions asked of the archives for pastoral and other personal reasons testify to the power of his words to transform hearts. Nouwen did lay down his life for his friends, and the harvest is, and will continue to be, rich indeed. As Robert Durback wrote after Nouwen's funeral: "This is not the end of Henri Nouwen's ministry. It's a new beginning. He's just gone underground."[1]

Note

[1] Robert Durback, "Ministry and Friendship–Pastor and Friend: Remembering Henri Nouwen," *Christian Century* 113, no. 29 (October 16, 1996): 957.

The General Files: Insight into Henri Nouwen's Pastoral Care of Social Activists

In addition to some prominent politicians and members of the Roman Catholic hierarchy, Nouwen also received personal letters, news bulletins, and updates from social activists, prisoners, radical protesters, and foreign missionaries from around the world. Indeed, the General Files can illustrate how often Nouwen was the nexus between such individuals and how he used his influence and extended network of contacts to introduce and endorse individuals in the social justice movement. These letters of support, guidance, and encouragement reveal another facet of Nouwen's spiritual ministry. Although he may not have spoken out publicly in his teaching or his published work on certain issues, through the medium of letters Nouwen quietly ministered to individuals actively struggling for nuclear disarmament, the AIDS crisis, poverty, and other social justice issues of his time.

14

How Not to Comfort a New Orleans Hurricane Survivor

Henri Nouwen's "Confession and Forgiveness"

Carolyn Whitney-Brown

This workshop at the Turning the Wheel conference explored an unpublished 1966 talk by Henri Nouwen to a Unitarian congregation near the University of Notre Dame.[1] Henri's talk, "Confession and Forgiveness," is a remarkably vivid and compact window into the development of Henri's foundational spirituality and convictions. It begins with Henri's description of visiting a friend in New Orleans in 1965, shortly after she had suffered terrible losses in Hurricane Betsy. To start the workshop, I prepared the participants in two ways: first, to become fully present; and second, to understand the origins of the questions explored in the workshop.

Throughout his life, Henri wanted people to own their experience, since that is where our authority lies. The workshop was designed to help participants "experience" Henri's early talk, not only to think about it. To help us become present to this experience, we heard a passage from Henri's 1983 foreword to Gustavo Gutiérrez's *We Drink from Our Own Wells*:

> To drink from your own well is to live your own life in the Spirit of Jesus as you have encountered him in your concrete historical reality. This has nothing to do with abstract opinions, convictions, or ideas, but it has everything to do with the tangible, audible, and visible experience of God, an experience so real that it can become the foundation of a life project. As the First Epistle of John puts it: "What we have heard, what we have seen with our eyes, what we have looked upon and our hands have touched—we speak of the word of life."[2]

Henri's 1966 talk would begin in his historical reality, and this workshop offered participants a "tangible, audible, and visible experience" of Henri's early insights. We did a few exercises to be sure that our ears and eyes and sense of touch—and also our sense of humor—were awake and ready.

Second, I wanted participants to understand what questions had brought me to this talk of Henri's. From 1990, while living in community at L'Arche Daybreak, I used to go to Henri for confession. I would seek out Henri after Mass or in his office. "Henri, could we find a time for a sacramental conversation?" I'd ask. Henri would beam his pleasure at the prospect and pull out his thick agenda book. He'd flip back and forth, becoming a bit agitated, complaining about how busy he was, how many people wanted to see him, murmuring about the preparations he still needed to make for some imminent trip that he regretted having scheduled. I'd listen sympathetically, then I would open my mouth to let him off the hook and say maybe this wasn't a good time, my need was not so urgent, we'd try again another time. Before I could get the words out, Henri would announce that he had two hours that afternoon or maybe the next day. He always found time within a day, and I would go off marveling at Henri's magical calendar, where time could always be found.

I will write elsewhere in more detail about my experience of confession with Henri. In brief, along with the affirmation that I was forgiven was the confidence that all my experience was useful, even essential in my life. That had something to do with the way Henri received my words; it was certainly easy to tell him anything, because the more difficult and painful my confession, the more excited he became that I had such significant and deep material from which to build my life and ministry.

This was a theme of Henri's life: the stuff we might want to burn or toss out of our lives and hearts is the fertile material that makes us who we are, that will enlarge our hearts, that will draw us into community with compassion and maturity. But it takes work and grace to make our compulsions and aggression and resentment and fear into useful material integrated into our lives. This experience was so unlike my other experiences of sacramental confession that after Henri's death I began to wonder how his understanding had evolved. I searched out the earliest writing I could find by Henri about confession.

After a New Orleans Hurricane

In the talk Henri gave in 1966, he began with a vivid story:

Very shortly after the hurricane and flood which destroyed a part of New Orleans, I visited a Mrs.O'Neill who lived in the middle of this stricken area. I found her alone, desperately looking at the damage done to her house, and although she used to be very open and talkative, now she hardly recognized me. She just sat there saying to herself: "I am superfluous. Since my husband died, I am only a burden for myself, my children, and my neighbors. There is only one thing left for me to do–to die."

Henri's story was so concrete that I wanted workshop participants to get inside the dynamic Henri described. Also, after several days of workshops and talks, I figured some participants would relish the chance to *be* Henri, and others to respond to him.

We set up groups of three: one person would take the role of Mrs. O'Neill, one would be Henri, and the third would be an observer. The "Mrs. O'Neills" began softly to rehearse their lines, settling deeply into the emotions and person Henri described. "It's 1965. You are thirty-three-year-old Henri Nouwen," I instructed the "Henris." "You have been ordained for eight years. You have just completed a program in clinical psychology at the esteemed Menninger Clinic in Kansas, where you have been writing case studies and offering diagnoses and care to a variety of people. You are both spiritually and psychologically trained, attentive and caring. You have come to a devastated area of New Orleans, where floodwater has destroyed much of the neighborhood, to seek out someone you know."

With the workshop participants in their roles, I continued with Henri's story:

How would you react to this situation? This is what I did. "You have no reason to be depressed," I said. "Look, you have children who love you and like to come and visit you; you have charming grandchildren who are happy to have a grandmother who can spend time with them. Your son is all ready to come and fix your house and there are perhaps few people who are so well off in this neighborhood as you are."

Now the groups ad-libbed. Each Henri tried to console in this way, while the Mrs. O'Neills responded with annoyance, sorrow, pain, and rejection. The observers interpreted what they were seeing: a lack of genuine engagement, an absence of listening, fearfulness in Henri of becoming too engaged.

We spoke of this experience, then listened to Henri's analysis:

I did not help her at all with these words. The only thing I did was to make her more depressed, to make her feel more guilty. My words to her were more an accusation than a consolation. "After all," I told her in effect, "My arguments for feeling good are better than your arguments for feeling bad." I had not even accepted her feelings, but immediately started fighting with her in a subtle competition of arguments. When I left, I left a lady more sad and depressed than before, more guilty because I had not even allowed her to feel sad in a sad moment.

Another Story

In contrast, Henri offers another story, of a young man he calls John. One of my friends at the workshop had kindly agreed to act the part of John for the group, and made vivid John's anguish:

> John is a man twenty years old. In one moment of his life, it just became too much for him. Everything, I mean. But he found the courage to talk. He is nervous and trembling; he has a strong, itching feeling in his stomach; he is extremely restless and cannot concentrate. He says, ". . . I cannot function any longer. The funny thing is, everybody likes me . . . but they don't know me." . . . Then he started to cry. The walls of his composure broke down and he exposed his deepest despair, his weakness, his hate and jealousy, his meanness and hypocrisy—his inner division. I did not know what to do. I only felt that he had told me about my own feelings as much as about his.

Henri's silence struck us. We were aware that Henri felt much closer emotionally to the young man than to the older woman. We all grasped the inner anguish articulated by this popular young priest and professor.

Looking back through the thirty years of self-revealing writings that would follow, this story of Henri's does not immediately seem remarkable. But in 1966 Henri is developing his professional life. He has not yet written a book. His reputation is just beginning to take shape. This public confession of his own inner division and fear is extraordinarily vulnerable and even risky for a young professor who wants to be taken seriously.

But it is a calculated risk. The point, as we will see, is that far from being taken seriously, Henri questions whether he wants to be "taken" at all.

> I present these two personal experiences to you to illustrate two essentially different forms of existence which I will call the "taking form" and the "forgiving form."

The Taking Form of Existence

> When you take a teacup by its ear you can hold it at a distance, you can look at it from all sides, you can make it an obedient instrument. . . . It is a risky thing to be honest, because someone might just take you by your weak spot and turn it against yourself. Our confession might destroy us. And when John says, "If my friends know how I really feel, they would not love me, but hate me," he speaks of a real possibility.

Why is Henri telling his audience this story of his encounter with John? Henri is modeling something here, in an exercise he will develop in his later writing and speaking: by naming his own inner anguish and "hypocrisy," he challenges his listeners to be aware of their responses. In being so self-revealing, Henri offers a framework for the individuals in his audience to observe and interpret what happens in them. Do they create distance and assume, in a taking form, that they now know Henri?

When Henri's *Road to Daybreak* was published in 1988, I heard harsh criticisms of the book as some readers responded to Henri's convoluted inner anguish with revulsion and even contempt. Years later, when I was asked to write an Introduction to a tenth anniversary edition of the book, I wanted to offer those readers a way into the book. I wrote:

> *The Road to Daybreak* can be painful to read, because here Henri lays bare so much of his inner life with great vulnerability. One can be tempted to read this judgmentally. . . . Or one can feel embarrassed for Henri that he is so exposed, or critical that what he reveals about himself is too personal. To read in this way may miss the meaning of this remarkable book. . . . If you can love the truth of Henri's struggles, perhaps you can love the truth of your own.[3]

Already in the mid-1960s Henri was formulating an analysis of the foundational dynamics of fear, domination, and manipulation. Henri's 1966 talk continued:

> In the world of this taking form, we operate in terms of power and are motivated by fear. We are armed to our teeth, carefully following the movements of the other, to hit back at the right moment and at the vulnerable spot. Often in a very subtle form we are victims of this world.

Henri at age thirty-three was positioning himself professionally. He was positioning himself in relation to academic expectations at Notre Dame, in relation to the framework of clinical psychology and case studies in which he was trained, and in relation to the post–Vatican II Roman Catholic Church in which he was an ordained priest. It was a complex and somewhat perilous terrain to negotiate, and Henri was ambitious.

All his life Henri was distressed by the thought of being taken, yet he did not let the risk paralyze him. Over and over he offered people the ammunition to dismiss him in a competitive taking mode, and the tools for freedom to hear him and themselves in a more forgiving and merciful mode. "But there is more," Henri continued. Before laying out his understanding of the forgiving form, Henri pushes his analysis to another level and invites his listener along.

The Irreversibility of Evil

The "more" to which Henri refers is the theological underpinning he sees as "deeper than psychology can reach." He identifies Thomas Merton's articulation of "the irreversibility of evil": "Evil, in this context, is something definitive, unchangeable. The only thing you can do with it is to cut it out, to eliminate, to uproot."

Henri, whose childhood was shaped by the tension and physical hunger of occupied Holland during World War II, identifies the political stakes inherent in this theological belief:

> The man who acted on this was Adolph Hitler, who firmly believed in the unforgiveableness of evil and the finality of sin. As Merton writes, "This is, indeed, fundamental to the whole mentality of Nazism, with its avidity for final solutions and its concern that all uncertainties be eliminated."

The Forgiving Form

In contrast, Henri articulates the "forgiving form of existence." Although throughout his 1966 paper he uses the framework of confession and forgiveness, he does not limit those words to the admission and merciful acknowledgment of specific wrongs. Rather, he explains, "This forgiveness is born out of the received confession—not so much of particular deeds, acts or events—but of ourselves."

The forgiving form moves the interaction from fear or competition to mature solidarity:

> Forgiving can only take place when the taking form is transcended, when all the fear is taken out of the confession. You may remember a few occasions in which you were able to show your weaknesses and pains, your bitter motives, your other dark side to someone you love. Perhaps it took a lot of courage to do this, but on the moment that you experienced that your sins were not only accepted but made into a common weakness, something new happened.

Henri then explores the concrete dynamic involved, and we hear an implied critique of some of his training in clinical psychology:

> Forgiveness is more than letting people talk-out. Aren't we a little simplistic if we speak about the cathartic effect of confession, as if all it is is a cheap form of chimney-sweeping, a talking-out cure, as if the mere fact of letting go has any meaning?

He continues, defining the limitations of simply analyzing personal history:

> Forgiveness is more than a form of self-understanding. If you are afraid to cross the road and someone helps you to understand that this is caused by a traumatic experience in your early childhood, the only result is that now you cannot cross the road, while knowing why you cannot. The problem remains that you still cannot cross the road.

Forgiveness, Henri insists, creates real change: "Forgiveness is more than understanding; it is mobilizing; and it creates a new life and does not stop by understanding the old one."

The Fellowship of the Weak

How does this mobilizing forgiveness happen? Henri sees the core of this dynamic in the community built through confessing weakness to another without fear:

> Forgiveness does not come about because I listen to your pains or because I can help you see how it all came about, but it only takes place when I can really say: "Your weakness is my weakness, your pain is my pain, your sin is my sin." Exactly in the sharing of weakness, forgiveness takes place. It is this fellowship of the weak that constitutes the core of the forgiving form of existence.

Already in 1966 Henri yearned to be part of community with vulnerability at its core. It would be twenty years before he would move to L'Arche Daybreak to live with people with intellectual and physical disabilities, people called core members because the weakest members create the core of community life. We also hear the commitment to the deep spiritual roots of peacemaking that would characterize Henri's later writing and speaking as he adds, "It is in this sharing of weakness that violence can be overcome."

Vices and Virtues

What is the "fellowship of the weak" that is created by the forgiving form of existence? It is not, Henri muses, about a moral stance of getting everything right:

> This fellowship of the weak is more than just tolerance. Perhaps it goes to that mysterious depth where we recognize that weakness and strength are so intimately related that by pulling out the ugly weeds we might

also pull out the fertile wheat. By trying always to have no vices, we might end up without any virtue.

In an unusual flash of humor, Henri goes on to describe what he means in concrete terms:

> Some people try so hard not to do certain things—not to curse, not to drink, not to smoke, and so to become perfect and saintly—that they become impossible to live with. They walk through life with so much self-control, that they seem to have swallowed an Easter-candle.

Finally, Henri names what he sees as a central problem: to give up all possibility of mistakes is to give up too much of being human: "They are never impatient, but also never passionate; never cold, but also never hot; never exaggerating, but also never inspiring." In other words, the virtues and the vices are not opposed. In fact, Henri seems to suggest that it is not entirely clear what is virtue and what is vice in an honest human life. He is way ahead of his time in his implied critique of moral binary oppositions. "I guess our spontaneous sympathy is with the weak," suggests Henri, adding self-revealingly, "especially with those who can live with their weaknesses without being crushed by their own guilt feelings."

The Reversibility of Evil

Henri returns to the theological underpinnings of the irreversibility or reversibility of evil, linking it directly again to violence and nonviolence, and to political action:

> The forgiving form of existence therefore, in contrast with the taking form, is based on the reversibility of evil. Evil is not final and unchangeable, but to be reverted in love. Gandhi's concept of non-violence was essentially based on his belief that forgiveness could change every enemy into a friend; that in hatred, love is hidden.

In Henri's book *Pray to Live*, published in English in 1972, this is explained further as he discusses Thomas Merton's affinity with Mohandas Gandhi. Henri names "one of the deepest of Merton's insights":

> The spirit of truth is the spirit of nonviolence. . . . Nonviolence stands or falls according to the vision of evil. If evil is seen only as an irreversible, clearly visible and sharply outlined tumor, then there is only one possibility: cut it out. And then violence is necessary. But when evil is reversible and can be turned into good through forgiveness, then nonviolence becomes possible.[4]

Henri goes on to quote Merton's passionate assertion that "a violent change would not have been a change at all. The only real liberation is that which liberates both the oppressor and the oppressed at the same time from the same tyrannical automatism of the violent process which contains in itself the curse of irreversibility."[5]

Some further context helps explain the importance of this question of the reversibility or irreversibility of evil to Henri. This talk was delivered a year after he had joined Martin Luther King, Jr., and thousands of others in the civil rights march from Selma to Montgomery.[6] The journey from Topeka to Selma and back and the march itself were pivotal experiences in his life. He was wrestling with specific experiences of both evil and community in his "concrete historical reality."

Concluding the Workshop

Henri worked these ideas out in more detail in his first book, *Intimacy: Pastoral Psychological Essays* (1969), acknowledging the necessity of some form of taking as expressing appropriate social boundaries:

> It is obvious that the taking structure is so much part of our existence that we cannot avoid it. Don't ask the telephone operator how she is feeling today. Don't start a conversation about the prayer life of the man from whom you want to buy some stamps at the Post Office. Don't ask your teacher about his sexual behavior. You destroy human communication because you want to play a game without rules, which means no game at all. . . . Our problem therefore is not how we can completely annihilate the taking structure of life but whether there is any possibility at all to transcend that structure.[7]

Henri does not urge his listeners to live only in the wide-open vulnerability of the forgiving form. He does expect that they will want to develop the honest self-awareness that the forgiving form requires, as he tried to model in his frank analysis of his encounter with New Orleans hurricane survivor Mrs. O'Neill. "Our life," he acknowledges, "is often a very painful fluctuation between these two modes of existence, the taking and the forgiving mode."

My experience of confession with Henri at L'Arche is illumined by this early talk. To Henri, our human problems and struggles were to be transformed and used, not removed. Nothing needed to be rejected. Henri's understanding was deeply coherent with the whole philosophy undergirding L'Arche, with its refusal to accept simplistic dichotomies of good and bad, useful and useless, normal and handicapped.[8]

Even in his early thirties Henri was working hard to live fearlessly and freely within his professional training as a priest and psychologist. Henri's life and writings witnessed that reflective human lives will be big, varied, and often full of contradictions. Throughout his life Henri had an affinity with a complex, multifaceted orientation to life.

By the end of the workshop we had shared many stories and personal responses to Henri's talk. The room had been full of laughter and deep emotion—and many words. It was time for silence, time to let our experience settle more deeply into our hearts. We ended the workshop by standing together, hand in hand, wordlessly soaking in the kindness and gift of our temporary community.

And on that afternoon nine months after Hurricane Katrina, we sent our love and solidarity to the people of New Orleans.

Notes

[1] Henri Nouwen, "Confession and Forgiveness," File 9, Item 5, Manuscripts–Short–Collected Sermons, 1960–1975, the Henri J. M. Nouwen Archives and Research Collection. All quotations are from this manuscript unless otherwise noted. I wish to thank Sue Mosteller, literary executor, for permission to quote Henri's unpublished notes.

[2] Henri Nouwen, "Foreword," in Gustavo Gutiérrez, *We Drink from Our Own Wells* (Maryknoll, NY: Orbis Books, 1984), xiv.

[3] Carolyn Whitney-Brown, "Introduction," in Henri J. M. Nouwen, *The Road to Daybreak: A Spiritual Journey* (London: Darton, Longman and Todd, 1997), xi.

[4] Henri Nouwen, *Pray to Live* (Notre Dame, IN: Fides Publishers, 1972), 66.

[5] Thomas Merton, quoted in ibid., 66.

[6] For Henri's description of that journey, see "We Shall Overcome: A Pilgrimage to Selma, 1965," in Henri Nouwen, *The Road to Peace: Writings on Peace and Justice*, ed. John Dear, 75–95 (Maryknoll, NY: Orbis Books, 1998).

[7] Henri Nouwen, *Intimacy: Pastoral Psychological Essays* (Notre Dame, IN: Fides Press, 1969), 34.

[8] I describe Henri's time at Daybreak in more depth in "Henri at Daybreak: Celebration and Hard Work," in *Remembering Henri*, ed. Gerald S. Twomey and Claude Pomerleau, 119–37 (Maryknoll, NY: Orbis Books, 2006).

15

Teaching with
The Inner Voice of Love

Kathleen M. Fisher

Anyone who teaches knows both the excitement and terror of the first day of class. The excitement comes from a new beginning, a fresh start on a new, if brief, intellectual journey. The terror comes from not knowing if the students will share that excitement; teaching always holds out to us the risk of disappointment. Our students, too, have a mix of emotions. Some are eager, clutching new notebooks and sitting in the front row. Others appear reluctant or timid, with downcast eyes and a barely audible "hello." Still others are excessively confident, striding into the room with a certain bravado or self-assurance. Most students are probably a mix of all these emotions and more. What makes them different from teachers, however, is that this is new territory to them. They are taking a course we may have taught many times, but for them it is a maiden voyage in the subject matter or the discipline or the faculty member. They are entering what Henri Nouwen calls "a new country."

Nouwen used this phrase–"a new country"–to describe the result of his spiritual journey through a crushing depression. In *The Inner Voice of Love* he writes with his trademark candor about his search for God amid the psychological and emotional battles of his life. He describes his struggle against "upward mobility"–the seductive pull of influence, success, affection, and praise. He concludes that he must relinquish the concern with success that drives this upward climb and embrace a desire for "downward mobility." Michael O'Laughlin, one of Nouwen's teaching assistants and biographers, described "downward mobility" as "a descent and a seeking out of others in the spirit of solidarity with those in need, in pain, and in affliction."[1] It requires the surrender of self-interest and self-determination in order to embrace a radical hospitality and humility toward others. Nouwen recognized this radical hospitality as the way of Christ and the only way to fulfill his deepest desire for God. In the last years of his life he would discover his own

145

"new country" among the members of the L'Arche Daybreak community in Toronto.

The work of education is much like entering a new country. Many students come to college primarily to secure a job. In preparing for careers they will be asked to demonstrate their knowledge of well-established facts and opinions. Thus, they tend to bring with them many truisms and convictions about history, God, science, politics, and morality. But if education is to expand their minds and hearts, which has long been the goal of liberal studies, it must not simply affirm what they already know and feel. Rather, it must draw them away from comforting beliefs into a place where theories and experiences can be tested, revised, renewed, or even discarded. For students, this often means opening themselves to people and ideas that challenge their view of the world. It means opening their eyes to a new vista.

Teaching in the mid-1980s, Nouwen challenged the expectation of intellectual and material comfort that seemed to permeate American culture. Many would argue that the material expectations of students have not changed much since Nouwen's days at Yale and Harvard. Even anecdotally, it does seem that students today are even more preoccupied with future financial security and view a college education as essential to that success. Consequently, the various forms of a liberal arts curriculum that colleges and universities require for the baccalaureate degree often feel to students distracting, boring, and irrelevant to their preparation for the "real world." In a 2006 interview, outgoing Harvard University president Lawrence Summers attributed this outlook to relentless activity and stress that makes this generation of students less inclined to reflect upon life's philosophical issues.

Yet, amid the career aspirations, there is often a glimmer of a spiritual longing for which students have limited language and the vaguest understanding. Teaching in a Catholic college, I meet students with assorted religious experiences and affiliations. Many come with a traditional Catholic upbringing that they now zealously defend or renounce. Others identify themselves as agnostic or atheist and boldly reject any religious orthodoxy. Still others hesitantly identify themselves as Christians but with a discomfited curiosity about non-Christian religions. So, the experience of a spiritual life is there but is not always acknowledged or consciously examined. It is part of their "new country."

So how do we reinvigorate the liberal arts to respond to a spiritual longing that is couched in the reasonable worries over how to make a living? It is, I think, a change of attitude more than it is a new and improved curriculum; this is where *The Inner Voice of Love* offers guidance.[2] Henri Nouwen kept this journal as a private record of his experience in a painful spiritual and psychological breakdown. He never intended for it to be published, much less applied as a philosophy of education, but his lessons in spiritual growth have much to offer the teacher's craft. His search for God traverses some of the same ground as a search for knowledge. So what follows are pedagogical ideas grounded in Nouwen's spiritual lessons, starting with the question, Why teach the liberal arts?

The longer I teach, the less satisfied I am with the traditional description of the liberal arts as a process of "freeing the mind from the shackles of ignorance." To break these shackles, the established academic model, in which I was educated, uses dualisms—true and false, subject and object, orthodoxy and heresy, faith and reason. It structures its pedagogy to encourage debate and argument, which imply only two sides of a given idea. How often do we find ourselves using phrases like "on the other hand," "two sides of the story," "as opposed to," or "in contrast"? It is an approach that by design separates ideas from experiences, thoughts from feelings, body from mind, often declaring one member of the pair superior to the other. This form of inquiry creates the perception that the liberal arts are a digression from career preparation—school is different from the "real world." Students' "real" lives are outside of the classroom, compartmentalized into dorm life, athletics, home, leisure, career, and friends, and nothing ties these experiences together in a meaningful way.

A more satisfying description of the goal of a liberal education resides in Nouwen's idea of a path toward a "place of unity," the core of our being "where all human sentiments are held together in truth."[3] In theological terms, this is where God dwells, primarily through the incarnation, and it is the place to which all human beings are called. Academic inquiry also seeks "truth" using its dualisms to winnow away false leads and eventually reveal the true path. But as the wars over political correctness and cultural values have shown, we cannot agree on what "truth" looks like, and perhaps this dispute is what gives intellectual life its vigor. Rather than viewing a liberal arts curriculum as an end in itself (truth), it should be viewed as a means of integration. If we interpret the curriculum as a way to put together the jumbled experiences of minds, hearts, and souls, students are more likely to find that place from which they can, as Nouwen writes, "feel, think, and act truthfully."[4] Such an education would drop the dualisms and integrate academic disciplines and pedagogies rather than divide them from each other. Then students could see that all human experience is a source of truth, not just the objectified, rationalized, dispassionate data we often privilege.

How might we pursue this ambitious goal of helping students find their integrity, especially when the time-honored approach to the liberal arts has tended to separate rather than integrate our intellect and emotion? What can we learn from the search for God that could guide our search for knowledge? Nouwen's struggle to realize an inner "place of unity" generated many lessons about the spiritual life. Four examples from *The Inner Voice of Love* impart wise counsel for education: seek community, set personal limits, recognize others' limitations, and respect the different aspects of one's personality.

First, seek community. If we treat teaching as a vocation (which Nouwen and many others do), then we must find our place in a community and learn to balance the demands of the calling with the gifts we bring to it. Writing about his role as a spiritual guide, Nouwen says, "When it is part of your vocation to offer your people a vision that will nurture them and allow them to keep moving forward, it is crucial that you give yourself the time and space to let that vision mature in you and become an integral part of your being."[5] Good teachers offer their students a "vision that will nurture them" and keep them "moving forward" along the path of intellectual and spiritual growth. However, if this "vision" is to be persuasive, it must be *lived* in a way students can witness.

The search for God, for knowledge, and for personal integrity all require a community that welcomes our presence and allows our solitude. It is reasonable to believe that people who love the intellectual life will seek some deeper communion with colleagues and students. But this communion has a dangerously seductive side. First, teaching is a profession of performers and critics full of praise and blame. Peer reviews, student evaluations, class observations, and tenure decisions all produce the uncertain and uneven mix of gratitude, disapproval, adoration, commendation, and rejection. They can expose our insecurities, leading us to seek "gifts and favors like a petulant child." Nouwen writes: "You want deep communion, but you end up looking for invitations, letters, phone calls, gifts, and similar gestures. When these do not come in the way you wish, you start distrusting even your deep desire for communion."[6] Like the spiritual quest, the results and rewards of teaching are not often immediate—we must place our faith in the future effects of what we do now. We may need peer and student praise to relieve the doubts about our efficacy.

As Nouwen worked to live out the gospel, he took courage from Jesus' words: "There is no one who has left house, brothers, sisters, mother, father, children or land for my sake and for the sake of the gospel who will not receive a hundred times as much . . . now, in the present, and in the world to come, eternal life" (Mk 10:29–30). Perhaps teaching requires the same trust that what we do or give for the sake of our students makes a difference, often unseen, in the present and in the future. Thus, we must not distrust our desire for some sort of communion, intellectual or spiritual, nor should we replace it with a desire for more immediate rewards.

The second lesson is to set personal limits. In the process of seeking community, we may become too open to others. Small colleges are particularly at risk here because of their commitment to personalized education. Liberal arts colleges regularly represent their campuses as student-centered environments where faculty excel in teaching, mentoring, and outreach. The teaching mission of most Catholic colleges, mine included, is described as "the intellectual, personal, and spiritual development of each of our students." Although this is a laudable goal, we must be vigilant in recognizing when our outreach becomes invasive or ineffective, particularly when we allow students too much access to our interior lives. Nouwen calls this "controlling your own drawbridge." He writes: "Never allow yourself to become public property, where anyone can walk in and out at will. You might think that you are being generous in giving access to anyone who wants to enter or leave, but you will soon find yourself losing your soul."[7] This often manifests itself in the belief that we need to be available fully and continuously to students, both emotionally and pedagogically. In the desire to make a difference in students' lives we may put no limits on when we will communicate with them in person, through email, or on the phone. We may become overly generous in granting extensions or interpretations of assignments, or excessively sympathetic to personal circumstances.

What I have learned is that such a set of porous expectations confuses students and reinforces their self-doubt and insecurity. It suggests that they cannot be responsible for themselves and think and act on their own initiative. Extreme generosity does not help students to become self-reliant or self-assured. Failure to control my "drawbridge," especially at the end of the semester when student demands are greatest, makes me tired, frustrated, and resentful of their needs. It taxes my mental and physical energy, and worse, it isolates students from the larger college community by encouraging their dependence on me. It deprives them of the gift of *interdependence.*

Teaching is something of a solitary act because we are generally masters of our own classrooms. Technology has ubiquitously redefined what it means to "be present" to someone, ironically isolating us even further from personal communication. So, advocating an even more deliberate retreat may seem ill-advised. But if we want to embody the virtue of small liberal arts colleges we must resist the impersonal; to do this we must make visible room in our professional lives for prayer, solitude, reflection, writing, and even absence. As Nouwen writes, "When you claim for yourself the power over your drawbridge, you will discover new joy and peace in your heart and find yourself able to share that joy and peace with others."[8] If we are going to carry out our educational missions with joyful energy, we need to develop a deep self-knowledge and a spiritual wholeness.

The third lesson from *The Inner Voice of Love* is to respect the limitations of others. Faculty often begin each semester with high hopes and a fresh syllabus with what they anticipate will be challenging but reasonable goals for their students. As the semester progresses and students continue to make the same mistakes or ask the same questions, faculty members may revise their pedagogy, sometimes extensively, assuming they have set the intellectual bar too high. By the end of the semester they may feel angry and disappointed when students fail to meet their expectations and desires for them. It is hard to avoid feeling as if the course failed in some way. But the only failure is in not recognizing students' limitations, both intellectual and personal. If they give up rather than give their best on the final exam, it is easy to view them as lazy. If they are late submitting the class project, they look irresponsible. If their grammar is no better than it was in the beginning of the semester, it must be because they just do not care. But the truth is that we know only a fraction of our students' lives, and the reasons for these unmet expectations are likely many and complex. They are not just lazy or irresponsible or indifferent. Too often I have discovered that a "recalcitrant" student has just lost a parent to cancer, or is battling depression, or is worried about getting a job, or is just tired and has run out of steam. Who has not faced similar circumstances in the shadow of someone else's expectations? Henri Nouwen would say that students are "confess[ing] their poverty in the face of [our] needs and desires."[9] We need them to succeed according to the standards we have set, and they may be telling us they simply cannot meet that need.

The fourth of Nouwen's lessons is to respect our individual personalities. Our spiritual, professional, and private selves possess multiple personalities in a healthy way. Two of them are what Nouwen calls our lion and our lamb. The lion of a teacher's persona is the authority he or she possesses in the classroom. It displays expertise and judgment, takes initiative and makes decisions, and can, at times, intimidate students. The "lamb" persona is a gentler side, the mentor rather than the authority figure. It is also the persona that needs support and affirmation, to be liked by students and respected by colleagues. It, too, can be intimidating if it offers more personal interaction than a student desires.

Nouwen warns about the danger of favoring one part over the other: "When you heed only your lion, you will find yourself overextended and exhausted. When you take notice only of your lamb, you will easily become a victim of your need for other people's attention."[10] In excess, the lion may become dictatorial, feeling the need to enforce standards or dispense information. The lamb may indulge students, spending too much time in office hours or trying too hard to appease their complaints about an assignment.

Of course, good teaching, like an honest spiritual life, requires the qualities of both lion and lamb. "The art of spiritual living is to fully claim both your lion and your lamb. Then you can act assertively without denying your own needs. And you can ask for affection and care without betraying your talent to offer leadership."[11] In teaching, this means giving students our best pedagogy and scholarship (the lion) with care and respect (the lamb). Believing there is good reason to study the liberal arts, we offer enough expert guidance to send them on their own way and then accept that they may choose a different path.

So, how do we deepen the desires of our students beyond material accomplishments without ignoring the very real need for financial stability? We might imagine a classroom through Henri Nouwen's eyes in three particular ways. First, we must resist seeing students as "poor, needy, ignorant beggars" coming in search of knowledge. Instead, Nouwen says, we must adopt an ethos of hospitality, treating them "like guests who honor the house with their visit and will not leave it without having made their own contribution."[12] He urges us to create in that room emptiness and space where change can take place, where students' talents and gifts can be revealed and affirmed.

Such a hospitable learning environment is not always comfortable; it does not indulge the desire for material success. In fact, it challenges students' natural inclination to be upwardly mobile. What Nouwen would say to them is this: "You know that what helped and guided you in the old country no longer works, but what else do you have to go by? You are being asked to trust that you will find what you need in the new country. That requires the death of what has become so precious to you: influence, success, yes, even affection and praise."[13]

Through subjects such as history, political science, theology, and literature we must teach them the urgency of "downward mobility"–the urge to respond to the deepest needs of our fellow human beings. We cannot redirect students' attention to these deeper needs simply by *imposing* the liberal arts upon them; the wistful longing for some golden age of education only serves to blind us to the particular circumstances of this generation. Instead, we must learn to *adapt* the gifts of the liberal arts to their legitimate concerns, at the same time turning them outward toward the concerns of others.

Second, as teachers we must see ourselves as part of a community, not as autonomous agents. A colleague and friend once remarked that teacher-of-the-year awards always troubled her because they imply that effective teaching is an independent achievement rather than a communal act in which many contribute to students' education. The search for God and the search for knowledge both need a grounding community; we must remain united to a larger body that cares about the successes and failures of our efforts and shares our desires to be good teachers.

Finally, we must continually nourish our souls in whatever ways suit us so that the wells from which we draw our talent and energy are always full. Prayer, writing, meditation, and reflection all strengthen us to work from our deepest calling, to give generously without being depleted, to approach our classrooms with a kind of love that recognizes our students' limitations and still challenges them to exceed them.

Teachers who approach the liberal arts with "the inner voice of love" will enter "a new country" distinguished by a pedagogical hospitality that welcomes the stranger, whether it is an unconventional idea or the student who poses it. The curriculum may not change, indeed need not change, but the view is dramatically different:

> Those you have deeply loved become part of you. The longer you live, there will always be more people to be loved by you and to become part of your inner community. The wider your inner community becomes, the more easily you will recognize your own brothers and sisters in the strangers around you. . . . The wider the community of your heart, the wider the community around you.[14]

This community's borders are flexible and its paths diverse as it challenges the social and academic values students have come to accept–namely, the belief that upward mobility is a worthy ambition best achieved through a college education in which they criticize their opponents until someone arrives at the truth. In the new country, teachers still teach sociology, chemistry, economics, and philosophy, but not as canonical ends in themselves; they reinterpret their subjects as paths to intellectual, moral, and spiritual knowledge and thereby redefine what it means to be an educated human being. The pressure of career orientation is stripping the liberal arts of their relevancy for this generation of students, but the desire for spiritual meaning is growing. If a liberal education is to respond to this paradox, it must help students cross into new intellectual and spiritual countries rather then stubbornly fortifying the existing borders.

Notes

[1] Michael O'Laughlin, *God's Beloved: A Spiritual Biography of Henri Nouwen* (Maryknoll, NY: Orbis Books, 2004), 138.

[2] Henri Nouwen, *The Inner Voice of Love: A Journey through Anguish to Freedom* (New York: Doubleday, 1996).

[3] Ibid., 14.

[4] Ibid.

[5] Ibid., 68.

[6] Ibid., 95.

[7] Ibid., 84–85.

[8] Ibid., 85.

[9] Ibid., 13.

[10] Ibid., 78.

[11] Ibid.

[12] Henri Nouwen, *Reaching Out: The Three Movements of the Spiritual Life* (New York: Doubleday, 1975), 89.

[13] Nouwen, *The Inner Voice of Love,* 21.

[14] Ibid., 59–60.

16

The Protreptic Henri

Christian Witness as Hospitality

James D. Smith III

It was a tremendous privilege to serve as a Harvard teaching fellow with Henri Nouwen in his final academic courses (spring of the 1984–85 academic year). Today, Henri's mentorship—as a unique human being, as a priest, and through his writings—continues to touch each spiritual and relational aspect of my life. One of the few physical keepsakes I have from that season is a half-sheet-size index card on which Henri drew a map. He had planned a gathering of friends at a local Indonesian restaurant and was inviting us to take part. His sketch of the streets of Cambridge, complete with arrows, corrected spellings, crossed-out entries, and the like demonstrated that his spiritual gift was not cartography. What made this piece priceless, however, was the inscription "For Jim and Linda" near the top, and the three emphatic arrows pointing to the restaurant, attached to the joyful exclamation "We are here!" It was vintage Henri. It was hospitality.

Hospitality remains one of the most significant themes in Henri Nouwen's life and literature. Through this attitude and action he prophetically modeled respect for the diversity of communities around him. In this essay I revisit a few expressions of hospitality in his writings, noting the global and interfaith importance of this concept and practice. I then draw on his unpublished Harvard lecture notes to depict witness to the risen Christ as, above all, a redemptive act of hospitality. Finally, I describe his personal and literary approach as protreptic, echoing early Christian invitations through writing and the offering of receptive space to the stranger, the outsider.

Henri's first major book was *Intimacy*, a collection of pastoral and psychological essays published during his Notre Dame years. In the chapter entitled "The Challenge to Love" he offered a particularly memorable insight: "Table and bed are the two places of intimacy where love can manifest itself in weakness."[1] As a Roman Catholic priest, candidly to place "the bed"—intimacy and sexuality—in such a prominent light was a remarkable act of personal engagement. Similarly, given the powerful role sexuality plays in the wounding or healing of human life, to place "the table" alongside it, even before it, was to elevate the practice of hospitality to focal importance. Offering one "a place at the table," by inspiration or design, shaping generations and cultures, remains a prophetic act of love and justice—in friendship, business, politics, and the Eucharist.

Beyond doubt, the most commonly referenced text devoted to hospitality in Henri's writings occurs in a work from his decade at Yale Divinity School. In *Reaching Out* he cites the spiritual movement from hostility to hospitality as that which determines the relationship with our fellow human beings. Over the past thirty years, insights and apothegms from this book have been utilized in countless moments and ways and need not be detailed here. Central to his discussion, however, Henri offers a working definition of hospitality: "The creation of a free and friendly space where we can reach out to strangers and invite them to become our friends."[2] He then turns to focus particular attention on three types of relationships: parents and children, teachers and students, and healers and patients. In this third category, a core Nouwen conviction appears: from the point of view of a Christian spirituality, every human being is called upon to be a healer.[3] This involves moving beyond a preoccupation with "the tools of the trade" (psychological, theological, professional) in surrender to the saving power of the Redeemer. "Words such as creating space, receptivity and confrontation, poverty of mind and heart were used to show that the spirituality of the Christian not only is rooted in the reality of everyday life, but also transcends it by relying on the gift of God."[4]

Some ten years after *Reaching Out* appeared, Henri was devoting himself to teaching at Harvard Divinity School and discovering (as the book title suggests) *The Road to Daybreak.* In the prologue to that work, reflecting on elements the Lord had used to guide his steps to the L'Arche community, he detailed the importance of a portentous (rather than pretentious) visitor. In the late 1970s, while still in New Haven, Jan Risse arrived at Henri's door bringing greetings from Jean Vanier. Surprised, and thinking he was being asked to do something, he finally realized he "hadn't shown much hospitality" and invited her to spend a quiet time in his apartment while he was off fulfilling academic duties. Upon his return, he discovered the table beautifully set, a meal in preparation . . . and his own confusion.

> "Where did you find all these things?" I asked. She looked at me with a funny expression and said, "In your own kitchen and cupboards. . . . You obviously don't use them too often!" It then dawned on me that something unique was happening. A stranger had walked into my home and, without asking me for anything, was showing me my own house.[5]

This experience of hospitality rewarded, with the guest bearing a gift through which the host discovers a true home, echoes the promise of shared hospitality bringing a blessing to each one.

Finally, during his years serving as a priest in the L'Arche community at Daybreak, Henri offered what many consider their favorite work, *The Return of the Prodigal Son.* In this reflection, inspired by Rembrandt's masterpiece painting of that biblical scene (Lk 15:11–32), there is the invitation to find oneself in a divine "story of a homecoming." Here it is made abundantly clear that our offering of hospitality to others is really a reflection of God's first love embrace and provision of a welcome for us. "I am not used to the image of God throwing a big party. It seems to contradict the solemnity and seriousness I have always attached to God. But when I think about the ways in which Jesus describes God's Kingdom, a joyful banquet is often at its center. . . . The invitation to a meal is an invitation to intimacy with God."[6]

The impact of the words, concepts and images of hospitality conveyed in Henri Nouwen's writings has been enormous. At the popular level, an Internet search for "Nouwen" and "hospitality" today yields 3,270 results! In a more specifically academic and pastoral vein, a few examples deserve particular mention. Arguably the finest recent work seeking to revive interest in hospitality as a Christian tradition and contemporary practice is Christine Pohl's *Making Room.* On the first page of her introduction, she quotes Henri's words: "If there is any concept worth restoring to its original depth and evocative potential, it is the concept of hospitality." She also notes the manner in which his reflections in *Reaching Out* are a point of entry for many current discussions on hospitality.[7] A publication of the Markkula Center for Applied Ethics at Santa Clara University addressed ethnic and religious tensions in the Holy Land: "According to theologian Henri Nouwen, hospitality is the creation of 'a space where the stranger can enter and become a friend instead of an enemy.' How apropos this goal seems for the very part of the world that originally gave birth to this concept–the Middle East."[8] This past year, historian and churchman Martin Marty explored the global, multicultural, and specifically interfaith aspects of this theme in *When Faiths Collide.* Though not specifically referencing Nouwen, in the chapter "The Risk of Hospitality" he advocates not settling for tolerance but rather the challenging priority of hospitality in a world beset by fear of the other, the stranger.[9] He reminds us of the rich New Testament materials supporting this commitment, as the Greek *xenos* as stranger or alien receives the welcome of *philoxenia,* hospitality, extended as an act of discipleship.[10] It was a message I shared in the spring of 2006 at a conference addressing religious extremism.[11]

In public discourse, hospitality may be described as an act of kindness, an ethical or theological virtue, or a strategy necessary to the survival of our species. Henri saw, and at times described, the value of all three. In his closing academic course, however, these memorably came together in his shared convictions and life. Renewed in his vision of the mission of Christ and confronted with the brokenness of the human family, he welcomed 250 students to his course "Introduction to the Spiritual Life." The opening words expressed his purpose:

A recent thirty-day retreat convinced me more than anything else that I should allow my teaching to have a quality of witness. Concretely, therefore, I want to be for you what John was for his listeners and readers: a living witness of the Risen Christ. I see this as a sort of spiritual hospitality. I want to invite you into my space, without taking the pictures from the walls or the books from the shelves. But I also want to leave enough room for you to walk in and out and around freely so that you can respond from your own place in life. Part of my struggle will be to find when and how my space becomes too crowded, or too empty to be truly hospitable. Only you can help me in discovering the right space. It is probably going to require much flexibility. . . . I am aware of the many pitfalls: proselytizing, manipulation, and even oppression. But acknowledging these pitfalls, I still feel strongly that "teaching spiritual things spiritually" also means to move from informing the mind to forming the heart and that it is not a neutral event but an event that involves us all in a deep personal way. If John wrote so that you may believe, I have to teach that same way. But I am deeply convinced that this is also the way to a deep respect for the great variety of experiences, histories, religious and cultural backgrounds among us. Just as the most personal often proves to be the most universal, so too what is most binding can prove to be most liberating. I hope and pray that what binds me most, my faith in the Risen Christ, can free you to make your own spiritual affirmations.[12]

Over the past year several of us who sought to support Henri during that final class have reflected together on the experience, grateful for his impact on our lives.[13] As a doctoral student then, and pastor in the evangelical tradition, I was already convinced of the importance of Christian witness. But I was all too familiar with the extremes of insensitive zeal on one side and inauthentic shrugs on the other. What Henri taught, by word and incarnation, placed biblical witness at the heart of Christian faith and biblical hospitality at the heart of witness. In exploring the Gospel of John, his desire to be "full of grace and truth" (1:14) opened new ground for me and for others, and continues to do so today.

I believe that in exploring the significance of hospitality and the dimension of witness in the life of Henri Nouwen, we find a valuable window not only into the content of his writings but also into their literary genre. Many of us have not only heard words appreciative of his work but other voices as well. There are those who have observed that "he never had a thought he didn't write" or "all his books are the same" or "he just wrote to win a popular audience." None of us is above legitimate and constructive criticism, and Henri received several varieties. What is proposed here is that the majority of his writings may best be understood as examples of a type of literature the ancients called protreptic.

No doubt this will be an unfamiliar term to many. What was a protreptic approach or use of language? In the broadest sense it was (and is) "invitation" discourse, a speech calling one, as the Greek root suggests, to "turn toward" purposeful life, and is essentially a literary form of hospitality. Whereas its related, and more familiar, genre, apologetic, emphasizes the defense of a credo through rigorous, logical argumentation, protreptic seeks to draw the neighbor forward by informed appeal. David Aune has recently revisited the role of this form in Greco-Roman culture: "The 'logos protreptikos' or 'speech of exhortation' is a speech intended to win converts and attract young people to a particular way of life."[14] Primarily found in school environments, it attracted adherents by exposing the errors of alternative ways of living and demonstrating the truth claims of a particular tradition or lifestyle. The central function was to encourage conversion, a change of life, through dissuasion and persuasion.

While relatively few of these writings have survived as full texts from the classical period, and there is some fluidity in these works, the main structural elements are fairly established. Protreptic literature offers a critique of prevailing ways of life and thought as unsound or unrewarding, an exposition of a particular stance as praiseworthy and defensible, and "a personal appeal to the hearer, inviting the immediate accepting of the exhortation."[15] In Christian expression, the hearer or reader was welcomed into a framework in which to weigh life options and discover the excellence of life in Christ. From the earliest Christian centuries, scholars have identified the *Letter to Diognetus* and the introduction to Justin's *Dialogue with Trypho* as examples of this approach. Perhaps the most interesting expression is the *Protreptikos* of Clement of Alexandria. As Eric Osborn has demonstrated, its function was as a handbook for Christians as missionaries, preceding formal doctrinal and catechetical teaching. Though an extensive analysis lies beyond the scope of our present discussion, Osborn's summary of the "good news" is helpful here:

At the centre of this economy is recapitulation in Christ, which includes correction and perfection of sinful humanity, inauguration and consummation of a new humanity in Christ. . . . His is the new song which brings life and which gives harmony to the universe reaching from centre to circumference (Protreptikos, 1.5.2). As the instrument of God (1.6.1), he opens eyes and unstops ears, he leads the lame and wandering to righteousness, and exhibits God to the foolish. He destroys corruption and death, and he brings divine love and grace to mankind. . . . By the act of God's champion, we are able to abandon the customs of our fathers as infantile and unworthy of mature men (10.109.3; 10.110.3). To cross over to the side of God is a change from ignorance to knowledge, from folly to wisdom, from debauchery to self-control, from injustice to righteousness and from godlessness to God (10.93.1).[16]

Many will readily identify in Henri Nouwen's writings distinct echoes of this early Christian approach. Rather than terse theological dogmatism or pop psychological narcissism, he engages life issues and exposes world views that have proven spiritually and relationally inadequate, even deadly. He then invites readers (who recognize themselves and their neighbors in this picture) to turn and discover fullness of life in the presence of God and find their true home as the beloved. In this foundational and transformational cause, offering simplicity of structure (for example, "threeness") is an asset, and presenting scripture and theology as redemptive answer more than speculative question is a virtue. Among works not mentioned above—in *Lifesigns*, for example—the obsession of productivity and the depression of sterility alike are revealed as dead ends to be laid aside in favor of a life-giving connection with Jesus Christ and the experience of fruitfulness.[17] In *Creative Ministry* one is presented with the choice of a routine professional practice of ecclesial tasks dependent on techniques or moving beyond this spiritual desert to following the living Christ.[18] A renewed interest in this classic genre, I believe, may be helpful in assessing the works of other authors as well.[19] It is surely no accident that, among the handful of writings Thomas Merton translated in the early 1960s, there was Clement's *Protreptikos*, presenting (in Merton's introductory words) "the challenge to pagan intellectuals summoning them to open their lives to the light of the Gospel, and to recognize in it the fulfillment of all the legitimate aspirations which Greek philosophy, even in Plato, was never able to satisfy."[20] Though Henri did not set out to imitate literary models such as Clement's, his own distinctive writings express a like spirit and endeavor. The Nouwen archives poster that many of us have expresses the common purpose: "I want my words to create space where people can meet God."

Having identified Henri Nouwen's overall literary approach as protreptic, inviting all to turn from false masters and discover wholeness and reconciliation in Christ, we return to his embrace of hospitality and find in it echoes of early Christian praxis as well. Scholars such as Carolyn Osiek have, in recent years, placed new emphasis on the role of house churches as the earliest Christian communities, and Henri delighted in gathering groups for worship and fellowship.[21] Gustav Stahlin, in the *Theological Dictionary of New Testament,* provides a stimulating study of the motivations for hospitality in this formative era, and many will recall Henri's custom of welcoming visitors, remembering his own seasons as a stranger.[22] Nouwen's reflections were shaped by interaction with onetime Yale Divinity colleague Rowan Greer, who carried his own studies of this practice of hospitality into the fifth century. For example Greer observes that John Chrysostom, as bishop and exegete, promoted the active virtue by commenting that "given to hospitality" (Rom 12:13; Homily 21) is a phrase used by St. Paul "to instruct us not to wait for those that shall ask it, and see when they will come to us, but to run to them and be given to finding them." Greer notes that institutions such as hospitals and hospices rose to offer Christian hospitality in late antiquity, as did the monasticism represented by Basil and Gregory of Nyssa.[23] Perhaps the crowning word belongs to Benedict of Nursia, who declared that "all guests who present themselves are to be welcomed as Christ, for he himself will say, 'I was a stranger and you welcomed me.'"[24] Henri's life, of course, was deeply informed by these words and others on the monastic culture.

This essay invites the fresh appreciation of a protreptic Henri. In life and literature, as a priest (*pontifex,* "bridge builder") he served Christ through personally creating space "at the table" for a remarkable array of people to meet God and prophetically writing to invite each one to be transformed through a relationship with the risen Christ. He respected the diversity around him less ideologically (for example, through revisionism and relativism) than in recognizing the variety of God's beloved peoples (e.g. embattled Sandinistas, Haitian children, handicapped adults, marginalized Ukrainians) and offering them love and life in the name of Jesus. In this, he drew deeply from early Christian faith and forms in offering authentic witness to a world sometimes called post Christian. As colleague Peter Weiskel remembers Henri's Harvard days:

The Carriage House provided ample space for Henri to practice his unique style of hospitality. He was able to connect with people quickly, and at a personal level. In his recent biography of Henri, Michael O'Laughlin confirms what I have always felt–that Henri's gifts of friendship, hospitality and community were rooted in a Eucharistic approach to life. The joy, suffering, sorrow, limitations, and hopes of our lives were for him gifts to be lifted up, celebrated and shared–at a common table that excluded no one.[25]

Notes

[1] Henri J. M. Nouwen, *Intimacy: Pastoral Psychological Essays* (Notre Dame, IN: Fides Publishers, 1969), 31.

[2] Henri J. M. Nouwen, *Reaching Out: The Three Movements of the Spiritual Life* (New York: Doubleday, 1975), 79.

[3] Ibid., 93.

[4] Ibid., 109.

[5] Henri J. M. Nouwen, *The Road to Daybreak: A Spiritual Journey* (New York: Doubleday, 1988), 1–2.

[6] Henri J. M. Nouwen, *The Return of the Prodigal Son: A Story of Homecoming* (New York: Doubleday, 1992), 113.

[7] Nouwen, *Reaching Out,* as quoted in Christina Pohl, *Making Room: Recovering Hospitality as a Christian Tradition* (Grand Rapids, MI: Eerdmans, 1999), 3.

[8] Miriam Schulman and Amal Barkouki-Winter, "Strangers into Friends," *Issues in Ethics* 11, no. 1 (Winter 2000). Available on the scu.edu website.

[9] Martin Marty, *When Faiths Collide* (Oxford: Blackwell, 2005), 124–48.

[10] See John Koenig, *New Testament Hospitality: Partnership with Strangers as Promise and Mission* (Philadelphia: Fortress Press, 1985).

[11] James D. Smith III, "From Religious Hostility to Hospitality: A Christian Perspective," presentation at the Religious Extremism and the Responsibility of Mainstream Religions panel, Harvard Club of San Diego (March 21, 2006).

[12] Henri J. M. Nouwen, "Introduction," lecture notes for Harvard Divinity School, HDS 2543: "Introduction to the Spiritual Life" (January 31, 1985), 3–5. My copy.

[13] James D. Smith III et al., "A Spiritual Mentor's Lasting Influence," *Harvard Divinity Today* 2 (Spring, 2006): 1, 10–14.

[14] David E. Aune, "Protreptic literature," in *The Westminster Dictionary of New Testament and Early Christian Literature and Rhetoric,* ed. David E. Aune (Louisville, KY: Westminster John Knox, 2003), 383–84.

[15] Ibid., 385.

[16] Eric Osborn, *Clement of Alexandria* (Cambridge: Cambridge University Press, 2005), 34.

[17] Henri J. M. Nouwen, *Lifesigns: Intimacy, Fecundity, and Ecstasy in Christian Perspective* (New York: Doubleday, 1986), 45–68.

[18] Henri J. M. Nouwen, *Creative Ministry: Beyond Professionalism in Teaching, Preaching, Counseling, Organizing, and Celebrating* (Garden City, NY: Doubleday, 1971).

[19] The writings of Boston College philosopher Peter Kreeft, for example, offer an occasion for such reflection. In the context of this essay, I also enjoyed conference conversations on the literary work of Fr. Ronald Rolheiser.

[20] Eric Osborn, *Clement of Alexandria, Selections from the Protreptikos,* trans. Thomas Merton (Norfolk, CT: New Directions, 1962), 11.

[21] Carolyn Osiek and David L. Balch, *Families in the New Testament World: Households and House Churches* (Louisville, KY: Westminster John Knox, 1997), esp. 38–39, 195–214. More recent publications also develop these themes.

[22] Gustav Stahlin, "Xenos," in *Theological Dictionary of the New Testament,* ed. Gerhard Friedrich, vol. 5 (Grand Rapids, MI: Eerdmans, 1967), esp. 15–25.

[23] Rowan Greer, "Hospitality in the First Five Centuries of the Church," *Monastic Studies* 10 (1974): 29–48. Of additional interest are the articles Nouwen offers in this same journal issue that anticipate themes soon to be refined in his *Reaching Out.*

[24] Rule 53.1, as cited in Timothy Fry, O.S.B., ed., *The Rule of St. Benedict in English* (Collegeville, MN: The Liturgical Press, 1982), 73.

[25] Peter Weiskel, "A Spiritual Mentor's Lasting Influence," *Harvard Divinity Today* 2 (Spring 2006): 11.

17

Named and Claimed as Beloved

Henri Nouwen's Contribution to a Spirituality of Youth Ministry

Michael Hyrniuk

Henri Nouwen will be remembered for many contributions as a spiritual writer. He touched on many important themes related to the spiritual life and to the work of ministry, such as solitude, silence, prayer, and hospitality. My intention here is to offer a few reflections on the way in which Henri Nouwen has contributed to the field of youth ministry over the last ten years. By way of background and context, I want to begin by saying a little about Henri's influence on me personally and then move to a description of the Youth Ministry and Spirituality Project (YMSP), which has occupied my attention and devotion for the last several years. It is through this project that Henri's vision of ministry has shaped a new approach to the Christian formation of young people and the persons who care for them. After looking at the specific ways in which Henri has influenced this project, I conclude with some thoughts and questions on the significance of Henri's life and thought for ministry in general and youth ministry in particular.

Henri and Me: Discerning the Questions

I do not remember precisely the first time I encountered Henri Nouwen's work. It is sort of like the first time you manage to ride a bike or get up on water skis. You do not always have a clear memory of the event, just the thrill of it. I find it significant that I discovered Henri as a teenager. I have vague memories of looking at a copy of *With Open Hands* as a high school student in Winnipeg. Or was it *Reaching Out?* I am not sure. What I do remember vividly, however, was reading *The Way of the Heart* in 1981, while I was an undergraduate at St. Michael's College in Toronto. I was eighteen years old and considering a vocation to the priesthood in the Ukrainian Catholic Church. I was fascinated with the desert fathers and planning to become one myself, even though I could barely understand the meaning of the Apothegmata. When I found *The Way of the Heart*, it was a revolution for me. I finally began to understand not only the meaning of this early monastic movement, but, more important, the meaning and power of the spiritual life in Christ. I can only describe it as coming home. As I began to explore Henri's other works, I found that he seemed to know and give voice to the deepest cry of my heart for meaning and for love. He seemed to know about my own pain, and doubt, and fears. In his vulnerability and openness, he could express my own insecurities, my own primal wound.

Henri also seemed to know the heart of God in a way I had never experienced. He spoke of God's first love and its perfect expression in the compassion of Jesus. This was a Jesus whose words and actions could illumine and save my life. Henri could speak to the spiritual life in a way that made it mysterious and attractive. His vision of the life of solitude, silence, and prayer was healing and inspiring. He gave me permission to be radical in my pursuit of God, to open myself completely to the power of the Spirit. His vision of ministry clarified my own sense of vocation. Henri revealed to me that to be a minister of Jesus Christ, a wounded healer and a prayerful witness to God's first love in the midst of a broken world, was the greatest thing I could offer. There was something about the simple, quiet, intimate way he wrote that gave me confidence that I was building on rock. It was as though he were there, right beside me, as a guide.

At twenty-two I joined the L'Arche community in Winnipeg, where I spent a total of five years. By then, I had also discovered Jean Vanier. Like Henri, his words felt real and authentic to me. His articulation of the mystery of community inspired me to taste this experience for myself. My friends and family thought I was crazy, wasting my life on handicapped people. But when it came to God, I tended to be pretty radical. I like to think that Henri and I joined L'Arche together. It was 1983, and he was also making his first visit to Trosly, where Vanier had founded the first L'Arche home. L'Arche was my first experience of ministry and pastoral care. It was wonderful and also very hard. Even though I never met him personally, I was delighted and grateful to have Henri accompanying me as he too discovered the gift and challenges of L'Arche. As I reflected on Henri's *Lifesigns, The Road to Daybreak*, and *The Return of the Prodigal Son*, I began to feel there was a larger challenge ahead for me. What he and Jean Vanier were articulating in L'Arche needed to be communicated to the larger world of the church and society. I sensed a call to this as a life mission.

I went on to do a master's and doctorate in Christian spirituality. Henri and Jean were still my two heroes, and my sense of vocation as a scholar and minister was nourished deeply by their witness. I used to say that I needed two advanced degrees to try to make sense of what I had learned from them and experienced in L'Arche. In September 1996, three years into studies for my Ph.D., I was forming my committee for my exams and dissertation. I was within a few days of finally realizing my dream and calling Henri to see if he would serve on my committee. I remember the morning when I walked into Bishops Hall at Emory University in Atlanta and a friend took me aside and told me the news of his death. We were all in shock and grief for days.

In the year 2001 I finished a dissertation focusing on spiritual transformation in the context of L'Arche. It was called "Growth in Communion" and was based on interviews with long-term assistants and a careful study of the lives and writings of Jean Vanier and Henri Nouwen. In this study I discerned a process of awakening and transformation in the journeys of L'Arche assistants that involved the healing of fear, guilt, and shame. As I read and reread Henri's incomparable work *The Inner Voice of Love,* I began to sense that this process of healing had significance for the spiritual life of those in other ministries as well. What Henri was describing was so elemental and so powerful that I felt it had to be interpreted for those involved in religious education, spiritual formation, and pastoral care.

Providentially, in 2001, I was given an invitation to do just that. I was asked to become co-director of the YMSP, a national program for the spiritual renewal of youth ministry based at the San Francisco Theological Seminary, in San Anselmo, California. I had been working with this project as a consultant for over three years and supporting its members in their quest to place contemplative spiritual formation at the heart of congregational youth ministry. They had just received funding for another phase of work and invited me to become their resident theologian. They wanted someone to articulate for their partner churches the theological meaning of spiritual transformation. They wanted someone to help interpret the experience of healing and conversion in a way that would illumine this path for young people and youth ministers. I said yes to this call, and that is how Henri Nouwen's witness became the foundation for a whole new way of youth ministry in the North American church.

Youth Ministry and the Journey of the Beloved: From Compulsion to Contemplation

The YMSP was formed in 1997 by a young youth minister named Mark Yaconelli who had experienced disillusionment, exhaustion, and burn-out in his efforts to save the souls of young people. Mark had been involved in youth ministry for several years. He was the archetype of the young, dynamic, charismatic, guitar-playing youth minister. His father, Mike Yaconelli, was the founder of Youth Specialties, one of the largest suppliers of youth ministry resources in the world. Mark grew up in the youth ministry "industry." He knew it inside and out. He also knew that in all of the high-voltage events, programs, activities, and resources something was missing. After making a spiritual retreat with Morton Kelsey, in which he was exposed for the first time to a number of ancient prayer practices, Mark began to wonder what would happen for youth if churches began to put contemplative spiritual formation at the heart of their youth ministry. What would happen to the kids, the youth ministers, the adult volunteers, and the churches if prayer and discernment began to inspire ministry instead of manic hyperactivity? The Lilly Endowment gave the project three successive grants over ten years to explore this question with the youth ministry leadership of ten denominations, twenty-six partner congregations, and several youth ministry organizations. It involved the formation of denominational and organizational executives, senior pastors, youth ministers, adult volunteers, and young people.

What was obvious to all of us in the YMSP was that youth ministry was dominated by two guiding agendas. The main agenda in the mainline and evangelical churches was to offer programs based on fun and games. We called it the entertainment model of youth ministry. The emphasis on entertainment focuses its attention largely on the planning and coordination of church-based recreational programs, events, and activities that attract the largest number of young people into church life. Familiar examples of this are pizza nights, lock-ins, movies, ski weekends, and mission trips. While acknowledging the goodwill and best intentions of parents and pastoral leaders to "do something for the kids," the emphasis on entertainment was also motivated by an anxious concern on their part to address young people's complaint that church is boring and irrelevant. There was an implicit, and occasionally explicit, attempt to compete with the dizzying array of social, recreational, and entertainment possibilities in a young person's life by offering a set of activities that promised to be "cool," fun, and exciting. There was a fear that unless the churches could offer compelling activities (along with hot pizza) to their young people, they would lose them to the influences of the world. Churches that offer entertaining activities usually engage a youth minister who is a young adult with the energy, dynamism, and charisma to attract and connect to teens. As one youth minister in our project put it:, "The key factor is numbers. It is to create a program that is more fun, more exciting and more interesting than every other game in town."

The other agenda, found more in the Roman Catholic and Eastern Orthodox Churches (and to some extent the Anglican/Episcopal Churches), is catechetical instruction. The focus here is on the faithful transmission of the beliefs and moral values of a given church tradition in the service of increasing doctrinal literacy. There is an overriding concern for sacramental instruction of youth at the appointed age and anxious attempts on the part of parents and church authorities to inculcate institutional identity and loyalty (becoming "good Catholics," for example) and regular, even if nominal, participation (becoming a "regular attender"). The youth minister is understood as an instructor or coordinator of educational programs for sacramental preparation. Charismatic personality is not as important as commitment to the correct communication of traditional beliefs, norms, and moral teaching.

What was clear to us at the YMSP was that whether focused on entertainment or instruction, or more often some blend of the two, most youth ministry in North America is driven by fear and anxiety. It may be fear that the church is losing its young people and is not attractive or relevant to their unique culture. It may be a fear that the young people do not know what to believe, or that young people need more guidance in forming moral values and virtues. In most cases youth ministry in North America is living, as Henri describes it, in the "house of fear" and not in the freedom of the "house of love." As he puts it, "When we consider how much our educational, political, religious, and even social lives are geared to finding answers to questions born of fear, it is not hard to understand why a message of love has little chance of being heard."[1] Youth ministry tends to be guided by questions born of anxiety rather than faith and trust. It is not simply the forms of ministry that need to be discerned but the "spirits" that underlie their creation. It is the presence of these "unclean" spirits of fear and anxiety that make a youth ministry born of the Spirit of love so difficult to realize.

The diagnosis of fear also applies to many of the people in youth ministry. Many youth workers fit Henri's description of the "compulsive minister"– very busy people with meetings to attend, visits to make, programs to run, and events to organize. It is not the busyness that defines the compulsive minister. It is the motivation. As Henri expresses it: "The basic question is whether we as ministers of Jesus Christ have not already been so deeply molded by the seductive powers of our dark world that we have become blind to our own and other people's fatal state and have lost the power and motivation to swim for our lives."[2]

In the light of the gospel's call to radical rebirth in the Spirit and an experience of abiding intimacy with God in the person of Jesus Christ, the mission of the YMSP is to support youth ministers in a transformation from anxiety-driven or compulsive ministry to a Christ-centered, Spirit-led ministry. It seeks to support them in moving from compulsion to contemplation. Rather than reacting anxiously to the consumer mentality among young people and their parents for more programming or fuller catechesis, it seeks to fulfill its mission by fostering Christian communities that are attentive to God's presence, discerning of the Spirit, and that accompany young people on the way of Jesus. This mission has focused not only the spiritual formation of youth but the souls of youth ministers.

One of our core questions in articulating a contemplative approach to youth ministry is this: What does it mean *experientially* for young disciples of Jesus to grow in the spiritual life? We took our bearings directly from Henri Nouwen, who speaks powerfully of the spiritual life as a process of "becoming the Beloved." For Henri, God's first love is always the starting point. This starting point is revealed most fully in the baptism and transfiguration, where the Father anoints and blesses the Son as his Beloved. Recall the words of the Markan narrative that describes Jesus' vision as he is coming up out of the water: "He saw heaven being torn open and the Spirit descending on him like a dove. And a voice came from heaven saying: 'You are my Son, whom I love; with you I am well pleased'" (1:11).

For us, as with Henri, it is the inner meaning of this event that is decisive. It is Jesus' experience of being named and claimed as the beloved Son of God in whom God takes delight. It is the awakening of Christ to his core identity as unconditionally beloved and uniquely beautiful and valuable in the embrace of the Father. Just as Jesus becomes fully self-aware of his identity as the Anointed One, the Christ, so too we believe that his followers, young and old, are invited gradually to shed the false identity that drives us compulsively and receive the very same anointing by the Spirit as one called to live in the peace and glorious freedom of the children of God. To know oneself as beloved is to enter into one's baptismal identity and vocation. It is to awaken to Christ-consciousness.

If Christ's baptism is considered the archetype of our own, the invitation we hear for youth and youth ministers in Henri's work is to enter for themselves experientially into the healing power of this sacrament. In *Life of the Beloved* Henri writes to his friend, Fred:

> Becoming the Beloved is the great spiritual journey we have to make. . . . Becoming the Beloved means letting the truth of our Belovedness become enfleshed in everything we think, say, and do. It entails a long and painful process of appropriation or, better, incarnation.[3]

At the YMSP we have heard and seen with our own eyes stories of this process of "becoming the Beloved." We have heard testimony like that of Will, who confessed to us, "I've been a youth pastor for twenty years and I've never heard or felt the gospel preached in this way." Or experiences like that of Sarah, who grew up as an adopted child and was filled with loneliness, shame, and anger all of her life. Her mother approached us after her attendance at our youth event and said: "I don't know what happened out there this summer, but my daughter is a different person. It's almost scary. She seems to be at peace now and has only kindness and gratitude for me instead of rage and contempt." Here are other testimonies we have received from project participants:

> "I have learned the words of grace: You are my Beloved. You are enough."
>
> —WALLACE, YOUTH MINISTER AND DENOMINATIONAL LEADER

> "I have heard the Spirit say to me—'I gave you breath. You are mine. . . . Take it in, live it out, unafraid.'"
>
> —LAURIE, ADULT VOLUNTEER

> "As I am growing older, God has given me an opportunity to let the deepest God-beauty emerge."
>
> —SID, PASTOR AND DENOMINATIONAL LEADER

> "Yes! Yes! Yes! Of course this is how it is! Loved and celebrated—embraced and cherished. What I knew in my head, felt once in a while in my heart, [is] now moving into my bones. I [have] soaked in it, lavished

in it without having to fight the 'Yes, but . . . ' temptation that so often
in my life I yielded to."

—Paul, pastor

"This changed my life. I can't say that I walked away committing my
life to Jesus, but I did feel love that I thought impossible."

—Nathan, youth

We believe that Will, Sarah, and other members of the YMSP have heard
their deepest name spoken by the Spirit, have put their trust in that voice,
and have been freed to live the risen life of the Beloved. They are experiencing a transformation in their core sense of identity as they "become the Beloved."

Henri Nouwen approaches this process of "becoming the Beloved" in a
eucharistic way through the movements of being taken, blessed, broken, and
given. We approached the process in a slightly different way, following the
journey of Christ as God's Beloved through three pivotal movements in his
life and ministry. In substance these movements are virtually the same as
Henri's description. They express the receiving and giving of love at the
heart of Christian conversion. In the first movement, as I have described,
Jesus is named as Beloved at the Jordan. In the course of the formation events
at the YMSP, we relied on Nouwen's *Way of the Heart* to help guide us in
creating space for solitude, silence, prayer, and rest in which to hear that
"inner voice of love" naming them as God's beloved. This was a process of
awakening to their inner beauty, their uniqueness, and the presence of God
within them. It was an invitation to let go of images of a judging or punishing
God and begin to explore a God who was not only safe but also one who
took delight in them.

In the second movement Jesus is claimed fully in his identity through the
temptations in the desert. Here, Satan attempts to distract and divert Jesus'
desire for God alone. He attempts to obscure and distort the name given to
him at baptism. He tempts Jesus to try to prove his identity as the Beloved by
miracles and spectacles or tries to seduce him with the promise of power.
Those of us in youth ministry know well the struggle with the temptations
that Henri so brilliantly interprets in *In the Name of Jesus*.[4] Youth ministers are
tempted to conform to the ideal images and standards of the relevant, spec-
tacular, and powerful youth ministry, that is, the "empowered" or "fully
equipped" minister that has all the right qualities and tools to bring kids to
Christ. Youth are also constantly seduced by peer pressures to be popular
and powerful in their own way. In the formation events at the YMSP, we
helped the members of our partner churches to identify the voices in themselves, in their churches, and in their culture that seek to seduce and distract
them from their identity as God's beloved. We used Nouwen's treatment of
the temptations to help them discern the spirits that were at work in their
lives and ministries and to find freedom from the voice of the "accuser" that

tempts them to prove their worth as persons and ministers. The movements of being named and claimed correspond closely to what Henri describes in the *Life of the Beloved* as being taken, blessed, and broken. They are experiences of knowing oneself as loved but also being tempted by forces within us that refuse or resist this love. We encouraged our ministers to heed the voice of the One who is always blessing and "reclaiming" them: "Fear not, for I have redeemed you; I have called you by name. You are mine" (Is 43:1).

The third moment in the journey of the Beloved is that of being sent. This moment is found in the fourth chapter of Luke's gospel, where Jesus begins his public ministry by announcing his mission of healing and liberation in his own synagogue in Nazareth: "The Spirit of the Lord is upon me, because he has anointed me to bring good news to the poor. He has sent me to proclaim release to the captives and recovery of sight to the blind" (Lk 4:18ff.; Is 61:1ff.). After his experience of being named and claimed as God's Beloved, after his trial and temptation in the desert, he is sent by the Spirit to name and claim others as beloved. He responds naturally and spontaneously to the call to share this "good news" with his own community in Nazareth. After forming ministers in an experience of being named and claimed as God's beloved in baptism, we followed Henri in grounding youth ministry in the power of the Spirit, who calls and sends the disciples of Jesus to share this good news with and to anoint others—especially young people—as the beloved of God. In *Life of the Beloved* Henri refers to this movement in a eucharistic sense of being given: "As the Beloved ones, our greatest fulfillment lies in becoming bread for the world. That is the most intimate expression of our deepest desire to give ourselves to each other."[5]

Henri Nouwen and the Contemplative Approach to Youth Ministry

Henri Nouwen has informed and inspired the work of the YMSP with his theology and spirituality of the Beloved. He has made a specific contribution to our work in his invitation to ministers to move beyond the identity of the "busy professional" toward an identity grounded in God's freedom and peace. Although his language is somewhat different than ours, in our spiritual formation we followed Henri in his principal conviction that the minister is most fruitful when he or she is a living witness to the deep inner joy and peace that flows from knowing oneself as beloved.[6] In this final section I would like to close with some summary reflections on how I see his contribution not just to our particular project but to youth ministry in general.

Henri's life and witness have inspired the renewal of youth ministry in three ways. First, by telling the story of his own intimate journey in relation to God, he has invited those in youth ministry to refocus their energy not only in the creation of ever-more-exciting activities, programs, curricula, and events for their kids but in the creation of space in their own lives for experiencing the power of God's love working in them and through them. As he put it so eloquently in *The Way of the Heart*, "Our first and foremost task is faithfully to care for the inward fire so that when it is really needed it can offer warmth and light to lost travelers."[7] Henri's openness about his own inner journey and his genius for articulating the deepest longings of the human heart have helped youth ministers to enter into an engagement with themselves in solitude, silence, and prayer. The notion of actually experiencing God's presence and power within one's deepest self is surprisingly new and sometimes threatening for many youth ministers, especially in the mainline Protestant and evangelical churches. Engagement with self and growth in self-knowledge are opening a new and profound experience of depth in the lives of these ministers and helping them to "re-source" their ministry in prayer, community, and spiritual guidance. Henri's capacity for speaking out of the place where God dwelled in him and leading others into that place has helped to lead youth ministers and young people to experience their inner life in Christ for the first time. Discovering this depth dimension of the self-in-God is the greatest gift that youth ministers can offer young people, but they can do so only if they have experienced it themselves.

Henri's second contribution is his honesty and vulnerability about his personal struggles and brokenness. He has given those in youth ministry permission to be real with themselves, with one another, and with their young people. He has given them the safety to own their own pain and darkness and to offer it up to God and to one another for healing. Henri's image of the wounded healer and his theology of weakness are especially helpful in youth ministry. Young people in particular are in a life stage in which the search for identity is of paramount importance. They are extremely self-conscious and seeking to be affirmed, confirmed, and encouraged by their elders. They are wondering whether they have value and worth, whether there is a place and a future for them in this increasingly complex and competitive world, and whether they are safely held as unique and beloved by some person or community beyond their homes and schools. Henri's own struggle with anguish, insecurity, shame, and self-doubt has given youth ministers the language to guide and support themselves in facing their own brokenness.

It has also been a great gift in accompanying young people in their own dark nights. His words speak directly to the heart of both youth ministers and the young people in their care when he says:

> Herein lies the core of my spiritual struggle: the struggle against self-rejection, self-contempt, and self-loathing. . . . But now I realize that the real sin is to deny God's first love for me, to ignore my original goodness. Because without claiming that first love and that original goodness for myself, I lose touch with my true self and embark on the destructive search among the wrong people and in the wrong places for what can only be found in the house of my Father.[8]

Henri's articulation of what it means to "become the Beloved" has opened up the possibility for youth ministers to become at home in the brokenness and beauty of their humanity and to minister out of that place in trust that they are enough. It has freed young persons to receive that core sense of identity in their lives at a developmental moment in which a life trajectory can be completely altered by an experience of the power of God's love.

Finally, Henri has spoken to the ministry of the church in the context of a larger movement of the Spirit that is working to bring about contemplative renewal of not just youth ministry, but all ministry. Not long after we began our first in-service formation at the YMSP, some of the senior pastors and priests from our partner churches remarked that everything we were teaching could be applied not only to youth ministry but to every ministry in their communities. One commented that this contemplative approach to youth ministry was going to involve a whole paradigm shift in his church and in the way it understood ministry to children, adults, the sick, the elderly—everyone. It could change worship, administration, staff relations, decision-making—everything. We nodded with great satisfaction. What we were holding up to them was the choice to move from a hyperactive, anxiety-driven ministry oriented toward numbers, dollars, and results to a Spirit-led ministry grounded in attentiveness, discernment, and responsiveness to God's Love manifest in human relationships. The criterion of good ministry in this new paradigm was not productivity but "fruitfulness" experienced through intimate relationships with ourselves, one another, and God. We pointed to Henri's vision of the church as a real possibility and not just the product of naive idealism. As Henri himself expressed it:

> Oh how important is discipline, community, prayer, silence, caring presence, simple listening, adoration and deep, lasting friendship. We all want it so much, and still the powers suggesting that all of that is fantasy are enormous. But we have to replace the battle for power with the battle to create space for the spirit.[9]

It is true that for youth, in particular, the most important dimension of life is relationship. Young persons tell us that they experience God not through high-voltage events or confirmation preparation, but through moments of deep encounter in solitude and community. We often tell church leaders that there is a gift hidden in the cry of young persons who call their churches back to authenticity and relationship. The numbers or the apparent "success" of church youth-ministry programs do not matter if the fruits of the Spirit are not being born in their young people. This applies equally to other ministries in the church. We refer constantly to Henri's vision of the "lifesigns" of intimacy, fecundity, and ecstasy as the true measure of effectiveness in ministry. If Christians are not growing in their capacity for experiencing these fruits in their lives in relation to churches that seek to accompany them on the way of Jesus and the Beatitudes, then they are not being formed in the Spirit of God. If our priests and ministers are burning out from a sense of anxiety, frustration, and isolation in their work, then they are not practicing Spirit-led ministry. Henri Nouwen has helped us to understand and live the one thing necessary as ministers–attending to God's loving presence in our lives and forming people to do the same.

Henri's desire to reinterpret the way of the heart revealed in desert spirituality, in the Latin American church, and in L'Arche is resonant with the witness of other major teachers of prayer and ministry. Thomas Merton, Thomas Keating, John Main, Joan Chittister, and Dorothy Day are other contemporary prophets who are calling the whole church back to ministry and community grounded in a deep contemplative experience of God's presence in our hearts. In the end, Henri Nouwen's unique contribution to this movement has been his theology and spirituality of the Beloved. It is the journey of "becoming the Beloved" that he shares in his writings that has helped those in youth ministry and in the churches generally to hear the inner voice of divine love in their own lives and to help young people to tune in to that voice as well. In an unwitting testament to his own enduring legacy, Henri writes:

> What I most want to say is that when the totality of our daily lives is lived "from above," that is, as the Beloved sent into the world, then everyone we meet and everything that happens to us becomes a unique opportunity to choose for the life that cannot be conquered by death.[10]

It is his witness to the healing power of this first love of God that invites all of us to live in the ecstasy of knowing who we are as the beloved daughters and sons of God in whom God takes delight. It is his witness that encourages us and that sends us in ministry to reveal that Love to others.

Notes

[1] Henri Nouwen, *Lifesigns: Intimacy, Fecundity, and Ecstasy in Christian Perspective* (New York: Doubleday, 1986), 17.

[2] Henri Nouwen, *The Way of the Heart: Desert Spirituality and Contemporary Ministry* (New York: Seabury Press, 1981), 21.

[3] Henri Nouwen, *Life of the Beloved: Spiritual Living in a Secular World* (New York: Crossroad, 1997), 39.

[4] Henri Nouwen, *In the Name of Jesus: Reflections on Christian Leadership* (New York: Crossroad, 1993).

[5] Nouwen, *Life of the Beloved,* 89.

[6] Ibid., 103.

[7] Nouwen, *The Way of the Heart,* 55.

[8] Henri Nouwen, *The Return of the Prodigal Son: A Story of Homecoming* (New York: Doubleday, 1992), 107.

[9] Henri Nouwen, *The Road to Daybreak: A Spiritual Journey* (New York: Doubleday, 1988), 184.

[10] Nouwen, *Life of the Beloved,* 108.

18

The Life of the Beloved Pastor

A Resource for Healing for the Parish Pastor

Rev. Christopher Cahill

A quarter-century ago Henri Nouwen observed that:

> The pressures in the ministry are enormous, the demands are increasing, and the satisfactions diminishing. How can we expect to remain full of creative vitality, of zeal for the Word of God, of desire to service, and of motivation to inspire our often numbed congregations? Where are we supposed to find nurture and strength? How can we alleviate our own spiritual hunger and thirst?[1]

By many accounts, pastors in American Protestant parish ministries are still under a great deal of stress. For example, in a recent study by the Pulpit and Pew project at Duke University, high on the list of reasons pastors leave local church ministry involuntarily are conflicts with congregations or denominational officials.[2] Another study conducted among pastors of the Lutheran Church (Missouri Synod) concluded that a high percentage of this denomination's pastors are on the brink of burn-out, ready to leave the ministry at a moment's notice.[3] The excellent Alban Institute publication *Clergy Self-Care* addresses some of these concerns, but such a book seems to be a rarity.[4]

For this parish pastor, who has struggled at times at the brink of burn-out and depression, none of these writers' answers satisfied the heart as deeply as Henri Nouwen's work *Life of the Beloved*.[5] This chapter explores some implications of the model suggested by Nouwen as a resource for healing for distressed parish pastors. Following Nouwen's outline, which is based on the actions of Jesus at the Passover and the celebrant in the Eucharist, I examine what it might mean for pastors to embrace the Belovedness of God and then consider what that Belovedness might mean for pastors to live as people chosen, blessed, broken, and given by God to the church.

What might it mean for parish pastors to accept that they are beloved of God? Quite often pastors are viewed as servants of God, of the word, or of the congregation. Indeed, the Lutheran formula for corporate absolution in the liturgy is "Upon this your confession, I as a called and ordained *servant of the Word* announce the grace of God to all of you." We say these words, I suppose, because we know that Jesus came not to be served but to serve, and we expect our pastors to follow his example.

This notion of pastors as servants is not without its problems. Taken to the extreme, pastors may be seen as hirelings of the congregation, serving at the whim of the church board. In a less extreme situation, ministry may be seen as simply the fulfillment of a series of tasks or accomplishments. Pastoral tasks are sometimes spelled out in the constitution and bylaws of a particular congregation; pastoral accomplishments are often particular achievements that go above and beyond what is required in the bylaws. This view of ministry leads to a performance orientation; in some congregations pastors need to maintain a constant level of achievement, described by the bylaws, in order to keep their job. In other congregations members have expectations of pastoral service that are not described in any document; in such places failure to meet these unexpressed expectations may also result in early termination.[6]

If we consider the metaphor of the turning wagon wheel that was the theme of the 2006 Nouwen-inspired gathering in Toronto, what I am speaking of here is attention to the rim. The pastoral duties and expectations outlined in bylaws are "where the rubber meets the road," at the rim of the wheel. This is the first place people look when their cars are not riding smoothly, and when there is distress in a congregation, people look first at the way the pastor is conducting the duties of the office. In a wagon wheel, the next place where attention might be focused is the spokes. This is the focus of most books on caring for clergy. "Look after your physical, emotional, mental health," we are told. "Take a day off/Do something different/ Re-prioritize your ministry," we hear. All these are important, because we do need to address cracked spokes before they break completely. Hardly anyone advocates paying attention to the hub, to the pastor's personal relationship with God. In fact, we seem to assume that because the wheel is attached to the hub, nothing is amiss.

Much is amiss, however, if pastors do not claim the belovedness they themselves have been given by the grace of God. The wheels of ministry then turn on faulty bearings such as success, popularity, and power.[7] The bearings are faulty because they are often seized with competitiveness or break under the strain of self-rejection and loneliness. If pastors claim their belovedness, however, their ministry is different. The pastors' true identity is not based on success, popularity, or power, but rather on this core truth: "You are my beloved!" This core truth is spoken from eternity to eternity by the One who is Eternal. This is the pastors' true identity, regardless of the way the rest of the world sees them.[8] This is what makes real pastoral ministry possible to begin with, namely, the eternal truth that pastors are the beloved of the Father, in the same way Jesus was and always is the Beloved of the Father.[9] This truth is what changes the way we can look at pastoral ministry. Where we once looked at pastoral ministry from the prevailing social perspective of competition, we look at it now from God's perspective of compassion.[10] Where we once looked at pastoral ministry from the internal perspective of insecurity, we can look at it from the external perspective of the offering of forgiveness. Where we once looked at pastoral ministry from the interpersonal stance of loneliness, we now see that the main focus of pastoral ministry is greeting one another's belovedness.[11] When we claim our own belovedness as pastors, we can understand that pastoral ministry is no longer characterized by pastors saying, "I'm better than you, but I'm lonely and insecure." Instead, pastoral ministry can be characterized by pastors saying, "Welcome, beloved of the Father, to a place where we can be together in compassion, forgiveness, and the Father's blessing!"[12]

At the Passover meal with his disciples, Jesus *took bread.* Thus, the first action in the Eucharist is *taking* or *choosing.* What might it mean for parish pastors to celebrate "being the beloved" by embracing their *chosenness* by Jesus?

During a recent retreat participants were asked to consider John 13 in a *lectio divina* exercise. This is the chapter in which Jesus washes the feet of his disciples on the night when he was betrayed. As I considered what this story might mean for me, it became clear that I was not to see myself as one of the disciples, nor was I to see myself as Jesus; instead, I realized "I am the basin and I am the towel." "I am the basin" means that I am not the servant of Jesus in my congregation. Instead, I am the vessel that Jesus will use so that he himself may be the servant for his people, and I pray that he will fill me with his grace so that he may accomplish his will among them. "I am the towel" means that I pray that Jesus will keep me wrapped closely about Himself while at the same time he uses me as his instrument for his service to others.

I have such a basin and a towel to remind me of this insight. There is nothing special about them—the basin is just a Corelle bowl from the Corning assembly line, and the towel is just like a stack of others on the WalMart shelf. Their uniqueness comes solely from the person choosing them, and from the use to which I put them. My uniqueness as a pastor has nothing to do with me and everything to do with the one who chooses me for this ministry: Jesus. My uniqueness as a pastor has nothing to do with what I think I can accomplish and everything to do with what Jesus wants to accomplish among his people.[13] For some people, these might be humiliating thoughts. For me, they are humbling because my focus is now on the One doing the choosing and not on my special qualifications for this office. I am "called and ordained" by Jesus to his ministry, not because I am such a great preacher and pastor but because Jesus loves his people and because he loves me. The ministry is not mine, it is his—his vision, his ideas, his goals. I rejoice that he loves me enough to allow me to share in his ministry among his people.

What should the pastoral ministry of his chosen one look like? For one thing, it should be a ministry that celebrates my chosenness with a life of thanksgiving. In everything I do and in everything that happens to me, I hope to be thankful that God has chosen me for this ministry. The pastoral ministry of chosenness should also have eyes that look beneath the surface of the world to see the truth of sin that infects it; it ought to have hands that uncover this sin and apply the balm of grace that can heal it; and the pastoral ministry of chosenness ought to speak that truth, not only bringing the darkness into the light but also shining the light of the gospel into places that would rather cower in darkness.[14]

At the Passover meal, Jesus took the bread and *blessed* it. This is the second action in the Eucharist. How might pastors embrace the *blessing* God has given them?

I sometimes wonder if things would have been different in my most conflicted days if, along with some of the other things people did for me, they had also blessed me. People prayed for me, listened to me, supported me, and more, but now I wonder how it might have been if they had blessed me, too. Henri Nouwen wrote that he ought to become the embracing father of both the prodigal son as well as the elder son.[15] He also wrote that he might enfold a blessing around another person and shelter that person within the folds of his robes.[16] But who blesses the embracing fathers? Who embraces the pastors and priests and enfolds them with blessings the way they enfold others?

In American evangelicalism and Protestantism a popular term these days is *accountability partners*. For some reason the notion that pastors ought to have someone to whom they are voluntarily accountable seems thrilling not only to congregations but to pastors as well. Several pastors that I know speak excitedly about their "accountability groups" and the strong relationships they have with the members of the group. For me, the term *accountability* implies confession without blessing, and maybe even without forgiveness. I think we pastors need to be more assertive in seeking to be blessed, and perhaps more quick to give blessings, too.

The rites of ordination and installation can be very important to the pastoral life here (in the Lutheran Church, the rite of installation is similar to the rite of ordination and is performed each time a pastor takes a new charge in a new parish). More than formalities or rituals, the rites of ordination and installation are the affirmation that the Lord of the church has already blessed this person into this office at this particular place. In the Lutheran Church the rite includes the laying on of hands by the other pastors and bishops present, but perhaps it should also include a blessing of welcome by the congregation that is explicitly stated (it is implicit in the worship service and the party or dinner that usually follows). Perhaps members of the congregation should also lay hands on the new pastor to bless him or her, as the clergy do. Nevertheless, whether or not the people physically enfold the pastor with their blessing is less important than knowing that Jesus blesses that pastor as well, a fact often lost in the excitement of ordination and installation day and often forgotten in the daily tasks of ministry that follow.

So how does the pastor claim the blessing that Jesus offers? Perhaps the most obvious way is to ask for it. I like the story of the Daybreak resident asking Henri Nouwen for a blessing and ultimately being enfolded in the flowing sleeves of his robe.[17] The picture is a wonderful one, but it began with her asking for the blessing. Of course, she had to demonstrate to him what she had in mind, but he was a quick study. Perhaps if the pastor is to ask for the blessing that Jesus offers, the best thing to do is to demonstrate it first, then ask for it. We pastors teach so many things to our people, but the giving and receiving of blessings do not seem to be on the list. If we taught blessing, practiced it, and did it regularly we might not have to ask—and we would receive blessings all the time.

Yet this physical act of blessing is not always available to us. Claiming the blessing of Jesus is something we want always readily available even if there is no one to enfold us at the moment. Henri Nouwen suggested that we can claim the blessing of Jesus through the dual practices of prayer and presence.[18] In both, Jesus is present with us; in both, we ask for his blessing; in both, he embraces us and enfolds us with it. I think of my little grandsons in this context. Sometimes, when the three year old wants something particular from me, he will climb up into my lap, snuggle down, and then ask for what he wants. That is prayer. Sometimes, when he wants nothing in particular, he just climbs up into my lap and snuggles down and does not ask anything—he just wants to be in my lap. That is presence. In both actions he is claiming the blessing that comes to him while sitting in my lap, snuggled down. In both prayer and presence we claim the blessing that Jesus has to offer us. The key for my grandson is to stop what he is doing long enough to climb into my lap for a while. The key for me as a pastor is to stop what I am doing long enough to be in prayer or in the presence of Jesus for a while, because it is only when I am doing nothing else that I have the time and the focus to claim the blessing Jesus wants to give me. Then, having claimed the blessing in prayer and presence, I am free to enfold that blessing around others.

After Jesus had taken the bread and blessed it, he *broke* it. This is the third action in the Eucharist. How can pastors transform their *brokenness* into ministry that heals and transforms others? I want to make a distinction here between a pastor who has been broken by Jesus and a pastor who has been broken by the congregation (or by individuals, or simply by stress).[19]

Numerous books on pastoral brokenness are available these days, with intriguing titles such as *Pastors in Transition: Why Clergy Leave Local Church Ministry*, *The Wounded Minister* (to be distinguished in title and approach from Henri Nouwen's *The Wounded Healer*), *Pastors at Risk*, and *It Only Hurts on Monday*. These address the myriad ways in which contemporary pastors suffer ministry-related stress. There are other books that seek to address and prevent stressful and painful situations, such as, *Leaders That Last*, *How to Keep the Pastor You Love*, and *Support Your Local Pastor*. For the most part these books point out that ministry-related stress arising from work with congregations inevitably leads pastors to believe that their ministry has become fruitless. This leads them to defensiveness, on the one hand, and to the need to make everyone happy, on the other. Most of these books offer psychological and sociological suggestions for preventing this kind of brokenness, or an array of solutions that promise to fix the brokenness once it has occurred. None of these books deals with the brokenness that Jesus brings or the desirability for beloved pastors to claim brokenness by Jesus as an integral part of ministry.[20] If we are to follow the paradigm suggested in *Life of the Beloved*, we must look for ways in which Jesus breaks his beloved, chosen, blessed pastors so that they can be given for the life of the congregation. Pastors ought to be asking themselves questions such as, What has Jesus broken me from? What does he still need to break me from so that I can resemble him more closely? and, How do I respond to the brokenness that he brings in such a way that I bring it under the blessing as his gift to his people?

Personally, Jesus has been breaking me from the influence of several lies common to many pastors, lies that affect our ministries deeply. One of these lies has been a twisted need to please other people. Some of my most painful ministry experiences came because one of my ministry goals was to keep everybody happy. This is not possible to do all the time. In fact, there are some people who were never happy with anything I did, yet I kept trying to win them over. Jesus has also been breaking me of the lie that equates worth with achievement. This is an especially difficult lie for American Protestant pastors to deal with, because there is a societal orientation toward success that leaks into the church in the form of "bigger churches equal more successful ministries." This lie leads to a third, a defensiveness that almost always occurred because I thought I had to defend my congregation's significance despite its size. This third lie also has roots in pride and self-approval, and the process of being broken of such a lie can be very painful.

The alternative to embracing the lies is to embrace the brokenness that Jesus brings to his beloved pastors. I love the eucharistic action of breaking a large host to be shared by all, because it is only when such a host is broken that God's people can share in the grace and blessing that it brings. In the same way, it is only when pastors embrace their brokenness that they can become the source of grace and blessing that Jesus intends for his people.[21] I want to caution pastors that following this train of thought may lead them in difficult and somewhat unpopular directions. First, pastors; who embrace their brokenness become increasingly dependent upon the love of God.[22] We do not usually want to know about such pastors: we would rather hear success stories of pastors with the largest congregations, wanting to know the secrets of their success so that perhaps we can replicate them in our own ministry. Embracing brokenness means we absolutely must give up all our dependency upon self-importance, achievements, approval, and accomplishments and becoming solely dependent upon the love of God.[23] Embracing the brokenness of Jesus means that pastors approach their congregations in the posture of confession rather than control, seeking forgiveness from those who are always seeking the proclamation of forgiveness from them.[24] We often want to see pastors who are successful, who speak at workshops and write books and have television ministries, but embracing the brokenness of Jesus means that pastors will have a new view of vocation. The vocation to pastoral ministry is the call to powerlessness, irrelevance, and humility—we remember that these were Jesus' affirmations of his own vocation when he was tempted by Satan in the wilderness with power, relevance, and popularity.[25] Pastoral ministry that has embraced the brokenness that Jesus brings means that to the world pastors appear to be powerless, irrelevant, humble, and in need of forgiveness—and therefore most able to be the gospel incarnate, the gift of God for the life of the congregation.[26]

Finally, after taking the bread, blessing it, and breaking it, Jesus *gave* it to his disciples. This *giving* is the fourth action in the Eucharist. In what ways can pastors function as the *given* of God to the congregations they serve?

I have come to realize that the pastor is the gift of God to the congregation. Please do not misunderstand what I am saying here. I do not say this in the same sense in which we sometimes speak of that particularly arrogant *macho* type of man who "thinks he's God's gift to women." When I say that the pastor is God's gift to the congregation, that is not meant in the spirit of arrogance but in the spirit of humility. This meaning of gift does not emphasize the intrinsic value of the gift but the relationship between the giver and the receiver. I have value on my own, because I am the beloved of God. Each pastor who serves a Christian congregation is the beloved of God—nothing can change or minimize that. But it is not because of my value to God as God's beloved that I have value to God as a pastor. If I have any value as a pastor it is because God loves this congregation. He gives it his word of truth to encourage and admonish it, to help the faith of individuals to grow and to help the church to grow as God's body. God gives individuals the sacraments for the forgiveness of their sins and the assurance, time and time again, of God's promise of eternal life. But God does not dump these means of grace in their lap and turn away, saying, "Make of these what you will." God also gives them a pastor who can tenderly and lovingly apply the balm of healing to this one, anoint another with the oil of gladness, and pour the cup of blessing over still another. This is the importance of the rites of ordination and installation for the congregation; these rites are the affirmation that God loves the congregation so much, enough to provide them with a living reminder of Jesus in their midst.

The pastor who is the beloved is given by God to the congregation to meet the needs of the congregation—not the congregation's need for a leader, administrator, or chief executive officer, but the congregation's core needs for forgiveness, for healing, and for blessing. The people gathered in a particular place are hungry and thirsty for the righteousness of Christ; the beloved pastor is the gospel incarnate, the bread of the world given to them by God so that they will know that God is feeding them. The beloved pastor is God's mission gift to a world drowning in hopelessness. The people come, Sunday after Sunday, because they know that there is one place in the world where despair and hopelessness do not reign and where their hearts may be fed and filled with gratitude for the gifts God gives.[27]

What does pastoral ministry that is the gift of God to the congregation look like? It does not look like the accomplishments of the pastor, measured in the size of the congregation's budget or in the number of filled seats in worship. Pastoral ministry that is the gift of God to the congregation looks like the presence of Jesus in the midst of his people, feeding them, giving them hope and blessing and affirming their own belovedness in the sight of the Father.[28]

What can the pastoral ministry of the beloved pastor look like? Let me begin by briefly outlining what the ministry of pastors who do *not* claim their belovedness might look like. When ministry is not based upon the certain knowledge that the pastor is the beloved of God, it can be characterized by fragility, loneliness, and self-rejection. The outward manifestation of these traits can be competitiveness, showing itself in a variety of ways. It may appear as a drive to "succeed"—to do more or grow a larger congregation or seem more important among one's peers and in the congregation. It may appear as a great smothering disappointment and depression when none of these goals is fulfilled. The underlying basis of such a ministry may not be the giving and receiving of blessing, but rather an emphasis on "mutual accountability." Finally, pastors who undertake this type of ministry will find themselves broken not by Jesus but by others. Such pastors might seek not to be the ones given by God to the people, but instead might seek to affirm their own self-worth in the approval of those they serve or in their own accomplishments, all the while adopting a posture of defensiveness that prevents them from truly being the gifts of God to the congregation.

Pastors who claim their belovedness have a ministry that looks entirely different. First, these pastors can greet the people of their congregations with compassion and forgiveness, knowing that it is the compassion and forgiveness of the Father that enables God to call the pastors beloved. Such pastors can affirm the belovedness of the people around them without fear that their own belovedness may be compromised. The ministry of these pastors and congregations can be characterized by a mutual sharing and claiming of belovedness rather than by accountability. Second, when pastors claim the belovedness that the Father offers, they understand that their ministry is not based on their election by the congregation or even approval by the bishop; it is based instead upon the choice of the Father. Since it is the Father who chooses them, these pastors can freely speak the truth in love, unmask the seductions of the world, and lead the people in thankfulness for God's grace to them all. The ministry of beloved pastors can overflow with acts of blessing as they affirm the blessing of the Father upon all the prodigals who come seeking redemption, for beloved pastors have themselves been prodigals who also know the blessing of the Father's love. While some of the actual tasks of day-to-day ministry may be difficult for beloved pastors, and certain members of the congregation may at times be less than cooperative, beloved pastors can know that real fruitfulness in ministry comes because Jesus has broken them of pride, selfishness, and ambition. Beloved pastors are able to see that truly fruitful ministry comes in those places in which the pastors themselves seem irrelevant and powerless. They know that the humility that flows from such a holy brokenness manifests itself in love, just as the brokenness of the Eucharist is the sign of the love of Christ for those who partake. Finally, the ministry of beloved pastors is a ministry of giving rather than accumulating and of compassion rather than competitiveness. In a world filled with resentment, hopelessness, and despair, the ministry of beloved pastors is a mission of hope that encourages gratitude to God, who wishes for all people to claim their belovedness.

Notes

[1] Henri J. M. Nouwen, *The Way of the Heart: Desert Spirituality and Contemporary Ministry* (San Francisco: HarperSanFrancisco, 1991), 12–13.

[2] See Dean R. Hoge and Jacqueline E. Wenger, *Pastors in Transition: Why Clergy Leave Local Church Ministry* (Grand Rapids, MI: Eerdmans, 2005).

[3] See Alan C. Klaas and Cheryl D. Klaas, *Clergy Shortage Study* (Smithville, MO: Mission Growth Ministries, 1999).

[4] See Roy M. Oswald, *Clergy Self-Care: Finding a Balance for Effective Ministry* (Herndon, VT: The Alban Institute, 1997).

[5] Henri J. M. Nouwen, *Life of the Beloved* (New York: Crossroad, 1992).

[6] In Lutheran pastor Don Abdon's sample constitution and bylaws for Lutheran churches, the first significant mention of pastors falls under Article 5, "Discipline in the Congregation," and deals with provisions for deposing a pastor from office: "Sufficient grounds for deposing a pastor . . . shall be persistent adherence to false doctrine, scandalous life, and willful neglect of official duties or evident and protracted incapacity to perform the function of the sacred office" (Don Abdon, *Organizing around the Great Commission* [Indianapolis, IN: Parish Leadership Seminars Inc., 1977], 10). In his suggested bylaws Abdon lists the following duties of the office of the pastor: "to proclaim to the congregation . . . the Word of God in its full truth and purity; . . . to administer the sacraments in accordance with their divine institution; to discharge toward all members of the congregation the functions of a minister and curate of their souls in an evangelical manner . . . ; to spiritually guard the welfare of the younger members of the congregation and adults during their preparation for acceptance of Holy Communion; to guide the congregation in applying the divinely ordained discipline of the church; to provide spiritual leadership and oversight in the educational agencies and the various adult and youth organizations within the congregation; to serve as an example by Christian conduct and to do all that is possible for the up-building of the congregation and for the advancement of the Kingdom of God" (ibid., 15). Individual congregational bylaws may include additional pastoral duties such as counseling, gaining new members from among the unchurched, and so on. This author has seldom seen a congregational constitution or bylaws that address the personal spiritual life of the pastor. While it is possible that congregations assume that pastors will have a strong personal spiritual life, the language of these documents might also lead one to conclude that a pastor may have

a weak, negligible, and mostly absent spiritual life and still be able to fulfill the functions of the office.

⁷ "During our short lives the question that guides much of our behavior is: 'Who are we?' Although we may seldom pose that question in a formal way, we live it very concretely in our day-to-day decisions. The three answers that we generally live—not necessarily give—are: 'We are what we do, we are what others say about us, and we are what we have,' or in other words: 'We are our success, we are our popularity, we are our power.' It is important to realize the fragility of life that depends on success, popularity, and power. Its fragility stems from the fact that all three of these are external factors over which we have only limited control" (Henri J. M. Nouwen, *Here and Now: Living in the Spirit* [New York: Crossroad, 1994], 188).

⁸ "Each time we claim for ourselves the truth of our belovedness, our lives are widened and deepened. As the beloved our lives stretch out far beyond the bound-aries of our birth and death. We do not simply become the beloved at our birth and cease being the beloved at our death. Our belovedness is eternal. God says to us: 'I love you with an everlasting love.' This love was there before our fathers and moth-ers loved us, and it will be there long after our friends have cared for us. It is a divine love, an everlasting love, an eternal love" (ibid., 194).

⁹ When Jesus was baptized, the voice of the Father said, "This is my beloved Son, in whom I am well pleased" (Mt 3:17; Mk 1:11; Lk 3:22). A sacramental view of baptism connects the baptism of the believer with that of Jesus (Rom 6:3–4) and applies the pronouncement of the Father about Jesus to the believer as well.

¹⁰ "When we take a critical look at ourselves, we have to recognize that competi-tion, not compassion, is our main motivation in life. We find ourselves deeply im-mersed in all sorts of competition. Our whole sense of self is dependent upon the way we compare ourselves with others and upon the differences we can identify" (Henri J. M. Nouwen, Donald P. McNeill, and Douglas A. Morrison, *Compassion: A Reflection on the Christian Life* [Garden City, NY: Doubleday, 1982], 19).

¹¹ "Community, then, cannot grow out of loneliness, but comes when the person who begins to recognize his or her belovedness greets the belovedness of the other. The God alive in me greets the God resident in you" (Henri J. M. Nouwen, *Turn My Mourning into Dancing: Finding Hope in Hard Times,* ed. Tim Jones [Nashville, TN: Word, 2001], 83).

¹² "The knowledge of Jesus' heart is a knowledge of the heart. And when we live in the world with that knowledge, we cannot do other than bring healing, reconcilia-tion, new life, and hope wherever we go. The desire to be relevant and successful will gradually disappear, and our only desire will be to say with our whole being to our brothers and sisters of the human race, 'You are loved'" (Henri J. M. Nouwen, *In the Name of Jesus: Reflections on Christian Leadership* [New York: Crossroad, 1989], 41).

¹³ "In [Jesus'] great tenderness, he chooses some of us—who are no better than others—human like us in their great fragility. He chooses some to whom he gives the ministry of forgiveness, to whom he says, 'You will forgive sins in my name; You will represent me in the sacrament of forgiveness'" (Jean Vanier, *Befriending the Stranger* [Grand Rapids, MI: Eerdmans, 2005], 81–82).

¹⁴ Nouwen's guidelines in the struggle to claim our chosenness: "First of all, you have to keep unmasking the world about you for what it is: manipulative, control-ling, power-hungry, and, in the long run, destructive. . . . Second, you have to keep looking for people and places where your truth is spoken and where you are re-minded of your deepest identity as the chosen one. . . . Third, you have to celebrate your chosenness constantly. This means saying 'thank you' to God for having chosen

you, and 'thank you' to all who remind you of your chosenness. . . . For me, [these guidelines] are the spiritual disciplines for my life as the chosen one" (Nouwen, *Life of the Beloved*, 62).

[15] Henri J. M. Nouwen, *The Return of the Prodigal Son* (New York: Image Books, 1994), 122.

[16] Nouwen, *Life of the Beloved*, 69ff.

[17] Ibid.

[18] Ibid., 75.

[19] In *Life of the Beloved* Nouwen suggests ways in which our brokenness is a result of living in a world that is itself broken and prone to breaking others. In the Eucharist it is not the world that breaks the bread, but Jesus. This section departs from Nouwen's discussion to try to follow the model of the Eucharist more closely.

[20] The following comments by Eugene Peterson occur in the context of a discussion about communion, not pastoral ministry per se, but they are to the point: "Our gifts don't remain what we bring. All too often we come to the Table with our best manners and a smug pose of impenetrable self-sufficiency. We are all surface, all role, polished and poised performers in the game of life. But the Jesus who saves us needs access to what is within us and so exposes our insides, our inadequacies, our 'cover-ups.' At the Table we are not permitted to be self-enclosed. We are not permitted to be self-sufficient. The breaking of our pride and self-approval is not a bad thing; it opens us to new life, to saving action. We come crusted over, hardened into ourselves. We soon discover that God is working deep with us, beneath our surface lies and poses, to bring new life. We cannot remain self-enclosed on this altar: 'a broken and contrite heart, O God, you will not despise' (Ps. 51:17): the body broken, the blood poured out" (Eugene Peterson, *Christ Plays in Ten Thousand Places: A Conversation in Spiritual Theology* [Grand Rapids, MI: Eerdmans, 2005], 209–10).

[21] "How can we live our brokenness? Jesus invites us to embrace our brokenness as he embraced the cross and live it as part of our mission. He asks us not to reject our brokenness as a curse from God that reminds us of our sinfulness but to accept it and put it under God's blessing for our purification and sanctification. Thus, our brokenness can become a gateway to new life" (Henri J. M. Nouwen, *With Burning Hearts: A Meditation on the Eucharistic Life* [Maryknoll, NY: Orbis Books, 1997], July 15).

[22] "From the moment I was helped to experience my interpersonal addiction as an expression of a need for total surrender to a loving God who would fulfill the deepest desires of my heart, I started to live my dependency in a radically new way. Instead of living it in shame and embarrassment, I was able to live it as an urgent invitation to claim God's unconditional love for myself, a love I can depend on without any fear" (Nouwen, *Life of the Beloved*, 100).

[23] "In a world that constantly compares people, ranking them as more or less intelligent, more or less attractive, more or less successful, it is not easy to really believe in a love that does not do the same" (Nouwen, *The Return of the Prodigal Son*, 103).

[24] "Just as the future leaders must be mystics deeply steeped in contemplative prayer, so also must they be persons always willing to confess their own brokenness and ask for forgiveness from those to whom they minister" (Nouwen, *In the Name of Jesus*, 64).

[25] Ibid.

[26] "The leaders of the future will be those who dare to claim their irrelevance in the contemporary world as a divine vocation that allows them to enter into a deep solidarity with the anguish underlying all the glitter of success, and to bring the light of Jesus there" (ibid., 35).

[27] "Life lived Eucharistically is always a life of mission. We live in a world groaning under its losses: the merciless wars destroying people and their countries, the hunger and starvation decimating whole populations, crime and violence holding millions of men, women, and children in fear. Cancer and AIDS, cholera, malaria, and many other diseases devastating the bodies of countless people; earthquakes, floods, and traffic disasters . . . [these are] the story of everyday life filling the newspapers and television screens. It is a world of endless losses, and many, of not most, of our fellow human beings walk with faces downcast on the surface of this planet. They say in some way or another: ' . . . We lost hope.' This is the world we are sent to live in Eucharistically, that is, to live with burning hearts and with open ears and open eyes" (Nouwen, *With Burning Hearts,* 88).

[28] "This has been, and continues to be, the experience of those who live a Eucharistic life. They see it as their mission to persistently challenge their fellow travelers to choose for gratitude instead of resentment and for hope instead of despair. And the few times that this challenge is accepted are enough to make their lives worth living. To see a smile breaking through tears is to witness a miracle—the miracle of joy" (ibid., 91).

19

The Legacy of Henri

Laurent Nouwen

The Henri Nouwen Retreat Center in the Netherlands is located in a large former military compound in the woods near the city of Hilversum, the city where Henri died ten years ago. Used in better days as an ammunition depot, one of the grim storage buildings is now in use as the retreat center. The center has limited comfort; there is no water, no toilet, no heating. However, it has a very large, smooth concrete floor, a forklift, and a coffee machine, which works when it is not freezing. What more can one wish for? Anyone coming to the center starts working right away. There is a lot of work to do, such as cleaning, sorting, packing, counting and storing. The center has only workers. Let me introduce you to some of the "retreatants."

Always present is Alfred, who just turned sixty. According to Alfred, he is on lifelong probation after early retirement from a chaotic twenty-year career as a civil servant. He is always in a very good mood, full of joy, except for one concern. He is very unwillingly a bachelor. The workers at the center provide Alfred with substantial but incompatible advice on how to find his great love and how to stay out of trouble.

Whenever free from his job as ticket collector on the bus, Siem attends our activities. His specialty is stuffing. Because of his preparedness to help, he is nicknamed Simon of Cyrene, after this marginal biblical person Simon. An issue of debate is whether or not Simon helped to carry the cross voluntarily or was forced to do so by the Romans. Siem had never seen the inside of a church and was not happy to be called a marginal biblical personality. But once, in Poland, we got him over the threshold of a church, and we followed the stations of the cross along the wall. We explained to Siem who the real Simon was and what he did. Now Siem is proud to be Simon.

Then there is Kees, a gentleman, day and night ready to help. He was formerly a human resources professional at the largest bank in the Netherlands. Kees continuously interrupts his hard work to give valuable professional comments on the style of management of the center. The greatness of his personality is evidenced by his acceptance of us ignoring all his comments.

We all miss Denis. Not that he was of any apparent use, but he was always full of energy and making trouble like a crisis manager in peace time. He never returned from last year's carnival down south. Recently he sent us a text-message that he is living somewhere south, taking care of Marije, who suffers from Korsakov's syndrome.

Next to these core "retreatants" of the center there are many other men and women volunteering to get all the goods organized. In the center we do not speak a lot. Actually we only speak during the short coffee breaks, provided the coffee machine works. The conversations are very down to earth and never directly about God, but you cannot have it all. The most serious question would probably be, "What would Henri think about all this?" We quote from his ordination card Matthew 9.38: "so ask the Lord to send laborers to his harvest."

Is this the harvest?

As soon as the truck is finally loaded and the big doors in the back are sealed, we are like a small family celebrating a miracle. How is it possible that we together, a bunch of totally inept persons, made this possible? We are all happy when wheels get rolling and we are off on the long road to the Ukraine.

It is a great honor for my family and me to be invited to this conference honoring the life of my brother Henri. I am very happy that my brother Paul and his wife Monique are with me. I am in the clouds that my son Raphäel—the healer of blind Tobias—is now next to me. He opens my eyes to the goodness of life. It is good to be together with you all, each so much a brother or sister to Henri. Coming back to Daybreak feels like coming back home, the home and family Henri left us. Many of you have known Henri personally, others maybe only through his writings, but all of us share his life as an inspiring gift. In essence we see his life as a real gift to us, as he awakened us to see and to live our own lives as a great gift. To experience our own life as a gift is not what the world is telling us and not even what church institutions are telling us.

The invitation to speak at the Turning the Wheel conference was okay, but the word *keynote* is frightening. In *The Way of the Heart* Henri is skeptical about "our wordy world" and our semantic existence. He advises us to live connected to silence and to speak from silence. We have to be very well aware of the enormous gap between, on the one hand, the quantity of spoken and written words by our small world of the outspoken, and on the other hand, the quantity of silenced suffering, poverty, and lack of basic necessities in the enormous world of the speechless.

Should I not remember the man in the gospel who said, "Lord, speak just one word and I will be healed"? Should I not keep my mouth shut and listen only to that one word? Often while driving the truck eastward toward the Ukrainian border, I am talking to Henri. Actually, most of the time I am complaining to him. If he had not written in his Ukraine diary that there was a spastic guy out there in need of an electric typewriter to get his poems on paper, our lives would have been different. We would not be hauling eastward second-hand computers, blankets, school furniture, clothing, shoes, wheelchairs, institutional kitchen equipment, and washing machines, all things he had forgotten to mention in his diary but turned out to be needed as well. Henri has no idea about the trouble one goes through gathering enough useful goods to get a truckload together.

Henri, listen: waiting for over twenty-four hours at the Ukraine border, and getting screwed by custom officers notwithstanding the ten bucks they already took out of my passport, does not really give me that particular feeling of living the life of the beloved. I shout to him: "Next time, you do it yourself, brother. You may be close to holy and I may be practical, but next time it will be the other way around."

But being totally unroadworthy, Henri stays away.

I am deeply grateful to Henri for writing that this guy in Ukraine needed to have this typewriter. If he had not mentioned this, there would not be this Henri Nouwen Retreat Center with Alfred, Siem, nicknamed Simon of Cyrene, and Kees, and we would not be missing Denis.

There is some irony in the fact that we gathered together in commemoration of Henri's life in an academic place, at a great university. If Henri had celebrated this tenth anniversary of his death, I wonder where he would have invited us. I am quite sure he would have invited himself to spend the day at your place, at your table, and shared your meal. He, the one who was always on the run, restlessly asked himself the questions: Is this the life I am called to live? God, who do you want me to be? Seeking answers to these questions brought him all over the globe to try to live yet another life. Somewhat all in vain, as he was called to live the not easy life of Henri Nouwen.

We all are impressed by Henri leaving his great academic career for his downwardly mobile journey to live together with persons with special needs at Daybreak. We are impressed because with this step downward Henri accepted the consequence of his search for God. He thought he could be of help there, and it turned out to be the other way around. Henri found in the Daybreak community acceptance of his own so special needs. He began by thinking of bringing core members closer to God, but slowly Henri discovered that it was the core members bringing Henri closer to God.

Am I, are we, in the world of words and power, still believing we bring God to the core members of this world, or do I, do we, and the world of power accept that we are to go intellectually, spiritually, and practically downward, and do we allow the core members of this world to bring God to us?

On one particular trip, crossing the border between Ukraine to Poland went faster than expected. I took a one-hour break at Premysl. I wandered a bit through the border town, full of ancient churches from Orthodox to Roman, nowadays the busy center of vodka and cigarette smuggling. I decided to visit the white monastery along the river San. I had bought some tulip bulbs there the year before. Dutch are always keen on tulips. Guest Sister Barbara opened the gate of the contemplative enclave. Seeing this nun in full battle dress always makes me wonder what the Western world has against Muslim women wearing the burqa.

Sister Barbara and I share a common vocabulary of approximately fifty words, two hundred gestures, and various spastic mimics. After a lengthy conversation about growing tulips, we discussed the dramatic poverty in Eastern Europe and later the life and books of Henri. She was very happy when I gave her another of his books, *Adam*, freshly translated into Cyrillic Ukraine. When we discussed the situation of Western theology and the newly appointed pope, she passed by those subjects as apparently irrelevant. Suddenly she said, very convinced, "Christ is living." She kept repeating this, looking me straight in the eyes: "Christ is living." As if that was the only relevant reality.

Walking away from the convent I try to work out Sister Barbara's "Christ is alive" credo. It may be true for her, it may be true for those living in enclaves, but is it a reality for me, for those living in the streets of this city, for all those living in the real world? But I do not feel comfortable, and her words "Christ is alive" stay with me. I have to think it over.

Like Henri, we face in our not too easy lives that same question: Is this the life I am called to live? This very question gave the conference its mission statement: "Henri Nouwen and Our Search for God." We are all working on that question throughout our lives. The "our search for God" issue is not only an individual and personal question. Basically, it is the most central issue for each individual, each group, and each culture. In essence our "search for God" is our search for an answer about the sense and meaning of our life, what we are living for, what it is all about. But does the issue of our search for God have real value? Being on a spiritual journey seems to be a national sport, like hot-air ballooning. "Oh, how wonderful! You are on a spiritual journey. Well, I am into French cooking." Often our search can become an introverted journey, embedded in our own fixed references and in a closed system of thoughts, judgments, and rules about morality. We accept this search and journey as long as the God we find does not come with real surprises and upset our lives.

Our inherent need to find the God of all meaning, the God who is the final result of our search, can be dangerous. Our inability to grasp God may cause us to create our own image of God, an image that will not disappoint us. We end up with the God who is "in the eye of the beholder," a God conformed to our lifestyle, a God serving our culture, a God not jeopardizing our economy and, since 9/11, a God cleared by National Security.

We have experience throughout history the disastrous consequences of humankind's created golden calves. We see again and again the brutal results brought about by the "God is on our side" believers and suffocations by the "we have found God" authorities. We have around the globe a wild diversity of hundreds of religions, hundreds and thousands of churches, mosques, holy places, and monasteries, each in the service of different and competing gods. It is certain that all those gods seem to drive us further and further apart. However, if we look at humankind, we have to realize that we are very united in one, worldwide church of not knowing and never getting a hold on God, the one and only God. It is in this church that I think Henri, the Catholic priest, lived.

It is sobering to realize that Henri found his own search for God counter-productive. Henri's over-conscious search for God left him with empty hands and brought him face to face with exactly the opposing question.

He wrote:

> For most of my life I have struggled to find God, to know God, to love God. I have failed many times but always tried again, even when I was close to despair.
> Now I wonder whether I have sufficiently realized that during all this time God has tried to find me, to know me and to love me. The question is not "How am I to find God?" but "How am I to let myself be found by him?"[1]

The rephrasing of the question "How am I to find God?" into "How am I to let myself be found by him" is rephrasing our lives from a desperate attempt to master God into a total surrender of ourselves, to being mastered by God.

The very issue in our lives is not whether or not we can successfully and with credibility answer the question "Do I believe in God and do I trust God?" Is that a relevant question? It is not. The fundamental challenge is to dare to live with the astonishing and miraculous inspiration and voice from within that, first of all and after all, God believes in us and God has put his trust in us. Exactly the same trust God put into that man from Nazareth standing in the Jordan River. To say it in Henri's circus theology: To give up our search for the catcher, but to live in full the life of the flyer Christ. Do not try to grasp the God you wish, but make the astonishing *salto mortale* God enjoys seeing you making.

The over 1,600 psychiatric patients in the psychiatric hospital Kulparkivska in L'viv, Ukraine, are housed in rusty beds, lucky if they have a urine-soaked mattress. The place was built a century ago for 350 patients. Now it is an overcrowded dump of human suffering on the outskirts of the city. Some patients are bound by ankles and wrists with cloth wraps to cold bed frames. Lusterless, hollow eyes stare from somewhere out of a sinister past. Here in this place time has come to a full stop. A mumbling sound is horrifyingly interrupted by a wild cry. I wonder about the many similar places scattered all over Ukraine. I wonder how many places like this must be hidden away in the forests of Eastern Europe. I wonder about those men in orange overalls, handcuffed, and in iron chains anonymously held or tortured in hidden prisons. I wonder how many places in this world are holding you and me, our brothers and sisters, our fathers and mothers, our son and daughters, our own existence locked up in desperation. I wonder how many places in this world are hells of illness, violence, hunger, rape, pain, and injustice. The crucifixion is ongoing. Jesus' last words, according to Matthew and Mark, is the question of very many around the world today: "My God, my God, why have you deserted me?"

Sister Barbara, what do you mean "Christ is alive"?

Yes, Henri was restlessly in search of God. Good advice for him would be: "Henri, you should take some time off and read a book by Nouwen." I doubt he did, but for sure he wrote yet another book.

Searching for God all his life, Henri realized toward the end that he had completely lost God. "I lecture about praying, but do not have time to pray. I speak about silence, but I am never silent. I teach everything about solidarity and spirituality. It brought me to the competitive top of the academic cathedral and it made me a speaker about God. But all of this brought me further and further away, further away from where I want desperately to get closer to."[2] After Harvard, Henri was, at Daybreak, put to work, real work, maybe the first real work Henri ever got to do. He had to give care to one person, to give this person food, to dress this person, and to provide this person with security. Henri lets us know: "This man, who I am given to take care of, this man who does not speak and who lives in silence and is so severely handicapped that his life depends on me, this man, Adam, reveals to me who God is. God is as present in Adam as God is present in Christ. Adam is brought on my path of life so that God could find me."[3]

Adam is as central in our community as Christ is during the Last Supper. Adam cannot survive if we around him do not make peace and come together to serve him. In Adam, Christ's life is at stake again. Adam had spoken less than a single word to Henri and had "healed" him. There are many men, women, and children in the world who we are given to take care of. There is a whole world of brothers and sisters who do not speak and who live hidden in silence. There are very many living next to us who are handicapped and dependent for their survival on us. Do we make peace for them to survive, or do we go to war for us to live peacefully? There are many Adams around, Adams brought on the path of our individual and collective life to reveal to us who God is. God is as present in those Adams next to us as God is present in Christ. We are invited to sit down with Adam and to share the bread and to share the cup. We are invited to start maybe our first real work, to feed the Adams, to dress them, and to provide them with security.

Sister Barbara, do I slowly start to see what you mean by "Christ is alive"?

The young South African black man between the white sheets in Sizenani hospice gives the white man a smile. The young black man is nearly a skeleton. He goes through a hell of pain, with his knees curled up, like a fetus. We support Elena Matseke in her work in her township Rethabiseng. Without giving a reason for it, she had asked me to visit this man. I stay there at the end of the bed, embarrassed, looking at him, and desperately searching for some words to say.

He takes the initiative. "Are you from Holland?" he asks me.

"Yes, I am," I say.

"When I am better, I will be playing for Ajax," he tells me, reminding me that besides tulips we are famous for a soccer team.

"Ajax is not doing very well. The team is waiting for you," I say to him.

Once more he shows me his yellow teeth. He cites the names of all the eleven angels playing in the team a world's distance away from his bed. The next morning I find the bed empty. The young black man is thousands of light years away. I want to dream that the young man has joined the team. Every day, five thousand young men and women south of the Sahara suffer in great pain and die of HIV/AIDS.

I am witness to yet another crucifixion; I hear here again, "Why have you deserted them," more convincing than "Christ is alive."

"Why have you deserted me?" God did not answer Christ. God did not take Christ from the cross. It became silent, very silent, and Christ died very, very alone.

God's answer comes in the ongoing resurrection of Christ, ongoing resurrection of the Beloved, the blessing surviving the cross.

Christ stays alive when God can find us, when we open our hands and hearts, our work and our spirit to accept, to claim and to embody again and again God's blessing: "You are my beloved." Come back from your journey, get your act together, and go for it. Make your hands and hearts the hands and hearts of the Beloved.

Christ arises by our lives, by the lives of our brothers and sisters, by the simple care for Adam and for all Adams.

The Beloved has not risen from death in a single past event to go in a dazzling upward mobility into heaven somewhere beyond the galaxies or into heaven somewhere out in space. The Beloved does arise in downward mobility to be present in our world, here and now, in every heartbeat, in every breath, in every second. Christ's resurrection brings God's kingdom to the very center of today's world and is not a yesterday or tomorrow dreamland. Not at the beginning or at the end of time, but right in the center of time, in the very axis of the turning wheel is where God is inviting us to resurrect the Beloved.

The children in the orphanage Zaluchia in the forests of the Ukraine are in really bad shape. They are all diagnosed to be mentally and physically disabled. In the Soviet days they were in category number four, the lowest category of existence. To keep order, the heavy-bosomed guardians tie the children of Zaluchia with ropes to a table leg, to a radiator or for hours on a bucket serving as a toilet. My God, my God, why have you deserted them?

It took a lot of time before the three angel-blue dressed sisters of St. Vincent de Paul were admitted to the orphanage as visitors. They came to live close to this desperate place and set up their mini convent in an uncomfortable house next to the orphanage. It had been a standard rule of the old system: category four meant no visitors. It took ten years for the director to figure out that there was no old system anymore, much to his regret. It took him some more years to figure out that there was no one except himself to say it was a standard rule. Now the three sisters are allowed to come in, only a few hours a day. They cannot change very much in the horrifying circumstances. The children are still suffering from their handicaps. But the sisters touch the children. They lift them up from the floor. They hug them. Miracles happen. One of the children began to smile, another one raised herself up and sat straight, and yes, one of them even started trying to walk. Christ is alive.

It is hard to accept fully that the center of spiritual inspiration is not our self-propelled search for God but the Beloved present in all those chosen, broken, blessed, and given Adams among us. They are the ones through whom God offers us his answer: I have not deserted you; my Beloved is alive. Just look and take care of my Beloved, provide my Beloved with food, get my Beloved dressed, and offer my Beloved security and peace; work in my harvest.

Another worker at our Henri Nouwen Retreat Center is our young friend Vitaliy. He cannot attend the truck-packing sessions in Holland as he is living on the other side of the border, on the other side of the border of opportunities, in L'viv, Ukraine. Vitaliy took upon himself the responsibility for the Henri Nouwen practice out there. Now he is working in the psychiatric hospital to humanize the situation for the patients, but also for the personnel. He is struggling with old, vested power and corrupted structures. He is not very welcome in his drive to change mentality and to improve the lives of the patients. He is ordered to clean the halls of the hospital or to take away the rubbish. But he is tolerant of all this and is renovating ward after ward, providing better beds, water baskets for the toilets, and a little space for recreational activities. Very, very slowly some first light comes into the dark place. When we get together with his family in its very small, one-room apartment, we really take life seriously. Vitaliy would have been much better off had he joined the army of millions of young Ukrainians working as cheap, illegal laborers in the West. But that is not an issue. We deliberate upon what to do for the children of Zaluchchia, for the patients of the psychiatric hospital, for the men in prison. We speak about the hopes of the Orange revolution and about the trouble of having running water only between six and nine in the morning.

Vitaliy did not meet Henri when Henri visited Ukraine fourteen years ago. He often asks me who Henri was. I tell him: Henri was a man befriended by Adam. Vitaliy jokes: Henri gave us many Adams, in Ukraine, in this world, and everywhere.

He asks me: When can the retreat center make the next truck ready?

As soon as we all get back from Henri's grave and this Henri Nouwen conference in Toronto with 250 participants, there will be 250 more truck drivers on their way to their Adams, I promise him.

Christ is alive and only alive.

Notes

[1] Henri Nouwen, *The Return of the Prodigal Son: A Story of Homecoming* (New York: Doubleday, 1992), 106.

[2] Translation of an excerpt from an interview given by Nouwen for *Overal et Nergens,* a Dutch television series produced by The Company Media Produkties, which aired in Holland in 1993.

[3] Ibid.

20

Aspects of Henri Nouwen's Social Ministry

Rev. Phillip N. Grigsby

Whenever I want to look up one of Henri's books, I usually look in the spirituality or inspiration section of the religious catalogue. I do not look in the contemporary issues or social justice sections. Henri Nouwen was both spiritual and inspirational with unquestionably profound gifts in both. His legacy grows as arguably one of the most profound spiritual leaders of the last century. I believe that his insights in the social justice arena were integral to his faith. His faith and his writings always led him somewhere beyond "the four walls," or with Jesus (in Hebrews), "outside the camp." Henri was not primarily a social activist, but he repeatedly wrote and lived the themes of compassion, inclusivity, and fecundity that inexorably led to work on social justice either by him or others. He hinted at what social compassion might look like. But at the time of his death, the book on peacemaking was still unpublished and his ideas on social compassion only at the beginning stage of an approach that he left to others to discover and begin to live into and out. This essay is intended as a modest but hopefully evocative compilation, articulation, and start of reflection on key themes in Henri's work that relate to social ministry and social justice. It is material that I have found useful personally and with groups. It is not complete. I am not an academic but an activist and organizer. But as I meet with congregations, it is a spirituality that I am called to practice and teach, that can afford the space to go beyond the "four walls" and "outside the camp." As James reminded Henri and us, "Faith without works is dead."

Perspective and Experience

Others can fill out this theme much more than I can in terms of personal experience with Henri through contact in person or with letters. I invite others who have experiences, to provide more insight into these aspects of Henri's life and work. My experience was more limited. I knew Henri during the Yale years. I returned from serving overseas in the Peace Corps in Sierra Leone, West Africa, and began to focus on urban ministry. My wife and I were fortunate to participate in a reflection group including those either in, or training for, community ministry of various types. Classmates involved in more radical social justice work than I included Art Laffin and Dean Hammer. In the mid 1970s, Henri celebrated ecumenical Eucharist, certainly not common in those days, and I was fortunate to attend these services.

After completing a call as the first staff member of a community ministry program in Norwalk, Connecticut, I directed Christian Community Action (CCA) in New Haven, which Henri supported financially. Walter Gaffney, who co-authored *Aging*, had worked for CCA for a time. The reflection group supported Walter and his wife traveling to Paraguay. Our group also hosted and encouraged Joel Filartiga when he visited New Haven to gain support for his work and struggle in Paraguay. I witnessed how Joel's presence with Henri led to a growing awareness and call to Central and South America. Joel's witness, especially as an artist, spoke powerfully to Henri.

Even in the New Haven years I was struck with how Henri could be present among such a wide range of people. He would be invited to speak to very conservative Roman Catholic orders, and yet he remained as pastor to groups (as articulated well by John Dear in *The Road to Peace*) involved in radical action.

Earlier Social Ministry/Social Justice Themes

We are all walking contradictions, but Henri more so than most of us. He combined such an extraordinary range of gifts, talents, and interests. All the biographies do well, with their varying perspectives, in describing this wide range. It is telling that Henri felt the call to visit Selma in 1965 and the funeral of Martin Luther King, Jr., in 1968 (see *The Road to Peace*). Reflecting on Selma, he wrote: "I knew that week had touched my soul far more than one year of study. And as my car sped through the night, I felt a newfound joy."[1] He reflected on the funeral in much the same way: "And here I rested, carried by people who kept on singing and praying, and I knew that out of my exhaustion, a new faith could grow, a faith in the possibility of nonviolent love. And while they carried away his body and started to move away from me, I felt a new joy, reassured that tomorrow was a new day with a new promise."[2]

While Henri's early *Creative Ministry* was designed more with the church in mind, some of the social justice themes he articulated later were first articulated here. In the section entitled "Organizing," Henri reflected on what we called then the "agent of social change." He stated that neither radical Christian reforms or Pentecostals are able to solve the problems of our society. The great task of the minister, rather, is to live and to help live in the tension between both and search for a synthesis. The Christian agent of social change is called upon to be a social reformer and a man who does not fall into the temptation of concretism. He does not worry about the results of his work because he believes that God will fulfill his promises and that it is only a temptation to desire to know exactly this will happen.[3]

Henri contrasted the Christian response and more prevalent means of social change used by secular society:

It is sad to see that we still believe that the best way to motivate others to offer their assistance is to show through books and photographs how inhumanely these people have to live. This certainly creates enough guilt feelings to make people open their wallets and give some money, thereby soothing their consciences for a while. But this is not a Christian response. That the exposure of misery can evoke not only pity but also aggression has become quite clear in concentration camps, in films about dying children in Biafra, and in the endless exposure of emaciated bodies by TV, radio and newspaper. As long as we want to change the condition of other people because we feel guilty about our wealth, we are still playing the power game and waiting for thanks. But when we start discovering that in many ways we are the poor and those who need our help are the wealthy, who have a lot to give, no true social agent gives in to the temptation of power since he has discovered that his task is not a heavy burden or a brave sacrifice but an opportunity to see more and more of the face of Him who he wants to meet.[4]

Not too much later, in *The Wounded Healer*, again written more for the church, Henri contrasted the "mystical way" and the "revolutionary way":

Is there a third way, a Christian way? It is my growing conviction that in Jesus the mystical and revolutionary ways are not opposites, but two sides of the same mode of experiential transcendence. . . . For a Christian, Jesus is the man in whom it has indeed become manifest that revolution and conversion cannot be separated in man's ache for experiential transcendence. His appearance in our midst has made it undeniably clear that changing the human heart and changing human society are not separate tasks but are as interconnected as the two beams of the cross. Jesus was a revolutionary, who did not become an extremist, since he did not offer an ideology, but Himself. He was also a mystic, who did not use his intimate relationship with God to avoid the social evils of his time, but shocked his milieu to the point of being executed as a rebel.[5]

In the same work Henri had his first full section on the theme of compassion. He wrote that "compassion must become the core and even the nature of authority."[6] In his conclusion Henri reflects on the role of the minister "to prevent people from suffering for the wrong reasons."[7] He notes that through a shared pain, "hospitality becomes community as it creates a unity based on the shared confession of our basic brokenness and on a shared hope."[8]

These early works and experiences provide the foundation for later important social ministry themes.

Was Henri Primarily a Social Activist?

John Dear collected a number of Henri's work related to social ministry themes and published them not long after Henri's death in 1999. In *The Road to Peace* Dear argues that "the essays on peace and justice gathered here in this collection are not side interests or posthumous footnotes to his great body of writing. They offer some of his most spiritual insights. They stand at the center of his thought."[9]

Deidre LaNoue rejects this in *The Spiritual Legacy of Henri Nouwen.* In commenting on whether or not "they stand at the center of his thought," she writes: "I do not agree. The center of Nouwen's thought was a personal relationship with God. He obviously believes that such a relationship would express itself through social activism, but this was not the center of his thought and work. Loving God and loving others as much as self was at the center of his work. Social activism was only one expression of these relationships at work."[10]

As more of a social activist than an academic, I see Henri's social activism as integral. Given his early call to Selma and Atlanta, I cannot see Henri without the social justice dimension. However, he was not primarily a social activist. But he was, like Karl Barth, always holding the newspaper in one hand and the Bible in the other. His faith was "both/and." Prayer led to engagement, and engagement led back to prayer.

What is different, of course, are the times in which he wrote and how they have changed. In the late 1960s and 1970s, New Haven was an activist place. The late Rev. William Sloane Coffin, Jr., was leading civil disobedience on Vietnam and the draft. New Haven was home to the Black Panthers' trial. The group I was to direct, the CCA, had "urban encounters" where white suburbanites encountered the Black Panthers and others in ways that led to dramatic change. The group I direct now in Schenectady emerged from the ferment of the times to "save the city" and "relate the resources of the churches to the human needs of the city."

The worry and challenge in those days were to keep up with the activism. The activists were busy; the kingdom was around the corner; the church needed to be relevant. We debated whether the world should set the agenda for the church. Then, as my mentor, Hank Yordon in Norwalk, used to say, ministers discovered prayer and left the demonstrations. The times shifted to quietism, a retrenchment. It was not that activists needed to be reminded that prayer was essential grounding for activism, but that there were fewer and fewer activists.

LaNoue helpfully concludes at the end of her section on activism that

> the self-centered spirituality that characterizes many Americans in the 1980s and 1990s seems to point to the fact that some American Christians today are dangerously close to practicing a kind of modern Gnosticism where the desire to know God and experience him results in a tendency to forget about or ignore one's obligation to love and care for others. Nouwen's thought concerning social activism is relevant and in keeping with the teachings of Scripture and the examples of many throughout the history of the Christian church, and it is a message that the American church needs.[11]

So while Henri was not primarily a social activist, the social justice implications were integral and, given the times, more necessary and urgent than when they were put forth originally.

The Link between the Personal and the Social

Theme 1: Compassion

In both his speaking and writing Henri moved between the personal dimensions and the social dimensions of his faith, as a short illustration from *A Cry for Mercy* illustrates:

> O Lord, look with favor on us, your people, and impart your love to us—not as an idea or concept, but as a lived experience. We can only love each other because you have loved us first. Let us know that first love so that we can see all human love as a reflection of a greater love, a love without condition or limitations. . . .
>
> If I can recognize you in the Sacrament of the Eucharist, I must also be able to recognize you in the many hungry men, women, and children. If I cannot translate my faith in your presence under the appearance of bread and wine into action for the world, I am still an unbeliever.[12]

Henri, in this excerpt, as in many other writings, moves from the first love to the love leading directly to love of neighbor.

Henri developed the theme of compassion in many writings. The earlier book *Compassion* sticks out by its larger biblical and theological focus and the art work. In what I have found as classic Henri, he and his colleagues articulated a series of three items in three sections. The impatient activist has to read the last chapter first!

Henri repeated many of the core themes around compassion in one of later works, *Here and Now* (1994). For example, he wrote about moving from competition to compassion, being the beloved, downward mobility, suffering with others, and self-confrontation.[13]

In the earlier work, as in the later, Henri contrasted competition (our normal approach) and compassion (not normal, who really wants to suffer with another?). We tend to shy away from suffering. The good news is that God is a God-with-us who takes on our suffering and the suffering of the world. The challenging biblical insight is a review of the passages where Jesus "had compassion (not pity) on them or moved with compassion." Henri pointed out that the term in Greek referred to the entrails or the guts. He commented further:

> The compassion that Jesus felt was obviously quite different from superficial or passing feelings of sorrow or sympathy. Rather, it extended to the most vulnerable part of his being. It is related to the Hebrew word for compassion, rachamim, which refers to the womb of Yahweh. Indeed, compassion is such a deep, central, and powerful emotion in Jesus that it can only be described as a movement of the womb of God. There, all the divine tenderness and gentleness lies hidden. There, God is father and mother, brother and sister, son and daughter. There, all feelings emotions, and passions are one in divine love. When Jesus was moved to compassion, the source of all life trembled, the ground of all love burst open, and the abyss of God's immense, inexhaustible, and unfathomable tenderness revealed itself.[14]

Therefore, compassion is not an optional element of faith. It is not something to do when you have some left-over time or energy. It relates to the core of faith, it is central to our faith (although as usual with Henri there are no footnotes or references).

The book gives a full exposition of voluntary displacement (later mobility) that he articulated elsewhere as well. Voluntary displacement is following our Lord, who left his ordinary place. It may mean dramatic or simply internal steps. Henri concluded:

> Thus voluntary displacement is part of the life of each Christian. It leads away from the ordinary and proper places where this is noticed by others or not; it leads to a recognition of each other as fellow travelers on the road and thus creates community. Finally voluntary displacement leads to compassion; by bringing us closer to our own brokenness it opens our eyes to our fellow human beings, who seek our consolation and comfort.[15]

Henri cautions against an activism that is not grounded in prayer and patience, or that does not reflect gratitude. However, in the end, compassion leads to action. Such action at times must include confrontation:

We are inclined to associate compassion with actions by which wounds are healed and pains relived. But in a time in which many people can no longer exercise their human rights, millions are hungry, and the whole human race lives under the threat of nuclear holocaust, compassionate action means more than offering help to the suffering. The power of evil has become so blatantly visible in individuals as well as in the social structures that dominate their lives that nothing less than strong and unambiguous confrontation is called for. Compassion does not exclude confrontation. On the contrary, confrontation is an integral part of compassion. . . . We cannot suffer with the poor when we are unwilling to confront those persons and systems that cause poverty. We cannot set the captives free when we do not want to confront those who carry the keys. We cannot profess our solidarity with those who are oppressed when we are unwilling to confront the oppressor. Compassion without confrontation fades quickly into fruitless sentimental commiseration.[16]

This could have been written yesterday! It is clearly a more radical perspective. Knowing some of the history of Joel Filartiga, the artist for the book, the work seems guided and sharpened by the drawings in it and what it reflected. Filartiga's art was born of real tragedy and the suffering he experienced in working with the poor, a voluntary displacement from one who was from the middle or higher classes. It was felt most keenly with the death of Joel's son at the hands of the secret police.

In a parallel article published in 1977, Henri links compassion to spiritual leadership. In beginning with the Sufi story he used from time to time about the Land of Fools, he contrasted the leader with compassion and without compassion. He utilized the themes of solidarity, displacement, and discipleship to describe the practice of compassion for spiritual leadership. Henri linked the "both/and" nature of prayer and action near the end of the article:

Our call to compassion is not a call to try to find God in the heart of the world but to find the world in the heart of God. That is the way of Paul, Benedict, Francis, Ignatius, Teresa of Avila, Martin Luther, John Wesley and all the spiritual leaders in the history of the Church. They all knew that the deeper our discipleship is, the deeper we enter into solidarity with the suffering world. There is nothing romantic, sweet, or easy about this. Those who think that this a way out—or even a copout—do not know what it means to have the mind of Jesus Christ. There is little doubt anyone who enters to any degree into discipleship with Christ not only does not avoid the pain of the world, but penetrates into its center. That is why a life of prayer connects us in the most intimate way with the life of the world, and why in its final analysis a life of compassion is a mystical life—a life lived in union with Jesus Christ.[17]

Theme 2: Inclusivity

Clearly from the above review of the theme of compassion, compassion is related and inextricably linked with the theme of inclusivity. Compassion links us in the life of faith with all people (and all of creation as well). Henri's thought and approach stretch all the limits and boundaries, probably to the breaking point. His was and is a radical inclusivity that expands the faith beyond any conventional limits.

I was impressed in looking through the archives to find an early private paper entitled "The New Mind," which addressed both compassion and inclusivity. While the article is somewhat complex, it begins with the fundamental contrast between the new mind and the old mind. The gift of the new mind is compassion. We need a conversion to live in the new mind; to be a Christian is to have a new mind (cf. Rom 2:16, 12:2).

The old mind is a conquering, acquisitive mind. The contrast is the new mind, where our real self is found in God:

Our identity is not attained, reached or conquered, but given. We are not what we can acquire but what is freely given by God. . . . We are in God. Our being is in God. The new mind is not the self standing over against God but the self finding itself in God as the source of all selfhood.

The new mind is the compassionate mind precisely because in it other people are no longer "over there" and hence difficult to reach but they are with us in God. The real conversion takes place when we realize, in the still point of our soul that in God there is no "over here" and "over there," there is *I* who wants and *they* who resist. . . .

As long as we work as if we have to unite divided people, as if there were no prior bond between them, we have forgotten who we are and have taken on our shoulders an impossible burden. The task given to us by the call to compassion is not to create unity between people, but to reveal and affirm the basic unity that underlies all difference. Our task is not to suffer with every human being but to give visibility in our concrete action to the reality that all human sufferings are suffered by God himself. In this old mind it was we who wanted to do it all. In the new mind, we are guided by the gentle hands of God, whose compassion exceeds all we could even expect.[18]

Also in the archives is a tape of a talk Henri gave at the Noroton Presbyterian Church in Stamford, Connecticut. He focused on what he believed to be the true qualities of life as a Christian: inclusivity and compassion. God created and introduced "covenant" that we come together. God's early covenant was with Abraham, Noah, David, and others. Then God created a new covenant, a new covenant for all people by sending God's only Son.. The covenant is inclusive, involving all places, all peoples, all races, all ages. In Jesus' cross, all humanity would be lifted to himself. The core of the new covenant is that all belong together. How do we live the truth that all are brothers and sisters? Life is an interruption of eternity. Inclusivity is to live with the heart of God and together with all people; no one is excluded.

Clearly Henri expanded all the boundaries.

Theme 3: Fecundity

Henri seemed to enjoy reclaiming old terms and making them provide insights. The results of compassion and inclusivity were fecundity, or fruitfulness. While others may see the task of ministry as to be faithful, Henri would use the term *fruitful,* or *to bear fruits.* He developed the theme in detail in *Lifesigns* in 1986. Beginning with John 15:5 ("Those who remain in me with me in them, bear fruit in plenty"), he acknowledged that "the word 'fecundity' is not used often in daily conversation, but it is a word worth reclaiming, for it can put us in touch with our deepest human potential to bring forth life."[19] In *Lifesigns* Henri articulated another of his core themes, moving from a house of fear to a house of love. He described the fruitful life as having three aspects: vulnerability, gratitude, and care.[20] A fruitful life means both giving and receiving, so difficult for us in our culture. The primary gospel story of gratitude is the multiplication of the loaves and fishes.

I was fortunate to experience and then save a copy of Henri's sermon on gratitude based on this story (preached on Thanksgiving in New Haven in 1980). As he did elsewhere, he contrasted the economy of scarcity with God's economy of abundance. The sermon is timeless:

> We are called to live grateful lives. And brothers and sisters, this is very very hard for us . . . and it's probably going to become harder and harder to survive in the uncertainties . . . and it is going to become harder and harder to survive in the coming decade . . . with unemployment, inflation, greater problems, greater fears, greater uncertainties . . . and it is going to be another real great temptation to hang on to what we have so at least we can survive. The power of our vocation is precisely to offer what we have in time of crisis. . . . Let the point of crisis be an invitation to proclaim the truth that God is a God of abundance and not of scarcity . . . and to keep giving away what we have our knowledge, our love, our property, whatever we can share, and to keep letting it be known that all is a gift.[21]

In one of his last articles, "Solitude, Community, and Ministry," Henri uses the path of Jesus going to the mountaintop, then gathering disciples, and then going out into the world in service. One flows to the other; it does not stop with solitude or community but leads to ministry. Ministry he describes as fruitfulness.

Henri never described any particular form of action. As one involved with urban ministry there are a variety of approaches: service, witness, advocacy, community, economic development, organizing, and so on. Each has its pros and cons. Ministry always leads somewhere:

What counts in your life and mine are not successes but fruits. The fruits of your life you might not see yourself. The fruits of your life are born often in your pain and in your vulnerability and in your losses. The fruits of your life come only after the plow has carved through your land. God wants you to be fruitful. . . . Our little lives are small, human lives. But in the eyes of the One who calls us the beloved, we are great–greater than the years we have. We will bear fruits, fruits that you and I will not see on this earth but in which we can trust. Solitude, community, ministry–these disciplines help us live a fruitful life. Remain in Jesus; he remains in you. You will bear many fruits, you will have great joy, and your joy will be complete.[22]

Social Compassion

Henri addressed the notion of social compassion in at least two writings. The first and earlier was a short interview in the 1984 compilation *Living with Apocalypse* by Tilden H. Edwards. The second was in the "Ecstasy" section of *Lifesigns* (1986). Both are illustrative.

In the interview Henri states that the primary resource for social compassion is the poor, who remind us of the "giftedness of existence in the mystery of God."[23] We need to remember and believe in the midst of protest that Jesus has overcome the world. Peacemakers must move from a scarcity mentality to one of God's abundance. The focus should be on spiritual disciplines that guide and sustain any witness. We do not have to worry or be unduly concerned; the value of the spiritual life is not about the numbers or breadth of those taking part. God calls a creative minority and is faithful even in the midst of persecution. The hope and assurance is that God suffers with all who suffer.

In the book chapter Henri again seeks to redeem a term and extends the term's use in a section entitled "Ecstasy and a New International Order." The extension is critical:

An ecstatic life which ignores the "powers and principalities" eroding creative international relations becomes an escapist life. Though the forces of evil infecting whole nations and peoples are often hidden, complex, and elusive, we are called, as Christians, to unmask and expel them in the Name of the God of love. That is the reason why we must continually search for a Christian spirituality which is global in the dimensions and unafraid to take seriously the dark forces at work on the international level.[24]

Nouwen recognized that applying this principle to global relations would be seen as naive. But our collective survival depends on it: "We must move out of the place of death wishes and death threats and search, as nations, for ways of international reconciliation, cooperation, and care."[25]

It requires bold steps:

> To speak this way is to dream great dreams; it is like composing a new symphony that, once created, sounds familiar. The Fifth Symphony of Beethoven now sounds as if it always existed. . . . It was not written in the stars, it had to be made. So, too, new ways must be found for nations to lift up their unity in global celebration, and praise the Creator in ecstatic, joyful song. Most people despair that such a peace is possible. They cling to the old ways and prefer the security offered by preparing for war to the insecurity of taking risks for peace. But the few who dare to sing a new song of peace are the new St. Francises of our time. They offer a glimpse of a new order that is being born out of the ruin of the old.[26]

During the 1990s, Henri would continue to speak on the theme of peacework as expressed in prayer, resistance, and community. The unpublished manuscript was written in 1983 and published in 2005 with a foreword by John Dear.[27] Henri wrote it as a spiritual resource for peacemakers in order to develop a spirituality of peacemaking:

> The main thesis of this book has been that this total belonging to Christ is not an escape from the world, but the only way to be in the world as peacemakers. Only by belonging to Christ and to him alone, that is, only by living as brothers and sisters of Jesus and sons and daughters of God, can we truly resist the devastating powers of evil and work together in this world to avoid a collective suicide.[28]

As John Dear comments, Henri's image of the house of fear is still, alas, timely and contemporary. Our situation is worse; therefore the need for conversation about social compassion becomes more urgent and necessary. But since we live in the light of that which is to come, and believe and trust that God desires peace and reconciliation, we can continue to live and work for peace in that confidence and joy, even in the midst of these times that are "out of joint."

In teaching on Henri's insights on compassion I have found that groups and communities are eager to extend the sense of compassion to communities, ecumenical settings, and beyond. Can it go further? Henri, in his challenging article "Christ of the Americas" in 1984, urged that the Parable of the Last Judgment be applied not just to individuals and communities but to nations.[29] I believe with the urgency of peace/war and energy issues, the times are coming again not only for discussion but for broad-based work and progress on social compassion. Our survival depends on it.

Notes

1 Henri Nouwen, *The Road to Peace,* ed. John Dear (Maryknoll, NY: Orbis Books, 1998), 95.

2 Ibid., 105.

3 Henri J. M. Nouwen, *Creative Ministry* (Garden City, NY: Image Books, 1971), 82–83.

4 Ibid., 84

5 Henri J. M. Nouwen, *The Wounded Healer* (New York: Image/Doubleday, 1971), 19–21.

6 Ibid., 40.

7 Ibid., 93.

8 Ibid.

9 John Dear, "Introduction," in Nouwen, *The Road to Peace,* xxix.

10 Deirdre LaNoue, *The Spiritual Legacy of Henri Nouwen* (New York: Continuum, 2000), 134.

11 Ibid., 139.

12 Henri J. M. Nouwen, *A Cry for Mercy: Prayers from the Genesee* (New York: Doubleday, 1981), 84, 109.

13 Henri J. M. Nouwen, *Here and Now* (New York: Crossroad, 1994), 116–32.

14 Henri J. M. Nouwen, Donald P. McNeill, and Douglas A. Morrison, *Compassion: A Reflection on the Christian Life* (Garden City, NY: Doubleday, 1982), 16–17.

15 Ibid., 74.

16 Ibid., 123–24.

17 Henri J. M. Nouwen, "Compassion: The Core of Spiritual Leadership," *Occasional Papers, The Institute for Ecumenical and Cultural Research* 2 (March 1977): 1–6.

18 Henri J. M. Nouwen, "The New Mind," Nouwen archives, box 178, 2118.

19 Henri J. M. Nouwen, *Lifesigns: Intimacy, Fecundity, and Ecstasy in Christian Perspective* (New York: Image/Doubleday, 1986), 43.

20 Ibid., 88.

21 Henri J. M. Nouwen, "The Mystery of Gratitude," unpublished sermon preached at Center Church, United Church of Christ, New Haven, Connecticut, November 27, 1980.

22 Henri J. M. Nouwen, "Moving from Solitude to Community to Ministry," *Leadership* (Spring 1995): 87.

23 "A Conversation with Henri J. M. Nouwen," in *Living with Apocalypse: Spiritual Resources for Social Compassion,* ed. Tilden H. Edwards (New York: Harper and Row, 1984), 15.

24 Nouwen, *Lifesigns,* 106–7.

25 Ibid., 113.

26 Ibid., 113–14.

27 Henri J. M. Nouwen, *Peacework: Prayer, Resistance, Community* (Maryknoll, NY: Orbis Books, 2005).

28 Nouwen, *The Road to Peace,* 124.

29 Henri J. M. Nouwen, "Christ of the Americas," *America* 150, no. 15 (April 21, 1984).

21

Contours of the Paradigmatic in Henri Nouwen's Pastoral Theology

Phil Zylla

> *The challenge of ministry is to help people in very concrete situations—people with illnesses or in grief, people with physical or mental handicaps, people suffering from poverty and oppression, people caught in the complex networks of secular or religious institutions—to see and experience their story as part of God's ongoing redemptive work in the world.*
>
> —HENRI J. M. NOUWEN, *THE LIVING REMINDER*

My first and only personal encounter with Henri J. M. Nouwen took place in Edmonton, Alberta, Canada, where he was scheduled to give a talk, "From Resentment to Gratitude," on one of his poignant core themes. I can still see him leading us in a rendition of St. Patrick's "Breastplate Prayer":

> Christ with me,
> Christ before me,
> Christ behind me,
> Christ in me,
> Christ beneath me,
> Christ above me,
> Christ on my right,
> Christ on my left . . .

That indelible impression of the integrative spiritual and pastoral insight of Henri Nouwen was augmented in a very deep way for me after the session, when I lined up politely with many others to talk to him. I was eager to tell him that I too shared his passion for ministry, for pastoral theology, and for integration. I was hoping that he might have something to say to me about the profound sadness I felt for my, at that time, two-and-one-half-year-old daughter, Chelsey, who was born with spina bifida and for whom I suffered deeply. He did not disappoint me. He turned to me as though I were the only person in the room and told me that Chelsey was my *vocation*, that I should reread his book *The Wounded Healer* and learn to speak of her and of my sufferings as a way to redeem them for good with God's help. This I have endeavored to do in my own work as a pastor and, now, as a pastoral theologian in an academic community. It is with this backdrop of his generous concern for all who suffered that, out of a debt of gratitude, I attempt to articulate what I am calling the contours of the paradigmatic in Henri Nouwen's pastoral theology.

Defining Pastoral Theology

At the core of the discipline of pastoral theology is a recognition that all Christian ministry is rooted in the faithful care of souls. Those of us who are called to this work in pastoral theology are constantly looking for ways to integrate the insights from the practice of ministry with the deeper reflection of theological inquiry rooted in our respective faith traditions. The Society for Pastoral Theology has defined its understanding of the discipline in its mission statement on its website:

> We understand pastoral theology as a constructive practical theological enterprise focused on the religious care of persons, families and communities. As such, it draws on interdisciplinary methods growing out of classical and contemporary theological traditions.

This is compatible with the definition of "pastoral theology" in the online *Catholic Encyclopedia*, which introduces the discipline with similar language:

> Pastoral theology is the science of the care of souls. . . . Pastoral theology is a branch of practical theology; it is essentially a practical science. All branches of theology, whether theoretical or practical, purpose [*sic*] in one way or another to make priests "the ministers of Christ, and the dispensers of the mysteries of God" (1 Corinthians 4:1). Pastoral theology presupposes other various branches; accepts the apologetic, dogmatic, exegetic, moral, juridical, ascetical, liturgical, and other conclusions reached by the ecclesiastical student, and scientifically applies these various conclusions to the priestly ministry.

Nouwen is uniquely postured as one of the key voices of contemporary pastoral theology with his deep pastoral and clerical commitments, his profound understanding of the dynamics of human interaction, and his continued integrative vision for pastoral and spiritual theology. As we engage the inimitable voice of Henri Nouwen, it is easy to become impressed with the many layers of integration in his writings. Yet, while this was his genius, it also marked his contribution as distinctive from all others in reference to what I am calling the contours of the paradigmatic. This essay is an attempt to honor the significant contribution of Henri Nouwen to pastoral theology and to understand how his work can inspire continued efforts in pastoral theology that are rooted in life with all of its complexity, depth, opportunity, and promise. Pastoral theology has always desired to enter into the depths of human existence and wrestle for understanding. Therefore, defining the nature of pastoral theology is a rather complex task. I think what comes close for me is expressed by Brazilian theologian Rubem Alves:

> God and the meaning of life are absences, realities for which we yearn, gifts of hope. . . . As the trapeze artist must leap out over the abyss, abandoning every point of support, the religious soul also has to leap out over the abyss, toward the evidence of feelings, of the voice of love, of the suggestions of hope.[1]

Nouwen's widely known love for the art of trapeze was undoubtedly related to his immense theological and pastoral vision. He always seemed to circle back to the ineffable mystery of God's presence and absence in the world and our participation in the life that God calls us to share. Pastoral theology, at its root, is caught up in reflection on these profound mysteries as they play out in the lives of ordinary Christians and the communities of faith in which they are called to be faithful. The distinctive contours of Nouwen's pastoral theology can be understood as embedded in a way of seeing the world that might best be described as the paradigmatic. In order to get at these contours, let me begin by outlining four levels of conceptualization in pastoral theology.

Levels of Conceptualization in Pastoral Theology

The first level may be called the *preceptual level* of conceptualization, and this must be understood as the basis for the other levels. At the preceptual level key principles or precepts are constantly applied until the habit of preceptual application becomes ingrained as part of the ministry context. The pastor or ministering person expresses the preceptual level in sermonic material, in case reports, and in various important communications about ministry development. Preceptual conceptualization directs ministry in ways that allow others to gain access to critical ideas.

The next conceptual level is the development of ministry models. *Models are developed from practiced precepts* that are placed in a coherent structure and can be explained to others. Over time, models are tested through trial and error in lived reality until a repeatable pattern or sustainable outcome can be described that others could use or imitate. Models, however, are seldom transferable to other contexts because they are often rooted in the contextual realities from which they come. Ministry models are constantly being revised, clarified, and updated as the contextual dynamics of ministry shift.

As the shifts in culture continue to affect the ministry context, a more nuanced and flexible structure is required to absorb the complexity. This leads us to the third level of conceptualization in pastoral theology, the paradigm. *Paradigms are flexible but settled sets of core convictions* that are derived from living with ambiguity, practicing displacement, and managing complex and often competing bodies of information. Paradox and simplicity combine in a poignant description of lived reality that has the feel of permanence. Paradigms have the simplicity that a child could accept but are layered with deep, symbolic understandings and function at the ontological level.

Most pastoral theology does not go beyond the paradigmatic level to the fourth level of conceptualization, the construct. *Constructs are the ontological condensation of tested paradigms.* In the constructive level the practice of paradigmatic conceptualization leads to settled convictions that are sifted through (discerned) over time and found to hold up in universal contexts. Constructs are cross-cultural, trans-generational, core insights that hold paradigms together and sustain the settled direction of a body of thought over long periods of time.

Four Contours of the Paradigmatic

The way I am using the term *paradigmatic* requires further clarification. The American Heritage Dictionary defines a paradigm as "a set of assumptions, concepts, values and practices that constitutes a way of viewing reality for the community that shares them, especially in an intellectual discipline." As a "way of viewing," the paradigm invites a nuanced integration of all the givens or assumptions being made within the context of that community. Paradigms function as a way of "sense making," taking very complex issues and ideas and folding them into a way of seeing or construing reality. Nouwen had a paradigmatic mind. He organized his grounding concepts in a way that allowed others to participate in his way of viewing the world and the spiritual dimensions of life.

In reflecting on common ministry practice, I am intrigued by the preference for the use of models rather than the more shaded and sophisticated next level of conceptualization, namely, the paradigmatic. I am convinced that the postmodern situation, in particular, requires the paradigmatic expression and approach to pastoral theology. Henri Nouwen was a person who was demonstrably ahead of his time, and I am convinced that by following the paradigmatic contours of Nouwen's thought we can see how this approach can be usefully expanded and developed as we carry on the pastoral theological enterprise in the twenty-first century. Allow me briefly, therefore, to describe four key dimensions of the paradigmatic, as I am using this term and as I see it demonstrated in the pastoral theological motifs of Nouwen's writings.

1. **Paradigms are both accessible and inaccessible.** At the core of the paradigmatic is accessibility without oversimplification. Paradigms are accessible because of their simplicity; they allow others to enter into the complexities and ambiguities they express without "solving" every aspect of the realities to which they point. They are inaccessible, however, in their capacity to describe the unmanageable bodies of (often competing) knowledge that they hold. These paradigms encompass more than they seem to and have elements of mystery, depth, and resilience in the face of many competing elements.

> - A paradigm moves with simplicity but is not simplistic.
> - The paradigmatic understanding allows for increasing insight and expansive reflection. Nouwen's own conceptions were often deepened, broadened, and rounded out with further confirmation. Very rarely did he abandon or give up on core ideas.

2. **Paradigms allow paradox to be expressed as lived reality.** At one level the paradigmatic conceptualization functions as an integrating matrix. Paradigms are ambiguous enough to contain elements that "don't make sense," yet are complete enough to resonate with lived reality.

> - The paradigm often treats seemingly less significant insights as core while never releasing the idea to which it is rooted or grounded.
> - Paradigmatic pastoral theology allows for interplay among core concepts.
> - At the root of the paradigmatic approach to pastoral theology is a trust of basic insights, which are not abandoned in favor of seemingly more sophisticated judgments.

With respect to this last point Dietrich Bonhoeffer makes a key distinction that clarifies paradigmatic reflection. He describes the fundamental difference between ethical language that is rooted in lived experience and ethical language that follows an abstract idea:

> Timeless and placeless ethical discourse lacks the concrete warrant which all authentic discourse requires. . . . It is often impossible to find fault with the process of abstraction and generalization or with theories advanced and yet they do not possess the

specific gravity [needed]. . . . The words are correct but they have no weight.[2]

3. **Paradigms give us the capacity to live with the questions.** The spiritual depth dimension is often "wait," "live with it," and is a call to pause with humility before offering the conclusion of the matter.

> • Patterned after the complexity of life, the paradigmatic approach to pastoral theology allows the idea to deepen and move into multifaceted layers of understanding.
> • The paradigmatic, in this sense, is deeply tied to the spiritual connotations of life and is prepared to hold mystery at its core.

4. **Paradigms are summary yet flexible frameworks that are deeply rooted in attention to the intricacies and complexities of life.**

> • Nouwen's approach involved careful meditation on the intricate, inner movements of the spiritual life (primarily his own) extrapolated into pastoral observations of his many experiences in the church, academy, and society.
> • Paradigmatic thinking in Nouwen's pastoral theology created vast opportunities for access to his ideas. His writings contain thousands of tributaries rooted in core concepts, each weaving another insight toward a single stream of thought, an integrative paradigm. This made his works immensely available to those who were interested in reflecting on their life situation.
> • The paradigmatic approach, while not exclusive to Nouwen, was his preferred way of framing Christian theological discourse and pastoral theology. It allowed the depth dimension to remain appropriately mysterious and elusive yet at the same time attainable within the realm of God's gracious and compassionate response to us as God's children.

The Paradigmatic Turn in Henri Nouwen's Pastoral Theology

There are "paradigmatic turns" in Nouwen's writings that allow greater theological reflection to occur. In most of these he was inviting a more integrative posture toward matters that seem to have settled into a firm commonplace understanding. Nouwen was sure that, with further light being shone on such settled ideas, a fresh perspective or paradigmatic turn was inevitable. By not despising the ordinary insight, Nouwen gathered seeds that would germinate into fluid and nourishing paradigms.

A good example of the paradigmatic turn in Nouwen is from *With Open Hands*. The subject of this book is prayer. He makes some ordinary remarks about the different forms of praying: petition, thanksgiving, and praise. He comments that often we "regard [petition] as less noble than prayer of thanksgiving and certainly less noble than prayer of praise."[3] This remark is not meant to be conclusive, thereby closing down dialogue, but rather to open up the common reflection on different types of praying. The reader, having thought about these forms of prayer, will likely reflect that this common conceptualization of prayer is a rather settled opinion on how things really are. Petition is considered to be the least noble of the prayer forms because it deals with self-interest, while praise is considered to be the highest form of prayer because it relates directly to the very character of God.

Nouwen then takes this rather settled and common conviction about prayer types into a paradigmatic turn. He reframes our understanding with a fresh conclusion:

> Thus, every prayer of petition becomes a prayer of thanksgiving and praise as well, precisely because it is a prayer of hope. In the hopeful prayer of petition, we thank God for God's promise and we praise God for God's trust. Our numerous requests simply become the concrete way of saying that we trust in the fullness of God's goodness.[4]

In this instance he uses a new theological category, hope, to introduce an integrative vision of the life of prayer, stating that "every prayer is an expression of hope."[5] Petition no longer serves as the lowest form of praying but rather is reintroduced as a prayer of hope. This demonstrates reliance on God and therefore stands together with the prayer of thanksgiving and the prayer of praise. The paradigmatic turn allows for three forms of prayer to be enfolded into a single category, the prayer of hope, under the rubric of the theological concept of hope, which he defines as "when you no longer accept things as they are now, and look ahead toward that which is not yet."[6]

Hope thus becomes the theological compass for the life of prayer. All of the categories of prayer are reframed within this rubric of hope. We see, in this particular case, that Nouwen is not trying to strip the reader of a settled conviction about the forms of prayer but rather to release readers to a new way of seeing, acting, and believing what prayer is. This allows their settled conviction to be integrated into a higher conceptual framework, the theological category of hope. This is at the heart of the paradigmatic turn in Nouwen. If we look carefully through his writings, we notice that this is one of his most concrete methods of practicing pastoral theology. He states this method early in *With Open Hands*:

> I came to see that praying had something to do with silence, with acceptance, with hope, with compassion and even with revolution. Then *I carefully sought out concepts and images which expressed* what I had experienced or would have liked to experience.[7]

The Parabolic Way of Seeing and the Paradigmatic

In *The Return of the Prodigal Son* Nouwen descends into the rich and complex parable of the return of the prodigal son to outline the contours of homecoming. Juxtaposed with the interior vision of Rembrandt's painting of this story, Nouwen proceeds to interpret the contours of our life and vocation by bringing into the light the various nuances of the way we see and understand our place in the world. In doing so, Nouwen demonstrates that the formative, parabolic way of speaking of Jesus is still vital for the way we envisage pastoral theological reflection in the twenty-first century. The paradigmatic structure of Nouwen's writings parallels the parabolic way of speaking in Jesus' teaching.

In *The Poet's Gift* pastoral theologian Donald Capps describes the connections between pastoral work and the parabolic way of speaking. He outlines the similarities of the poetic word form of contemporary poets with the parabolic word form of Jesus, noting:

Like the parable, the poem is an extended metaphor, the meaning of which is expressed by the poem itself. Like the parable, one does not look outside the poem for the "point" of the poem, since the poem is the point. Too, like the parable, the poem is necessarily open-ended. Its goal is not to tell a complete story, as a novel does, but to use a life episode– often one that is seemingly unimportant or that other, less perceptive eyes would have overlooked–to inspire or even prod the reader to look at life in a different way. Like Jesus' parables, poems are usually considered unorthodox, if not radical, precisely because they challenge our usual and routine ways of perceiving and construing our life experiences, enticing us into viewing them from a different angle or slant.[8]

At the core of Nouwen's acuity is this apparent link with the poetic or parabolic word form. It was not simply that Nouwen understood the hermeneutical structure of the parable (although he certainly demonstrates this in *The Return of the Prodigal Son*), but rather that he replicated the parabolic way of seeing the world in the interior structure of his works. This is another way to describe the paradigmatic in Nouwen's pastoral theology.

The paradigmatic, like the parabolic way of seeing the world, requires searching out the depths of ideas, turning these on their head, as it were, and exploring the terrain they imply. By using this parabolic method Nouwen, like a poet, was able to open up possibilities of life and plumb their depth until something fresh crystallized in his thinking.

For an example of this parabolic way of construing the world, consider Nouwen's play on the idea of homecoming and of leaving home in *The Return of the Prodigal Son:*

Implicit in the "return" is a leaving. Returning is a homecoming after a home-leaving, a coming back after having gone away. The father who welcomes his son home is so glad because this son "was dead and has come back to life; he was lost and is found." The immense joy in welcoming back the lost son hides the immense sorrow that has gone before. The finding has the losing in the background, the returning has the leaving under its cloak. Looking at the tender and joy-filled return, I have to dare to taste the sorrowful events that preceded it. Only when I have the courage to explore in depth what it means to leave home, can I come to a true understanding of the return.[9]

In this way Nouwen reflects on homecoming in light of the underside of "home-leaving." This method allows him to pick up fragments of reflection and insight that linger around the lived reality of "homeness" in all of its radiant complexity. It returns such insights as these: "The way home is long and arduous";[10] "I am keenly aware of how full my inner life is with this kind of talk [long dialogue with absent partners]";[11] "Many of my daily preoccupations suggest that I belong more to the world than to God";[12] "The farther I run away from the place where God dwells, the less I am able to hear the voice that calls me the Beloved, and the less I hear that voice, the more entangled I become in the manipulations and power games of the world";[13] and "One of the greatest challenges of the spiritual life is to receive God's forgiveness."[14]

Nouwen understood that the fundamental structure of the parable serves the paradigmatic design of pastoral theological reflection. Thus, he uses the hermeneutical essence of the parabolic word form to "get at" the underside or the deeper contours of the spiritual life. The paradigmatic turn imitates the parabolic way of seeing the world that is embedded in Jesus' parables. The paradigm functioned in Nouwen's writings in a similar manner to the parabolic way of construing the world in Jesus' teaching. The following table describes more completely the connection between the parabolic world view and the paradigmatic in Nouwen's pastoral theology:

Parable	*Paradigm*
upside-down view	view from temporal reality
kingdom idea or concept	central insight or core concept
surprise	sudden turn or return
poignant interpretation of life	pathway for understanding life
simple idea	root or inner core idea
multiple ways into the story	many entry or access points

Henri Nouwen and the Discernment of Root Concepts

The paradigmatic approach to pastoral theology depends on the decisions one makes with respect to the root ideas from which the paradigm flows. Henri Nouwen had a unique gift of *discernment*, which comes from the Latin term meaning "to sift through." At the core of his pastoral theological vision was this serious attempt to go to the *root idea* from which all the other ideas flow or to which they are related. Brazilian theologian and philosopher Rubem Alves reminds us that all such core thinking is radical, stating, "We do not want to be radicals—indeed this word has acquired an almost obscene connotation; we have forgotten that to be radical means simply to go to the root of things."[15]

In this sense the paradigmatic approach to pastoral theology is highly integrative around core concepts that are rooted in life. Few of Nouwen's books demonstrate this as powerfully as *Reaching Out*. In this volume Nouwen explores the opening question, "What does it mean to live a life in the Spirit of Jesus Christ?"[16] In order to "get at" the contours of this foundational inquiry, Nouwen explores the polarities that govern our life situation in three movements: the movement from loneliness to solitude; the movement from hostility to hospitality; and, finally and most important, the movement from illusion to prayer, the core of life with God. How does he discover these as opposed to other grounding concepts?

According to Simone Weil the function of language "is to express the relationship between things."[17] If we are to speak meaningfully of the deeper experiences of God in our life and in the life of our faith communities, which was at the core of Nouwen's pastoral theology, we need to pay careful attention to how language may express the deeper contours of our searching.

This capacity for rooted language, articulation of a depth dimension, and discerning judgment about which concepts are at the origin of life was central to the efficacy of Henri Nouwen. One might ask, in this respect, how the discovery of the "true north" concepts selected by Nouwen is achieved.

Deep at the root of Nouwen's paradigmatic understanding was a sustained, engaged, and profound ontological participation in ultimate reality. Paul Tillich describes the necessity of being rooted in ultimate reality when he states: "Ontology presupposes a conversion, an opening of the eyes, a revelatory experience. It is not a matter of detached observation, analysis, or hypothesis."[18] Notice, in particular, Tillich's insistence on the proximity of ontology and "an opening of the eyes" as a basis for speaking about ultimate reality. Much of our language in formal academic theology seems to lull us to sleep, to "closing our eyes." Detached observation, calculating analysis, and dry hypotheses fail to break through. What is needed are word forms that participate in the reality to which they point, word forms that express the depth dimension of reality and open up the soul. In order to offer such meaningful expression one must be immersed in ultimate reality. Paul Tillich insists that only those who are "involved in ultimate reality," who have encountered "it as a matter of existential concern, can try to speak about it meaningfully."[19]

In fact, this is the most demanding discipline of the pastoral theological paradigms articulated by Henri Nouwen. He would have used the term *theological reflection* to state engagement with ultimate reality and the holistic integration of the heart, body, and mind. Theological reflection, for Nouwen, was a deep living of life in the Spirit and the courageous reflection on that life as a continuing discernment. Hence, he states in *In the Name of Jesus:*

> Just as prayer keeps us connected with the first love and just as confession and forgiveness keep our ministry communal and mutual, so strenuous theological reflection will allow us to discern critically where we are being led. Few ministers and priests think theologically. . . . Real theological thinking with the mind of Christ, is hard to find in the practice of ministry. . . . Thinking about the future of Christian leadership, I am convinced that it needs to be a theological leadership. For this to come about, much—very much—has to happen in seminaries and divinity schools. They have to become centers where people are trained in true discernment of the signs of the times. This cannot be just an intellectual training. It requires a deep spiritual formation involving the whole person—body, mind, and heart.[20]

The integrative vision of Henri Nouwen had this singular capacity to live in ultimate reality and to discern carefully the basic or root concepts that required engagement. Nouwen referred to this in *The Wounded Healer* as "sensitive articulation," a concept that went far beyond his pastoral ministry to the core of his writing method and the structural support for the paradigmatic turns in his thinking. Sensitive articulation was the true axis of Nouwen's pastoral theological paradigms. He describes the crucial concept of articulation:

> The key word here is articulation. The man who can articulate the movements of his inner life, who can give names to his varied experiences . . . is able to create space for Him whose heart is greater than his, whose eyes see more than his and whose hands heal more than his.[21]

In order to create this space, the ministering person must engage in life and the deeper contours of that existence, learning to articulate sensitively and carefully the essence of these experiences in such a way that others can move forward in their journey. Nouwen describes this core engagement of ultimate reality as

> a deep human encounter in which a man is willing to put his own faith and doubt, his own hope and despair, his own light and darkness at the disposal of others who want to find a way through their confusion and touch the solid core of life. In this context preaching means more than handing over a tradition; it is rather the careful and sensitive articulation of what is happening in the community so that those who listen can say: "You say what I suspected, you express what I vaguely felt, you bring to the fore what I fearfully kept in the back of my mind. Yes, yes—you say who we are, you recognize our condition."[22]

Spirituality of Ministry and the Paradigmatic

It is virtually impossible to separate the vital spiritual vision rooted in Christian spirituality in Henri Nouwen from his more critical pastoral insight and his pastoral theology in general. In *The Living Reminder* he states his assumptions about the integrative connection between spirituality and ministry:

> We have fallen into the temptation of separating ministry from spirituality, service from prayer. Our demon says, "We are too busy to pray; we have too many needs to attend to, too many people to respond to, too many wounds to heal. . . . But to think this way is harmful. . . . Service and prayer can never be separated. . . . In this book I want to explore the connection between ministry and spirituality and show how service is prayer and prayer is service.[23]

It would not be an overstatement to say that for Henri Nouwen, the integrative insight for ministry is the life of prayer. To dwell with God, to commune with God, and to abide in God's presence are at the very core of life itself. The prayer life is a way of being in the world as one who attends to the voice of God. For Nouwen, this is the heart of the vocation of all believers. In *Reaching Out*, he weaves the paradigmatic concept of "reaching out" in three polarities, the most important being the polarity that "structures our relationship with God," the polarity between illusion and prayer.[24] Within the vicissitudes of life we move along these polarities, but at the core is the life of prayer. Nouwen describes the role this polarity plays in his paradigmatic scheme:

> We need the willingness and courage to reach out far beyond the limitations of our fragile and finite existence toward our loving God in whom all life is anchored. . . . Solitude and hospitality can only bear lasting fruits when they are embedded in a broader, deeper and higher reality from which they receive their vitality. . . . They are rooted in the most basic movement of the spiritual life, which is the movement from illusion to prayer. It is through this movement that we reach out to God, our God, the one who is eternally real and from whom all reality comes forth.[25]

I want to go further than I did in my earlier remarks about the parabolic word form to note carefully the perceptive use of paradigmatic scriptures as the connecting point of many of Nouwen's root ideas. Passages such as the *kenosis text* of Philippians 2:1–8, the temptation of Jesus in Matthew 4, the reinstatement of Peter in John 20, and the metaphor of the vine in John 15 are all carefully woven into the fabric of Henri Nouwen's pastoral theology.[26] This is a crucial aspect of his work, because it allows Christians from every tradition to engage in the pathways of his theological reflection from the common standpoint of the Christian scriptures. The interpretation of these elements was constantly being worked into his soul and sensitively articulated through his writing. However, it must be stated that Nouwen's paradigmatic approach was deeply rooted in scripture and these tested ideas created an alignment with his pastoral theological insight, the remarkable and comprehensive spiritual vision that illuminated everything he wrote and served as the guide for the paradigmatic structure of his work.

Concluding Insights

In closing I might remark briefly on how the paradigmatic approach to pastoral theology introduced by Henri Nouwen might shape the future of pastoral theology in the twenty-first century.

- The "postmodern turn" requires continued attention to ambiguity, depth, and the universal experiences that form the basis of our life. Nouwen gave us a method for exploration of the basic themes of pastoral theology with his paradigmatic approach.
- Theological integration requires flexible paradigms that will allow dialogue to mature between disciplines and between theological systems. The paradigmatic serves this interdisciplinary enterprise well.
- Paradigmatic thinking allows for a rooted perception to be "sensitively articulated" without a determined dogmatism or rationalistic interpretation of life.
- Pastoral and spiritual theology are driven by the human need for meaning, understanding, and integration. This was instinctive for Henri Nouwen, and his fruitfulness ought to inspire those of us who continue to teach pastoral theology to take our cues from this.
- The paradigmatic structure of Nouwen's thought gives those of us who are committed to the work of pastoral and spiritual theology a way forward where being precedes doing; this is the approach that will bear the greatest fruit. Fecundity, not productivity, is the criterion for effective pastoral theology in the twenty-first century.[27]

The paradigmatic approach to pastoral theology introduced and perfected by Henri Nouwen will continue to inspire the work that must be done in future generations as we discern the deeper meanings of the spiritual life. Clearly Nouwen's legacy will continue in the field that rooted his original insights. I close with a simple note of gratitude for the inspiration of this creative mind on our discipline.

Notes

[1] Rubem Alves, *What Is Religion?* (Maryknoll, NY: Orbis Books, 1984), 90.
[2] Dietrich Bonhoeffer, *Ethics* (Minneapolis: Fortress Press, 2005), 270, emphasis added.

[3] Henri J. M. Nouwen, *With Open Hands* (New York: Ballantine Books, 1972), 39.

[4] Ibid., 46.

[5] Ibid., 37.

[6] Ibid.

[7] Ibid., xi, emphasis added.

[8] Donald Capps, *The Poet's Gift: Toward the Renewal of Pastoral Care* (Louisville, KY: Westminster/John Knox Press, 1993), 2.

[9] Henri Nouwen, *The Return of the Prodigal Son: A Meditation on Fathers, Brothers, and Sons* (New York: Doubleday, 1992), 34.

[10] Ibid., 51.

[11] Ibid.

[12] Ibid., 42.

[13] Ibid., 47.

[14] Ibid., 53.

[15] Rubem Alves, *Tomorrow's Child: Imagination, Creativity, and the Rebirth of Culture* (New York: Harper and Row, 1972), 5.

[16] Henri J. M. Nouwen, *Reaching Out: The Three Movements of the Spiritual Life* (Garden City, NY: Doubleday, 1975), 14.

[17] Simone Weil, *Gravity and Grace* (London: Routledge and Kegan Paul, 1952), 3.

[18] Paul Tillich, *Theology of Culture* (New York: Oxford University Press, 1964), 65.

[19] Ibid.

[20] Henri J. M. Nouwen, *In the Name of Jesus: Reflections on Christian Leadership* (New York: Crossroad, 2002), 85–86, 90.

[21] Henri J. M. Nouwen, *The Wounded Healer* (Garden City, NY: Image Books, 1979), 38.

[22] Ibid., 39.

[23] Henri J. M. Nouwen, *The Living Reminder: Service and Prayer in Memory of Jesus Christ* (New York: Seabury Press, 1977), 12–13.

[24] Nouwen, *Reaching Out,* 18.

[25] Ibid., 112–13.

[26] See Henri J. M. Nouwen, Donald P. McNeill, and Douglas A. Morrison, *Compassion: A Reflection on the Christian Life* (Garden City: NY: Doubleday, 1982), chap. 2; Nouwen, *In the Name of Jesus,* 12; and Henri J. M. Nouwen, *Lifesigns: Intimacy, Fecundity, and Ecstasy in Christian Perspective* (Garden City, NY: Doubleday, 1986), 55ff., 85ff.

[27] "I may have come to the theoretical insight that being is more important than doing, but when asked to just be with people who can do very little I realize how far I am from the realization of this insight. Thus, the handicapped have become my teachers, telling me in many different ways that productivity is something other than fecundity. Some of us might be productive and others not, but we are all called to bear fruit; fruitfulness is a true quality of love" (Nouwen, *Lifesigns,* 64).

22

When You See, You See Direct!

Turning the Wheel to Sharpen Your Sight

John S. Mogabgab

Editors' note: This talk was given on May 20, 2006, at the closing of the Turning the Wheel conference. References to the conference have been left intact.

We were hurtling through the Dutch countryside toward the Vincent van Gogh Collection at the Kröller-Müller Museum in Otterlo. The atmosphere was soft and heavy from rain the previous night. Patches of water lay on the road like puddles of quicksilver. Henri Nouwen was driving, always a concern for passenger and public alike. In the distance a car on a side road slowly approached the intersection with the main road on which we were traveling. Suddenly Henri wrenched the steering wheel to the left and stomped on the brake pedal as if to avoid an imminent collision with the other vehicle. When I had regained sufficient breath to speak, and with all the calmness I could muster, I asked Henri why he had done that. Matter of factly, he explained that the approaching car had appeared very close and did not seem to be stopping at the intersection. Moreover, all the ice on the road made it clear that if he had not braked and veered to the left, an accident was very likely. Still working on my breathing, I commented that the threatening car was quite far down the road and that what appeared to be ice was actually water. Henri then confessed that problems with his eyesight made things appear closer than they really were.

Henri's eyes made things appear closer than they really were. This led Henri to unusual and sometimes alarming behavior in the driver's seat. But what was a potential problem on the road to the Van Gogh Collection became, on

219

the road to intimacy with God, a wonderful gift that always amazed me. To
the eyes of Henri's heart, God often appeared closer than God does to others. The spiritual landscape Henri inhabited, and through which he guided
so many, was thick with parables of the kingdom.

I was working in Henri's office at Yale Divinity School the day Bob
Durback, who later edited *Seeds of Hope*, came to visit him. They had become
friends several years earlier when Henri helped Bob with discernment about
his vocation. It happened that the Red Cross was holding a blood drive in
the Divinity School common room, and Henri had gone there to participate.
We found Henri on a gurney at the far end of the room. Bob eagerly approached the patient and, without explanation, cried out, "When you see,
you see direct!" Clearly there was a story behind this unique greeting! I never
learned the story, but I have been challenged and quickened by those words
ever since Bob spoke them. For me, they express something deep and enduring about Henri's spiritual legacy. Perhaps they also give voice to his invitation to us as we leave this conference. This legacy and invitation are about
the cultivation of spiritual sight, and I would like briefly to explore it under
three headings: noticing, turning, and loving.

Noticing

There is an old joke that goes something like this: "My friend says I'm
getting forgetful. Funny, I don't remember forgetting anything." Can something like this be happening with our capacity to see? "Funny, I didn't notice
not seeing anything." Recently I saw a picture of a United States serviceman
sunning himself in a rubble-strewn yard in the Baghdad Green Zone. Huge
concrete blast walls enclosed the yard. The height and thickness of those
walls surely prevented that soldier from seeing much of the city around him.
I wonder if we do not sometimes experience the world as impenetrable as a
blast wall, hardened by tragedy, suffering, outrages great and small, with
thick overlays of cultural or religious assumptions and psychological projec-
tions that stand formidably between us and what is really happening. What
are we really able to notice?

"Behold," calls God to the people, "I am doing a new thing; now it springs
forth, do you not perceive it?" (Is 43:19). The Bible is filled with the call to
behold: "Behold! I bring you tidings of great joy" (Lk 2:10); "Behold! I tell
you a mystery! (1 Cor 15:51).[1] Maggie Ross, the Anglican solitary, has pointed
out how central the call to behold is in scripture: "It signals shifting perspective, the holding together or even conflating of radically different points of
view. . . . Our settled accounting of ordinary matters is shattered and falls
into nothing as light breaks upon us."[2]

"Look," Henri exclaimed, "there is a woman begging over there!" We
were walking across Boston Common on our way to Leonard Nimoy's one-
man play about Vincent van Gogh, told through the voice of his brother,
Theo. The woman seemed quite far away to me, but to Henri she was as

close as his heart. "Look," Henri said to each of us, "you are the beloved daughter of God, and you are the beloved son of God!" This was for Henri the first truth about us, the truth beyond all biological, cultural, and psychological truths that accumulate around our identity. This was for Henri the deep truth that shines through all the pain and sorrow and anger and fatigue that cloud the face of humanity, the ancient truth wandering in the public square of human community, begging to be noticed and affirmed.

Henri invites us to be beholders of God in the world. This involves us in a movement from seeing opaquely to seeing transparently, a movement he writes about in *Clowning in Rome*.[3] In that book and in this conference the commission we receive from Henri is to see and to help others see, to participate in God's work of making manifest the "mystery that has been hidden throughout the ages" (Col 1:26). To take part in this work, however, requires turning.

Turning

Turning the Wheel is the title of this conference. When I think of Henri behind the steering wheel of a car, I realize that he might have had two reasons to turn the wheel. (Well, three if you count jerking the wheel to avoid real or imaginary collisions!) The two reasons I have primarily in mind are, first, turning the steering wheel to gain a new and more revealing perspective on something. Second, Henri might also turn the wheel to approach something and, possibly, enter into a relationship with what he has noticed. Fresh perspectives and new relationships—these are aspects of the cultivation of spiritual sight to which Henri draws our attention. They are part of the trajectory of Henri's legacy for the twenty-first century. So let me explore them a little.

One of the New Testament texts to which Henri often returned was Romans 12:2: "Do not be conformed to this world, but be transformed by the renewing of your minds, so that you may discern what is the will of God—what is good and acceptable and perfect." These few words gather up so many facets of Henri's teaching, so much of his own struggle to live in but not of the world. The great question Paul puts before us here is simply this: How can we notice anything truly new if we see only with the eyes of the world? If our sight is shaped by the world, then we will see only what the world sees. And the world has seen it all. "What has been is what will be, and what has been done is what will be done; there is nothing new under the sun. Is there a thing of which it is said, 'See, this is new'? It has already been, in the ages before us" (Eccl 1:9–10). This is the voice of the tired, disillusioned world. More often than I would like to admit, it has become my voice as well. Perhaps you are familiar with it too. This voice insinuates itself into mind and tongue so subtly that before we are aware of it our sight has lost its capacity to see direct, to see through the blast wall of the world's pain and disillusionment into the deep mystery of God that is closer than we think.

Henri understood that in order to resist conformation to the world he had to turn the wheel. He had to drive off the road the world had so nicely paved and painted with directional markings. So he began to write about and then to live the disciplines of voluntary displacement and downward mobility. His several extended stays in the Trappist Abbey of the Genesee, his later immersion in the barrios of Lima, Peru, his sojourn with the circus and his fascination with the Flying Rodleighs, and his final years in L'Arche Daybreak all were expressions of this off-road journey to gain fresh, authentic, transforming perspectives on the traces of an elusive, enigmatic God.

One night, after a long day of travel, Henri and I arrived very late at the almost deserted parking lot of the New Haven airport only to find shadowy figures roaming around dressed as R2D2 and 3CPO, the *Star Wars* androids. I was for getting to the car as quickly and unobtrusively as possible, but with great excitement and enthusiasm after such a long day, Henri urged: "Come on! Let's go over there so we can see better what's happening!" I believe Henri still calls out something similar to us today. His invitation is to step out of our accustomed place in the world, to turn the wheel to the left or the right. As we leave this conference, will we be alert for the nudges that suggest an alternate route, a fresh vista that will reveal something new and important for us to notice in the landscape of God's kingdom already among us?

Turning makes possible a new angle of vision. It also may involve more than that. If we turn toward what we have noticed, we must be prepared for a claim to be made upon us. Indeed, we must be open to the possibility of a relationship we had not expected or even wanted. This was the experience of the good Samaritan, who turned toward the injured man by the side of the road. Three people in that story see the hurt Jew—a Pharisee, a Levite, and a Samaritan—but only one really notices him. Seeing is here tragically disconnected from noticing that something is happening before their eyes that lays claim to their attention and concern. As I ponder this story, I wonder how often I have turned away from a person, a situation, a possibility, or a problem because I believed myself to be too busy, too tired, too fearful, or too inadequate to risk the onset of a relationship.

The Samaritan is ready to risk a relationship with the injured Jew. He notices that here is a person in need of his assistance. Moreover, he notices without distinction. The fact that he is a Samaritan and the other is a Jew, a distinction of monumental significance in that time, is eclipsed by compassion.

Henri liked the story about a rabbi of old who asked his students how they could tell that night had ended and morning was on its way. "Is it when you can look at a tree in the distance and tell whether it is a fig tree or a peach tree?" asked one student. "No," said the rabbi. "Is it when you can look at an animal and tell whether it is a sheep or a dog?" asked another. "No," answered the rabbi. "Well, then, what is the answer?" asked the students. The rabbi paused and then said, "It is when you can look on the face of any man or woman and see there the face of a brother or sister. Because if you cannot do that, then no matter what time of day it is, it is still night." Morning dawned fresh and clear that day along the road from Jericho to Jerusalem. The sun of compassion enabled a Samaritan to notice in the face of a Jew the countenance of a brother. When you see, you see direct!

Henri turned toward and embraced the wounded aspects of his own humanity. In many of his writings, and notably in *The Wounded Healer*, he encouraged us to recognize that "when we become aware that we do not have to escape our pains, but that we can mobilize them into a common search for life, those very pains are transformed from expressions of despair into signs of hope."[4] Henri's willingness to accept and affirm his personal brokenness also allowed him to wrap his arms around the wounded other and, through his baptismal union with the risen Christ, to embrace the whole wounded world within the boundaries of his own wounded heart. When we return home from this gathering, will we be more prepared to turn toward what we notice with compassionate attentiveness? Will we be ready to embrace the many vulnerable and wounded people we encounter with the gaze of love?

Loving

"Do you love me?" Jesus earnestly asks Peter this question not once but three times after they have eaten their shore breakfast along the Sea of Tiberias (Jn 21:15–17). Each time Jesus asks Peter, we witness a profound act of love on the part of Jesus. Each repetition of the question gives Peter an opportunity to undo one of his denials on the night Jesus was arrested. Jesus sees the heart of Peter and knows Peter needs to hear this question and to answer it from his heart. Henri turned to this text in John's Gospel frequently. It was a touchstone passage of scripture for him because, I believe, Jesus' question to Peter, which is also Jesus' question to each of us, allows us to claim freedom from our past failures and betrayals, and prepares us for the messy uncertainty of love. "Very truly, I tell you," Jesus says to Peter and to us, "when you were younger, you used to fasten your own belt and to go wherever you wished. But when you grow old, you will stretch out your hands, and someone else will fasten a belt around you and take you where you do not wish to go" (Jn 21:18). The freedom to love sometimes means the freedom to let someone else turn the wheel of our life's direction, guiding us to where our love is most needed.

"Do you love me?" Jesus' question echoes down the ages, whispering its urgent invitation amid the noise and bustle and despair of the world. "He comes to us," observes Albert Schweitzer, "as one unknown."[5] The invitation is to love him in all his distressing disguises, and in loving him, learn how to notice him and turn toward him ever more freely. Michael Downey describes well the relation between loving and seeing, a relation Henri's spiritual legacy challenges us to develop and deepen: "Our gift and task is to learn how to see anew each day, learning how to look. Christian faith is a whole way of life, a way of seeing by loving. The more we see, the more we love. The more we love, the more we see. Refining, purifying our eye allows us to see each and everyone, everything and every living creature, deeply. To read the world and all that is in it with love."[6]

When you see, you see direct!

Notes

[1] All scripture quotations are from the New Revised Standard Version Bible.

[2] Maggie Ross, "Barking at Angels," *Weavings* 21:1 (January/February 2006): 15.

[3] Henri J. M. Nouwen, *Clowning in Rome* (Garden City, NY: Doubleday/Image Books, 1979).

[4] Henri J. M. Nouwen, *The Wounded Healer* (New York: Doubleday, 1972), 93.

[5] Albert Schweitzer, *The Quest of the Historical Jesus*, trans. W. Montgomery (London: A. and C. Black, 1910), 403.

[6] Michael Downey, *The Heart of Hope: Contemplating Life, Awakening Love* (Boston, MA: Pauline Books and Media, 2005), 57.

23

A Call and a Blessing

Reflections for the Closing of the Conference

Sue Mosteller and Gord Henry

Editors' note: This talk was given on May 20, 2006, at the closing of the Turning the Wheel conference. References to the conference have been left intact.

Gord Henry:

> Henri and I were good friends.
> Henri was like a father to me.
> We travelled together and spoke together.
> Sometimes I talked to Henri about my life.
> He helped me with my temptations.
> He made a tape for me.
> When I go into my room to pray, I play my tape.
> Henri was grateful, so grateful.
> What I liked about Henri? He blessed me.

Sue Mosteller:

David, one of the men in our L'Arche Daybreak community, is a man who "sees direct." He has an incredible gift to say what he sees and hit the nail on the head. One night, sitting in the living room with David, I said wearily, "Dave, I'm so exhausted! Do you think you could carry me upstairs to bed?" David thought a moment, hit his knee with his hand, and replied, "I could, but I'd need a crane!"

Another time, in a full car en route to a meeting in Erie, Pennsylvania, we had a long period of silence. In order to make conversation I began, "Wow! I'm so glad they got my guitar to fit in the other car so I'll have it at the meeting." No one spoke, so I went on. "You know, they might ask me to play and make music for the meeting!" Silence. I pushed ahead. "If they do, you know, I'll be on the stage and everyone will clap for me." I could see Dave in the rearview mirror, processing all I was saying. Finally, because I was only learning guitar at the time, I said, "You know, I can play 'Long Long Ago.'" Dave didn't stop for breath before he replied with emphasis, "Yes! And you should play it far, far away!"

The conference is closing now, and prior to leaving, it is time to "see direct" what the meaning of this event might be. I will gather a few gems from the keynote speakers to remind us of the gift of some treasured insights, directed not for consummation but for radical discipleship.

This conference was not meant to be primarily about Henri Nouwen or about the many people who spoke here. The conference was for and about you and me in our search for God, in our finding God, and in renewing our passion for announcing the good news by our lives. So let us endeavor to "see direct" and identify with the voices calling us to more.

Carol Berry pointed us to the lives of two beautiful, courageous, and fragile men, Vincent van Gogh and Henri Nouwen. Both suffered profound anguish, and both became wounded healers. But they did not allow suffering to overcome their passion, nor did they choose to play the victim. Rather, they allowed their anguish to fuel their genius, and they clung to the inner spark, the inner spirit at work in them. Their lives reveal their attraction to identify with the ones who were different from them, going beyond fear and finding beauty and courage and love in their unlikely teachers.

We must ask ourselves if we embrace a similar path in our own lives. Both those men knew that life is a sowing, not a reaping, time. How about you and me? Let us allow our inner aspirations to be inspired by these two brothers and go forth to sow the seeds of love around us wherever we are. Let us not wait to be healed but reach out as wounded healers in a world that waits for love. Let us hope that our suffering—mostly undeserved—can be the fuel for *our* genius.

We are beloved daughters and sons of a living God and called to become more and more beloved mothers and fathers, loving others and taking responsibility to be compassionate and forgiving of all. We were not here as consumers of a nice gathering and nice speeches. We are beloved and called to share this good news with others.

Laurent Nouwen introduced us to those who are tempted to say with Jesus, "My God, my God, why have you forsaken me?" We met the inmates of the psychiatric hospital in Lviv, Ukraine, in unthinkable conditions, without mattresses or respect or dignity. How can we be present? The children in orphanages in the forest of Eastern Europe, tied to the radiators or bed posts, languish in loneliness and agony, cry out to us somehow to introduce them to love and care. And we touched the life of a young man dying of AIDS in South Africa who represents countless brothers and sisters, alone and in need of support, love, prayers, and compassion.

Laurent's response is to be present, to offer support, and to call others to the Henri Nouwen Stichting in Holland where everyone works to collect furniture, bathroom and kitchen equipment, and other useful items—and to drive these things to those in need in Ukraine.

It is not enough for you and me to know about it. These are our brothers and sisters in the human family who need dignity, love, and support. It is not enough for us to consume the news of refugees, those injured through terrorism, the homeless, the abused, and the victims of violence. Each of us is strongly called to ask, "How, in my life situation, will I become present, offer support, and involve others? How will I grow in my passion to be a man or woman of God?"

We are beloved daughters and sons of a living God and called to become more and more beloved mothers and fathers, loving others and taking responsibility to be compassionate and forgiving of all. We were not here as consumers of a nice gathering and nice speeches. We are beloved and called to share this good news with others.

Michael Higgins "saw direct" and told us straight that we do not have our own, private, entrepreneurial spiritual life. Our life is bigger, much bigger, and linked with many others everywhere. Michael, echoing Henri, asked what we are to do with the inner wound. He called us to become transparent and unafraid of scorching self-revelation.

Is it possible that you and I learn from Thomas Merton, Donald Nicholl, Henri Nouwen, and so many others how to disempower the destructive forces of the inner wound and choose to become wounded healers? What are we to do with our failures, our depression, our inability to forgive, our resentment, our overwhelming addictions, and our anger? Michael pointed the way. He reminded us to struggle to see and to accept the wound as Henri saw it—"a gift in disguise" and "a gateway to my salvation."

We are beloved daughters and sons of a living God and called to become more and more beloved mothers and fathers, loving others and taking responsibility to be compassionate and forgiving of all. We were not here as consumers of a nice gathering and nice speeches. We are beloved and called to share this good news with others.

Finally, Mary Jo Leddy reminded us of the challenge of living in a culture that wants us to make God smaller and cut God down to size, so that our private lives will remain undisturbed. She urged us to allow God to be God and a God of surprises! She challenged us to claim the truth of our primary identity—beloved of God. She described how a knock comes to her door and she very often faces a refugee who asks, "Please help me." She knows the scene, and she knows the improbability of that person—or of herself—getting through the unjust system that militates against those who are different. But she listens and makes another effort, another call, to prevent a deportation or enable the entrance into the country of spouses and children of loved ones already here. She shared her passion and her motivation by telling us, "Life cannot be taken for granted. Your life becomes significant, weighty, consequential."

We are beloved daughters and sons of a living God and called to become more and more beloved mothers and fathers, loving others and taking responsibility to be compassionate and forgiving of all. We were not here as consumers of a nice gathering and nice speeches. We are beloved and called to share this good news with others.

So, friends, we have been inspired and called. The response is in our hands.

David, my friend at Daybreak, likes to respond when the phone rings. He is very friendly and has many questions for the caller. If someone asks, "May I speak to Sue, please?" Dave may answer, "How did you meet Sue?" He goes on from there, requesting to know where the person lives and works and finally what he or she wants to talk with me about. One time an assistant from Daybreak, Joe, went to Boston for the weekend, and he called home to tell us about a change in his travel plans. Dave answered the phone, and the operator said, "I have a collect call from Joe for anyone. Will you accept the charge?" Dave replied, "No. Joe isn't here." After a moment the operator tried to explain, "Please listen. I have a collect call for someone there *from* Joe. Do you accept the charge?" Dave thought a moment and then said, "No, Joe is in Boston. He's not here." This time in the pause, Joe himself jumped in and urgently said to David, "Dave, just say 'yes.'" The operator promptly cut in and said, "Please sir, if you don't want to pay for this call, please do not speak to your party!" A long pause ensued. Finally, Dave spoke, "Oh, Joe, there's a call here for you. What should I do?"

We, like David, are being called. All that we received is not just for us but for others—our brothers and sisters—and for our world. Like Dave's, our call is a collect call, because our lives are times of sowing and not reaping.

We are beloved daughters and sons of a living God and called to become more and more beloved mothers and fathers, loving others and taking responsibility to be compassionate and forgiving of all. We were not here as consumers of a nice gathering and nice speeches. We are beloved and called to share this good news with others.

To help us in our response to this wonderful news, Gord Henry would like to offer us a blessing. And even the blessing is not just for us, so let us, in our hearts and minds, gather those we love around us. And let us think of those in our past that have touched our lives in joy and in pain. Bring them here in your heart. Let us go beyond and gather all our brothers and sisters in the human family and bring them to this moment with us. Let the blessing flow through you to all those with whom you are called to walk the journey of life. Please stand and hold hands together.

Gord Henry: Blessing

> I know that God loves me.
> When God asks me to open my heart it means that I am
> to come closer to God.
> So, I bless you in the name of the Father, the Son, and the
> Holy Spirit.
> Go home, and be grateful.

Conclusion

Jonathan Bengtson
and Gabrielle Earnshaw

In his lifelong effort to describe the spiritual life, Henri Nouwen used a variety of creative devices: Rembrandt's paintings, the life of Vincent van Gogh and Thomas Merton, stories from the Zen masters and desert fathers, biblical and other traditions, and poetic metaphors, such as the trapeze and the clown. Perhaps the most used of all was the motif of travel, which spans his writing from at least 1974 to a month before his death in 1996. His book titles often referred to the traveling life (*The Road to Daybreak*, *Sabbatical Journey*, *Bread for the Journey*, *Walk with Jesus*, and *Show Me the Way* are some examples), and he frequently described the spiritual life as a movement from one state to another—from loneliness to solitude, from resentment to gratitude, and from the house of fear to the house of love, to name just a few instances from his writing. The wheel was a particularly rich image for Nouwen, one that he used to convey different aspects of Christian spirituality depending on the questions he was asking for his own spiritual life. An early use of the image comes from *Aging*. He writes: "This is what the large wagon wheel . . . teaches us. . . . No one of its spokes is more important than the others, but together they make the circle full and reveal the hub as the core of its strength."[1] In this passage which foreshadows books to come, Nouwen used the wheel to describe three aspects of the spiritual life: life is a circle (as opposed to a straight line based on linear time); young or old, able or disabled, we all have an equal place in God's world; and sorrow as much as joy gives life its meaning and fullness. Nouwen's words echo those of Ralph Waldo Emerson, who wrote in his essay "Circles": "Our life is an apprenticeship to the truth, that, around every circle another can be drawn; that there is no end in nature, but every end is a beginning; that there is always another dawn risen on mid-noon, and under every deep a lower deep opens."[2]

In 1994, in *Here and Now*, Nouwen used the wheel image again, this time about the paradoxical nature of the contemplative life: "The wagon wheel shows that the hub is the center of all energy and movement, even when it often seems not to be moving at all. In God all action and all rest are one."[3] It is in this further reflection for *Here and Now* that he offers an explanation for his attraction to wheel imagery and puts even stronger emphasis on living life from the center. He writes: "I have always been fascinated by these wagon wheels with their wide rims, strong wooden spokes and big hubs. These wheels help me to understand the importance of a life lived from the center. When I move along the rim, I can reach one spoke after the other, but when I stay at the hub, I am in touch with all the spokes at once."[4] In this classic passage, Nouwen likens the hub to his own heart, to the heart of God, and to the heart of the world and reiterates that only by remaining in his own center can he feel communion with the world and find the energy to move out of the center to help others.

Given the rich meaning attributed to the wheel by Henri Nouwen, it seemed an apt centering image for the title of our conference and now the title of this volume. We hope you have been inspired by the writings herein. It is our sincere desire that Henri's notes, essays, letters, recordings, and manuscripts deposited here at St. Michael's College become increasingly a living, breathing extension of the legacy that Henri left us all and that you are entrusted to carry forward in new and creative ways in your own lives. To achieve this, we are exploring the possibility of taking part in a Nouwen-inspired spirituality center, that would bring people together, like spokes in wheel, in order to renew faith in a loving God, build community, and foster hope and courage to reach out and care for others.

In one of the last interviews he gave before his death on September 21, 2006, Nouwen sketched a wheel and proceeded to use it once again to describe the spiritual life. This sketch is now in the archives, and in spite of the ten years that have passed since he drew it, one can almost see him leaning

forward in his chair, reaching out with his whole being to the interviewer, eyes ablaze with conviction and passion to convey his insights, won with so much difficulty. *You see, you see,* he might say, dramatically and emphatically piercing the center of the wheel, *it is from the center that we find our energy, and the courage to move out to touch the spokes and find our common humanity.* It is a message we still need to hear today.

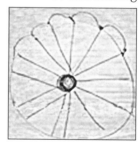

Notes

[1] Henri Nouwen and Walter Gaffney, *Aging: The Fulfillment of Life* (New York: Doubleday, 1974), 13.

[2] Ralph Waldo Emerson, *Essays: First Series* (New York: T.Y. Crowell and Co., 1891), 220.

[3] Henri Nouwen, *Here and Now: Living in the Spirit* (New York: Crossroad, 1994), 26.

[4] Ibid., 25.

Contributors

Nathan Ball is currently a trustee of the Henri Nouwen Legacy Trust. He supports the Henri Nouwen Society in the areas of planning and development and is the executive director of the L'Arche Canada Foundation. He is a longtime member of the L'Arche Daybreak community and was a close friend of Henri's for more than ten years. He lives close to Toronto with his wife and their four children.

Jonathan Bengtson has been the chief librarian of the John M. Kelly Library at St. Michael's College in the University of Toronto since 2004. Previously, he held various senior positions in academic, research, and nonprofit libraries in the United States and the United Kingdom.

Rev. Christopher Cahill has been a pastor in The Lutheran Church-Missouri Synod for over twenty-five years and pastor at Christ the King Lutheran Church in Lodi, Ohio, for more than sixteen years. He received the Doctor of Ministry degree from Ashland Theological Seminary in the area of spiritual formation, focusing on the spiritual formation of pastors.

Gabrielle Earnshaw is the archivist for the Henri J. M. Nouwen Archives and Research Collection and curator, special collections, at the John M. Kelly Library at the University of St. Michael's College. She holds a B.A. in history from Queen's University and an M.A.S. from the University of British Columbia. Gabrielle is part of the team conducting oral history interviews with the Henri Nouwen Oral History Project. She sits on the Nouwen Legacy Trust as a non-voting member. She lives with her husband and son, Heiko, in Toronto.

Kathleen M. Fisher is an assistant professor of theology at Assumption College in Worcester, Massachusetts, where she teaches courses in scripture, church history, and medieval Christian literature.

Constance Joanna Gefvert is a professed member of the Sisterhood of St. John the Divine, an Anglican monastic community in Canada. She holds B.A., M.A., and Ph.D. degrees in literature and a D.D. degree from Wycliffe College in the Toronto School of Theology. She served as the elected leader of the sisterhood for over ten years. Currently she serves as director of development for the sisterhood, is an adjunct faculty member at Wycliffe, does spiritual direction, and leads retreats. She is preparing to be ordained a priest in the Anglican Church of Canada.

Rev. Phillip N. Grigsby is a minister in the United Church of Christ and a graduate of Yale Divinity School (where he shared a group experience with Henri Nouwen). Since 1986 he has served as urban agent/director of the Schenectady (NY) Inner City Ministry, an ecumenical coalition of fifty-eight congregations that seeks "to relate the resources of the churches to the human needs of city." He has led seminars on Henri Nouwen in various settings, in part from work supported by The Lilly Endowment.

Wil Hernandez, Ph.D., works with The Leadership Institute, a nondenominational organization that focuses on integrating spiritual formation and leadership development. He is also affiliated with Spiritual Formation Alliance where he serves as its southern California coordinator. Wil regularly teaches a course on the spirituality of Henri Nouwen as an adjunct professor at Fuller Theological Seminary. He is the author of *Henri Nouwen: A Spirituality of Imperfection* (Paulist Press, 2006).

Michael Hryniuk, Ph.D., is a theologian, writer, teacher, and consultant in the field of Christian spirituality and contemplative formation. From 1997 to 2004 he served as the formative evaluator and co-director of the Youth Ministry and Spirituality Project, a national research and teaching initiative based at San Francisco Theological Seminary that promoted contemplative spirituality in the field of youth ministry among mainline Protestant, evangelical, and Catholic churches. He was recently appointed to serve as executive director of the Henri Nouwen Society.

Rev. Gregory Jensen is a priest of the Greek Orthodox Metropolis of Pittsburgh. He is by profession a psychologist of religion, specializing in human and Christian spiritual formation. With his wife, he currently lives in Pittsburgh, where he serves as the Orthodox Christian chaplain at the University of Pittsburgh and Carnegie Mellon University. A scholar/researcher with the Palamas Institute, he provides consulting services in spirituality, spiritual formation, catechetics, and pastoral ministry for a broad range of Christian communities.

Paul Johansen is the senior pastor of Good Shepherd Community Church (Scarborough), a community he has served for over fifteen years. He has studied religion and theology at the University of Toronto, Tyndale Seminary, and the Wheaton College Graduate School. He describes Henri Nouwen as one of his most influential spiritual and pastoral mentors. Paul met Henri personally during a wonderful, random encounter in the late 1980s.

KangHack Lee is a Ph.D. student in the area of Christian spirituality at the Graduate Theological Union in Berkeley, California. He has worked as a staff member in courses of the Spiritual Life and Leadership program and in the Diploma program of the Art of Spiritual Direction at San Francisco Theological Seminary. He was an associate pastor at Dail Presbyterian Church in Korea. He lives with his wife and two children in Berkeley.

Peter Naus is the chancellor of St. Jerome's University in Waterloo, Ontario, Canada. He taught psychology at the university from 1973 until his retirement in 1996. His prior appointments were at the University of Notre Dame and the Catholic University (now Radboud University), Nijmegen, the Netherlands. He received his training in psychology at the Catholic University and became friends with Henri Nouwen. Peter was one of the contributors to *Befriending Life: Encounters with Henri Nouwen* (Doubleday, 2001), a collection of reflections on Henri by his friends and associates, edited by Beth Porter and published by Doubleday.

Michael O'Laughlin was one of Henri Nouwen's teaching assistants at Harvard University. There he earned a doctorate in New Testament and church history. He is the editor of Nouwen's *Jesus: A Gospel* (Orbis Books, 2001). He has written a number of articles about Nouwen and his legacy as well as two Nouwen biographies, *God's Beloved* and *Henri Nouwen: His Life and Vision* (Orbis Books, 2004 and 2005). O'Laughlin is a spiritual director with an office at the Healing Center in Arlington, Massachusetts.

Anna St. Onge previously worked as archival assistant at the Henri J. M. Nouwen Archives and Research Collection and as project archivist for the Sheila Watson papers. She is currently the temporary curator of special collections and archivist of the Nouwen archives at St. Michael's College. She holds a master's degree in archival studies from the University of Toronto's Faculty Studies and the Book History and Print Culture collaborative program at Massey College.

Emily Pardue is an ordained Baptist minister and founder of JAIA Sister Ministries, Inc. She holds doctor of ministry and master of divinity degrees from Ashland Theological Seminary, where she is currently an adjunct professor. Her focus is spiritual formation, and she is author of *The Drama of Dance in the Local Church* (Xulon, 2005).

James D. Smith III served as a teaching fellow at Harvard Divinity School in Henri's final academic courses. He is associate professor of church history at Bethel Theological Seminary, offering "Christian Spiritual Life: Henri Nouwen" on the San Diego and St. Paul campuses. He also is a Lecturer at the University of San Diego and ministers as care pastor at College Avenue Baptist Church.

JoAnn Ford Watson is the H. R. Gill Family Professor of Theology at Ashland Theological Seminary in Ashland, Ohio. She is a member of the Henri Nouwen Society. She is an ordained minister in the Presbyterian Church USA. She holds a Ph.D. from Northwestern University and an M.Div. degree from Princeton Theological Seminary.

Carolyn Whitney-Brown and her family were part of the L'Arche Daybreak community from 1990 to 1997. Carolyn received her Ph.D. from Brown University and trained in spiritual direction in the Ignatian tradition at St. Beuno's in Wales and Loyola House in Ontario. Carolyn is a writer and artist who has taught religious studies at St. Jerome's University, Waterloo, and continuing education at St. Michael's College, Toronto. She contributed a chapter on Henri Nouwen to *Remembering Henri* (Orbis Books, 2006). The Whitney-Brown family lives on Vancouver Island.

Jeremy Wiebe is a Ph.D. candidate at McGill University. He has lectured in ethics at McGill and is currently an adjunct faculty member teaching philosophy at St. Stephen's University in New Brunswick. His primary areas of research are religious ethics, continental philosophy, and Paul Ricoeur.

Phil Zylla, is the academic dean and associate professor of pastoral theology at McMaster Divinity College in Hamilton, Ontario. Prior to that he served as the principal to the Associated Canadian Theological Schools of Trinity Western University in Langley, B.C. Phil has served as a congregational minister in various parts of Canada for seventeen years. He lives in Ancaster, Ontario, with his wife and their two daughters.

Keynote Speakers

Carol Berry currently teaches art at the acclaimed Long Trail School, in Dorset, Vermont. Since 2002 she has been an adjunct faculty member in the area of visual art at the Graduate Theological Union through the Pacific School of Religion and the Center for Arts in Religious Education in Berkeley, California. Berry immigrated to the Unites States thirty years ago from her native Switzerland. She earned a B.A. degree from the University of Missouri and an M.A. in art education from California State University at Northridge. Carol met Henri Nouwen at Yale University where she attended Henri's class on the compassion of Vincent van Gogh. For the last ten years she has been refining her understanding of Vincent van Gogh's work, its impact upon Henri Nouwen's life, and how the compassionate way of Henri and Vincent van Gogh can reach us today.

Gord Henry lived at home with his sister and two brothers in Port Credit, Ontario, for the first eighteen years of his life. Then, in 1972, he moved to the

L'Arche Daybreak community. He has welcomed and introduced hundreds of house assistants into the community and has given them his confidence, his love, and his prayers. Gord has grown in stature and wisdom over his almost thirty-five years in community. Gord is an experienced speaker, and he traveled on many occasions with Henri Nouwen and assisted him in his talks and lectures. Gord presently works in the woodworking shop at Daybreak known as the Woodery. He was a principal worker in designing and decorating the true and colorful masterpiece that became Henri Nouwen's coffin in 1996.

Michael W. Higgins is president and vice-chancellor of St. Thomas University, Fredericton, New Brunswick A nationally distinguished scholar and teacher, he is the author of many books, including *Heretic Blood: The Spiritual Geography of Thomas Merton* (Stoddart, 1998) and *The Muted Voice: Religion and the Media* (Novalis, 1999). His most recent work is *Stalking the Holy: In Pursuit of Saint-Making* (Anansi, 2006), timed to appear with the CBC Ideas airing of the series of the same name. He is a regular contributor to CTV's Canada AM as well as CBC's Sunday Edition. For twelve years he was editor of *Grail: An Ecumenical Journal.* Higgins is the former president of St. Jerome's University.

Mary Jo Leddy received her doctorate in the area of philosophy of religion at the University of Toronto and is an adjunct professor at Regis College. She was the founding editor of *The Catholic New Times* newspaper and is active in various human rights and peace groups. Leddy has written and co-written eight books, including *Reweaving Religious Life* (Twenty-Third Publications, 1990), which won a first place award from the Catholic Press Association of America, and *Radical Gratitude* (Orbis Books, 2002). Leddy is the director of Romero House Community for Refugees, and her numerous awards and scholarships include The Governor General's Bronze Medal, the Canadian University President's Award "Outstanding Woman of 1978," the Ida Nudel Human Rights Award, The Canadian Council of Christians and Jews Human Relations Award, and, most recently, the Order of Canada. She is also the recipient of five honorary doctorates.

John S. Mogabgab is founding editor of *Weavings: A Journal of the Christian Spiritual Life,* a publication of Upper Room Ministries. He was Henri Nouwen's teaching and research assistant at Yale Divinity School, and he currently serves on the board of the Henri Nouwen Society

Sue Mosteller, has been a member of the Sisters of St. Joseph in Toronto for fifty years. Missioned in the early years of L'Arche in Canada, she has lived and worked in L'Arche Daybreak near Toronto for more than thirty years, serving in leadership there and in the International Federation of L'Arche. She published *My Brother My Sister* (Griffin House, 1972), about Jean Vanier and Mother Teresa. Sue was one of the people to welcome Henri Nouwen when he joined the L'Arche Daybreak community in 1986. She replaced him during his sabbatical year as pastor of the community of L'Arche Daybreak. In 1996 she wrote *A Place to Hold My Shaky Heart* (Crossroad), describing her experience of living in a Christian community. Her latest book is *Light through the Crack: Life after Loss* (Doubleday, 2006). Upon Henri Nouwen's sudden death in 1996, Sue became literary executor of his estate. She is presently living at L'Arche Daybreak and working with the published and unpublished works of Henri Nouwen.

Laurent Nouwen is the younger brother of Henri Nouwen. After thirty years of practice in the law, Laurent founded the Henri Nouwen Foundation in the Netherlands shortly after Henri's death. The foundation organizes an annual spirituality lecture series and sponsors a spiritual manuscript competition. Convinced that Christian spirituality makes sense only if it materializes in practice, the Henri Nouwen Foundation coordinates numerous projects in the Netherlands, Ukraine, and South Africa aiming to humanize living conditions for the poor and the marginalized in society. Following Henri's footsteps in Ukraine, the foundation provides substantial material and financial support for prison ministry, for improvement of psychiatric hospitals, and for the care of the handicapped.

Paul Nouwen is the elder brother of Henri Nouwen. He studied law at the University of Leiden in Holland and received his degree in 1958. He worked for the largest insurance company in Holland, Nationale-Nederlanden (which later merged with ING), where he soon became director and where he remained for twenty-seven years. In 1987 he was asked to become director general of the Royal Dutch Touring Club, which is similar to the American Automobile Association in the United States. After retiring, he started his own management and consulting firm for government, companies, and other institutions. Paul sits on the boards of several charitable organizations, including the board of Musea, to raise funds for charitable works, especially prison ministry. He and his wife live in Rotterdam.